OXFORD ENGLISH DRAMA

General Editor: MICHAEL CORDNER
Associate General Editors: PETER HOLLAND · MARTIN WIGGINS

THE PLAYBOY OF THE WESTERN WORLD
AND OTHER PLAYS

JOHN MILLINGTON SYNGE (1871–1909), Irish poet, playwright, and essayist, was one of the key figures, along with W. B. Yeats and Lady Gregory, in the creation of Dublin's Abbey Theatre. Trained as a musician and a linguist, he spent several years studying music and literature in Germany and France before being encouraged by Yeats to become involved in the creation of an indigenous theatre for Ireland. His first completed play, the sombre tragedy *Riders to the Sea*, was written in the summer of 1902, along with the one-act comedy *The Shadow of the Glen*. These were rapidly followed by four others, *The Tinker's Wedding*, *The Well of the Saints*, and *The Playboy of the Western World*. His book *The Aran Islands*, describing his visits to the west of Ireland, was published in 1907. *Poems and Translations* and further travel essays were published posthumously; his unfinished first serious attempt at playwriting, *When the Moon Has Set*, was not published until 1968. Engaged to the Abbey actress Molly Allgood for whom he wrote the role of Pegeen Mike in *The Playboy* and the title role of his last play, *Deirdre of the Sorrows*, Synge died of Hodgkin's disease before they could marry.

ANN SADDLEMYER is a Professor of English and Drama and Master of Massey College in the University of Toronto. She has published extensively on Irish literature, Canadian drama, and theatre history. Her two-volume edition of *The Collected Letters of John Millington Synge*, which received an award from the British Academy, was published by Oxford University Press in 1983 and 1984. She is currently working on a biography of George (Mrs W. B.) Yeats.

MICHAEL CORDNER is Reader in the Department of English and Related Literature at the University of York. He has edited editions of George Farquhar's *The Beaux' Stratagem*, the *Complete Plays* of Sir George Etherege, and *Four Comedies* of Sir John Vanbrugh. His editions include *Four Restoration Marriage Comedies* and he is completing a book on *The Comedy of Marriage 1660–1737*.

PETER HOLLAND is Professor of Shakespeare Studies and Director of the Shakespeare Institute, University of Birmingham.

MARTIN WIGGINS is a Fellow of the Shakespeare Institute and Lecturer in English at the University of Birmingham.

OXFORD ENGLISH DRAMA

J. M. Barrie
Peter Pan and Other Plays

Aphra Behn
The Rover and Other Plays

George Farquhar
The Recruiting Officer and Other Plays

John Ford
'Tis Pity She's a Whore and Other Plays

Ben Jonson
The Alchemist and Other Plays

Ben Jonson
The Devil is an Ass and Other Plays

D. H. Lawrence
The Widowing of Mrs Holroyd and Other Plays

Christopher Marlowe
Doctor Faustus and Other Plays

John Marston
The Malcontent and Other Plays

Thomas Middleton
Women Beware Women and Other Plays

A Mad World, My Masters and Other Plays

Richard Brinsley Sheridan
The School for Scandal and Other Plays

J. M. Synge
The Playboy of the Western World and Other Plays

John Webster
The Duchess of Malfi and Other Plays

Oscar Wilde
The Importance of Being Earnest and Other Plays

William Wycherley
The Country Wife and Other Plays

Court Masques
ed. David Lindley

Eighteenth-Century Women Dramatists
ed. Melinda Finberg

Five Romantic Plays
ed. Paul Baines and Edward Burns

Four Jacobean Sex Tragedies
ed. Martin Wiggins

Four Restoration Marriage Plays
ed. Michael Cordner

Four Revenge Tragedies
ed. Katharine Maus

London Assurance and Other Victorian Comedies
ed. Klaus Stierstorfer

The New Woman and Other Emancipated Woman Plays
ed. Jean Chothia

The Roaring Girl and Other City Comedies
ed. James Knowles and Eugenen Giddens

OXFORD WORLD'S CLASSICS

J. M. SYNGE

Riders to the Sea
The Shadow of the Glen
The Tinker's Wedding
The Well of the Saints
The Playboy of the Western World
Deirdre of the Sorrows

Edited with an Introduction and Notes by
ANN SADDLEMYER

OXFORD
UNIVERSITY PRESS

OXFORD
UNIVERSITY PRESS

Great Clarendon Street, Oxford OX2 6DP

Oxford University Press is a department of the University of Oxford.
It furthers the University's objective of excellence in research, scholarship,
and education by publishing worldwide in

Oxford New York

Auckland Bangkok Buenos Aires Cape Town Chennai
Dar es Salaam Delhi Hong Kong Istanbul Karachi Kolkata
Kuala Lumpur Madrid Melbourne Mexico City Mumbai Nairobi
São Paulo Shanghai Singapore Taipei Tokyo Toronto

with an associated company in Berlin

Oxford is a registered trade mark of Oxford University Press
in the UK and in certain other countries

Published in the United States
by Oxford University Press Inc., New York

First published as a World's Classics paperback 1995
Reissued as an Oxford World's Classics paperback 1998

British Library Cataloguing in Publication Data

Data available

Library of Congress Cataloging in Publication Data

Synge, J. M. (John Millington), 1871–1909.
The playboy of the western world & other plays / J. M. Synge.
p.   cm.—(Oxford World's classics)   1. Ireland—Drama.   I. Title.   II. Series.
822'.912—dc20   PR5532.P5   1995   94–34336

ISBN 0-19-283448-7

5 7 9 10 8 6 4

Printed in Great Britain by
Clays Ltd, St Ives plc

CONTENTS

ACKNOWLEDGEMENTS

As with my other work on John Millington Synge, I am indebted to the late Mrs Lilo Stephens and the Synge and Stephens families for their assistance and encouragement. Permission has been graciously granted by Miss Anne Yeats and Macmillan & Co. Ltd. for W. B. Yeats's Prefaces to *The Well of the Saints* and *Deirdre of the Sorrows*. I wish to thank also all those individuals and institutions who have through the years placed their knowledge and material at my disposal and whom I have had occasion to thank by name in previous editions of Synge's plays and letters. I hope they will realize how continuous their assistance has been throughout the years, and will accept my ongoing gratitude.

INTRODUCTION

Each work of art must have been possible to only one man at one period and in one place.'¹ This entry from an early notebook aptly describes not only John Millington Synge's personal aesthetic but also his contribution to the Irish dramatic movement at the beginning of the twentieth century. For there is more than a grain of truth in William Butler Yeats's assertion that the Abbey Theatre was 'Synge's theatre',² despite the heroic efforts of Lady Gregory and himself to keep it alive after their colleague's early death in 1909. Certainly in terms of numbers and variety Lady Gregory's contribution was immense; a good deal of Yeats's energy also went into 'theatre business, management of men'.³ But it was Synge's plays that provoked the greatest controversy and first received professional productions in other languages. And it is to Synge that critics now most frequently turn as the forerunner of contemporary dramatists such as Samuel Beckett.

It was not always so. When Yeats and Lady Gregory first met in 1896 and conceived the idea of a literary theatre which would encourage a national movement of the arts, thereby, in Lady Gregory's famous phrase, restoring to Ireland its native dignity, Synge was attempting to establish a career in Paris. He had originally planned to be a violinist and composer, and studied first at the Royal Irish Academy of Music, then for a year in Germany. But by 1895 he had switched his allegiance to languages, moving beyond the Irish and Hebrew he had studied at Trinity College to incorporate German, French, and Italian, with the vague intention of becoming European correspondent for various Irish and English journals. More important still, perhaps influenced by the courses he was taking at the Sorbonne and his reading of contemporary writers, he attempted some poetry

---

¹ Unless otherwise stated, all Synge's notebook entries are published in vol. ii of the *Works, J. M. Synge: Prose*, ed. Alan Price (Gerrards Cross: Colin Smythe, 1982), 347–51.
² Quoted by Joseph Holloway, *Joseph Holloway's Abbey Theatre: A Selection from his Unpublished Journal Impressions of a Dublin Playgoer*, ed. Robert Hogan and Michael J. O'Neill (Carbondale: Southern Illinois University Press, 1967), 172.
³ W. B. Yeats, 'All things can tempt me', *Collected Poems* (London: Macmillan, 1952), 109.

and impressionistic essays of his own. Always the student, he recorded in his diaries some visits to the theatre, but many more to art galleries; contemporaries recall his keen knowledge of the techniques of painting and print-making. Inevitably he was drawn into the group of Irish expatriates in Paris, and through them for a time dabbled in the study of socialism, nationalism, feminism, and even spiritualism—activities which were anathema to his staunchly Unionist, strictly Evangelical widowed mother, who nevertheless supported, even when she could not sympathize with or understand, her youngest son's determined individualism.[4]

Finally, late in 1896, these various interests conspired to introduce Synge to William Butler Yeats. Yeats's description of this meeting in the introduction to *The Well of the Saints* is well known, though it is probably oversimplified: 'I said: "Give up Paris. You will never create anything by reading Racine, and Arthur Symons will always be a better critic of French literature. Go to the Aran Islands. Live there as if you were one of the people themselves; express a life that has never found expression." '[5]

But Yeats's description of Ireland's westernmost islands struck a responsive chord: Synge was recovering from an unhappy love affair, was writing very little, and publishing less; classes at the Sorbonne had rekindled an interest in the currently popular Celtic movement; he was beginning to experience the first symptoms of the Hodgkin's disease which would eventually kill him; perhaps most influential of all, an uncle had been pastor on the islands some years before.

Even so, he moved with typical caution into the literary and nationalist circles made available to him by Yeats. Not for almost two years, in 1898, did he visit the Aran Islands for the first time and on the way back meet Lady Gregory at Coole. A few months later he ensured his continuing Europeanism by taking a permanent room in Paris, to which he returned every winter for the next five years. But from now on his time in Ireland would no longer be restricted to County Wicklow, where his mother regularly spent the summer months. For four more years he returned to Aran, renewing his knowledge of the Irish language and recording his experiences in

[4] See *The Collected Letters of John Millington Synge*, vols. i and ii, ed. Ann Saddlemyer (Oxford: Clarendon Press, 1983, 1984) for the most comprehensive biographical information. Unless otherwise indicated, all quotations from Synge's letters are from this edition.

[5] 'Mr Synge and his Plays', in *J. M. Synge: Plays Book I*, ed. Ann Saddlemyer (Gerrards Cross: Colin Smythe, 1982), 63.

numerous small notebooks. Back in Dublin he took an active interest in the experiments of the Irish Literary Theatre and the productions of a small nationalist company led by W. G. Fay. Inevitably he himself tried his hand at writing drama, first in verse, then with the ill-fated *When the Moon Has Set*, in which he rehearses with a more successful ending the saga of his courtship of a young woman rigidly adhering to the narrow faith he had earlier rejected.

Neither Yeats nor Lady Gregory would sanction the production of this first immature play, even though Synge revised it at least three times and left it among his papers at his death.[6] And nobody was prepared for the sudden outburst of creativity which, in the short space of six years, produced five more plays, a volume of poems, and two volumes of travel essays. During 1902 alone Synge began two verse plays set in County Wicklow, conceived the scenarios of several more, revised *When the Moon Has Set*, wrote *Riders to the Sea* and *The Shadow of the Glen*, embarked on *The Tinker's Wedding*, and produced various essays, reviews, and poems. Later that winter he sketched yet another verse play and began *The Well of the Saints* and *The Playboy of the Western World*. Ideas for plots flocked to his mind as he worked painstakingly at *The Playboy* and contemplated *Deirdre of the Sorrows*, a subject which had interested him as early as 1901, when he embarked on a translation of the Irish text while on the Aran Islands. In addition, as the only one of the three Directors now residing near Dublin, he became increasingly involved in the day-to-day running of the theatre, frequently serving as intermediary between a hasty-tempered Yeats and the equally temperamental company members.[7] Finally, when he became engaged to the actress Maire O'Neill (Molly Allgood), his fortunes were permanently tied to the Abbey Theatre and his years as a traveller and student in Europe were over.

It is not surprising, therefore, to find close relationships in the treatment of material and ideas in Synge's work, while at the same time observing a natural development in theatrical techniques. For although he brought with him the sensitivity to form and rhythm of

---

[6] The play was published for the first time in its final one-act form in *J. M. Synge: Plays Book I*, ed. Ann Saddlemyer (London: Oxford University Press, 1968). The earlier two-act version, with an introduction by Mary King, has since been published in *Long Room* (Dublin: Trinity College, 1982).

[7] *Theatre Business: The Correspondence of the First Abbey Theatre Directors*, ed. Ann Saddlemyer (Gerrards Cross: Colin Smythe, 1982) provides a detailed account of the early years of the dramatic movement.

a trained musician, the keen ear of a natural linguist, and an awareness of colour and line fröm his study of the visual arts, Synge had shown little interest in theatre before his meeting with Yeats. Even then it was several years before he attended the early productions of the Irish dramatic movement. But since boyhood he had travelled the roads of County Wicklow, relishing the idiosyncratic speech of the tramps and people of the glens and listening sympathetically to their stories. Out of that appreciation of their heightened sensitivity to the changing moods of nature and the harsh conditions they endured, Synge developed his own aesthetic, a blending of romantic pantheism and ironic realism. That mingling of what he described in his diary as 'humanity and this mysterious external world' accounts for much of the individuality of his writing. It accounts also for his insistence that all the notes must be played between tragedy and humour, for him the two poles of art and the mark of its sanity. As he expressed it in his Preface to *Poems and Translations*: 'There is no timber that has not strong roots among the clay and worms. Even if we grant that exalted poetry can be kept successful by itself, the strong things of life are needed in poetry also, to show that what is exalted, or tender, is not made by feeble blood. It may almost be said that before verse can be human again it must learn to be brutal.'[8]

It is equally clear from his notebooks and worksheets that Synge's original concepts and the incessant revising and meticulous polishing of each passage took place in the study, not on the stage. He rewrote each scene over and over again, polishing the phrasing, balancing the dialogue, clarifying the action, until he had achieved the strong stage play he required. Although he did most of his work at the typewriter, lettering the various drafts as he went along, he frequently jotted down phrases and related ideas, sometimes entire scenes, in one of the small notebooks he always carried with him; these fragments would then be worked into the fabric of the play. When he finally read the finished work to his colleagues, no revision beyond minor verbal alterations in rehearsal was possible; even the suggested alteration of a single passage would have upset the delicate balance of the whole. In an important sense, then, although Synge undoubtedly learned much from his experience as a Director of the theatre and adviser to

[8] *J. M. Synge: Poems*, ed. Robin Skelton (Gerrards Cross: Colin Smythe, 1982), p. xxxvi. For a discussion of Synge's theory, see Ann Saddlemyer, 'A Share in the Dignity of the World: J. M. Synge's Aesthetic Theory', in *The World of W. B. Yeats*, ed. Robin Skelton and Ann Saddlemyer (Dublin: Dolmen, and Seattle: University of Washington Press, 1965), 241–53.

would-be Abbey dramatists, play-writing remained for him very much the private composition of the lyric poet or musician, writing as much or more for the ear than the eye, imposing a balance of mood, tone, and colour on the material he distilled from the life about him rather than allowing characterization alone to control plot. In a letter to Frank Fay, one of the brothers responsible for the training of the company, he commented: 'The whole interest in our movement is that our little plays try to be literature first—i.e. to be personal, sincere, and beautiful—and drama afterwards.'

This does not mean that Synge did not become a practical man of the theatre. In a remarkably short time the musician and dilettante student of languages and literature turned into an alert producer, pointing his directions with an intimate knowledge of the stage, and punctuating rhetorically with an ear for the speech rhythms of the actor. But just as the dialogue was a distillation or selection from peasant speech rather than the idiom itself,[9] so the rhythms remained very much his own. Maire nic Shiubhlaigh, who created the roles of Nora Burke in *The Shadow of the Glen* and Bride in *The Well of the Saints*, recalls:

At first I found Synge's lines almost impossible to learn and deliver. Like the wandering ballad-singer I had to 'humour' them into a strange tune, changing the metre several times each minute. It was neither verse nor prose. The speeches had a musical lilt, absolutely different to anything I had heard before. Every passage brought some new difficulty and we would all stumble through the speeches until the tempo in which they were written was finally discovered. I found I had to break the sentences—which were uncommonly long—into sections, chanting them, slowly at first, then quickly as I became more familiar with the words.[10]

If the actors were plunged into a new, completely artificial though recognizable language, their roles were even more demanding, at times bewildering. Nothing in the plays of the early theatre movement prepared them for the people Synge created, and so there is a gradual increase in stage directions as the playwright came to grips with the problems of realizing his characters on stage. Because *The Tinker's Wedding* was not produced in his lifetime there are fewer written instructions, but *The Well of the Saints* provides rationalization for each change of mood. Then, by the time of *The Playboy of the Western*

---

[9] Alan Bliss summarizes this method and its effect in 'The Language of Synge', *J. M. Synge Centenary Papers*, ed. Maurice Harmon (Dublin: Dolmen, 1972), 35–62.
[10] Maire nic Shiubhlaigh and Edward Kenny, *The Splendid Years* (Dublin: Duffy, 1955), 42–3.

World, he had realized the necessity of choreographing not only every movement (note, for example, how the actress playing Pegeen is even told when to lick a stamp) but also each change in facial expression. Again, his worksheets are illuminating as he carefully plotted the 'currents' and 'crescendos' for each individual scene, as can be seen in these charts for early drafts of *The Well of the Saints* and *The Playboy of the Western World*:[11]

Analysis Well of Saints

Act I	1. Martin and Mary	Exposition of characters and psychics
	2. +Timmy crescendo narrative	comedy
	3. +girls current more Martin excitement	
	4. +Saint	
	5. minus Saint	
	6. quarrel	tragic
II	Timmy and Martin no current	comic
	2. Martin and Molly Love current	traPoetical
III	Martin and Mary current of reawakened interest	
	2. plus crowd current to make Martin recured	

[Analysis Playboy]

Act I	1 Pegeen and Shawn current her loneliness crescendo	comedy and locality

[11] These and other draft materials are published in the Appendixes to *J. M. Synge: Plays Books 1 and 2*.

Act I	2	Ditto and 3 men current keeping of Shawn climax	Molièrean climax of farce
	3	Ditto and Christy current (a) to find out his crime (b) to keep him exits climaxed by Shawn's	savoury dialogue
	4	Pegeen and Christy current (sub)—growing love interest	Poetical—to be very strong
	5	Ditto and Widow Quin current taking off of Christy	Rabelaisian—to be very strong
	6	Pegeen and Christy short finale	diminuendo ironical
II	1	solo Christy	character
	2	Christy and girls current (sub) of flattery	comedy
	3	Ditto and Pegeen short episode	comedy
	4	Pegeen Christy current his worked fear leading to second love stage	Poetical
	5	Shawn and Christy current Shawn's effort to get rid of him and Christy's pride	comedy
	6	Christy and Widow Quin current his getting away from her	comedy and character
	7	Ditto and Old Mahon current *opposition?*	stationary comedy

	8	Widow Quin and Christy
		current her effort to win him
		    her going over to him
		    his thanks etc.
			Poetical

III	1	Philly and Timmy and Old Mahon current Mahon	plot in comedy

III	2 interlude Mahon and Widow current she tries to get him off	Rabelaisian
	3 Christy and Pegeen current marriage hopes?	Poetical make her play round him a little at first to get the hook into him?
	4 Ditto and Michael James current opposition	Rabelaisian
	5 Ditto and crowd current Christy swears	drama
	6 Ditto and Old Mahon	drama
	7 finale	to be an elaborate mélange

When Synge wrote *Riders to the Sea* and *The Shadow of the Glen* he had still not seen the Fay brothers' company perform. But he had spent many weeks on the Aran Islands over the preceding five years, and he knew every inch of the Wicklow glens. With Yeats's support, both plays were immediately accepted by the small Theatre Society. Because alterations in staging were required for *Riders to the Sea*, the little Wicklow play, originally entitled *In the Shadow of the Glen*, was presented first. And with that production the long battle between Synge and the Irish nationalists began. The story of Synge's struggle—or rather Yeats's, for Synge did not actively participate beyond an insistence in the press that the original story had come from his old Irish teacher on Aran—has been fully documented elsewhere.[12] It seems likely, as Yeats and Lady Gregory always suspected, that the criticism was part of a premeditated nationalist attack on the entire theatre movement which began over Yeats's *The Countess Cathleen* in 1899, and was to flare up again over *The Playboy of the Western World* in 1907. But it is clear also that the Dublin audience, trained on traditional melodrama at the old Queen's Theatre and led to expect another 'Celtic' play in the Yeatsian tradition, were hardly prepared for the shock of reality to which Synge subjected them, a reality further emphasized by the produc-

[12] See *Laying the Foundations, 1902–1904* (Dublin: Dolmen, 1976) and *The Abbey Theatre: The Years of Synge, 1905–1909* (Dublin: Dolmen, 1978), both compiled by Robert Hogan and James Kilroy, for contemporary documents surrounding the productions of Synge's plays.

tion: Dan Burke's cottage was scrupulously copied from life and Synge, who knew well the actual building and site (Harneys' cottage in Glenmalure), could describe to the producer Willie Fay the exact setting:

His power of visualisation was perfect. . . . If I asked him, 'Was Dan standing where he is on the right, behind the table, when he said these lines?' he would say, 'No, he was on the right-hand side of the table with his hand on it.' He was a great joy to work with, for he had a keen sense of humour and plenty of patience, and above all he knew what he wanted, and when he got it said so.[13]

In the same play, that power of visualization created many amusing echoes between what the audience saw on stage and what it heard.

Similarly, *Riders to the Sea* was produced with as much authenticity as possible, Synge going so far as to order thick flannel and pampooties, the traditional Aran footgear, from the west. This fidelity and simplicity of design, developed for the most part in Synge's two shorter plays, combined to create the style of acting and production which became known as 'the Abbey method'. Although Lady Gregory was to make far more use of 'the Folk Play' than Synge, clearly his early work was the inspiration for, as much as it was the product of, the new movement in Irish drama. It is hardly surprising, therefore, that the audience, taken off guard by the realism of the productions in front of them, should accept literally the words and situations presented there. Eventually this method hampered Synge as well, for by the time he came to produce *The Playboy* his own theories had become more sophisticated, and neither the company nor the audience were trained to follow him.

Even before he had seen *Riders to the Sea* on stage, and perhaps as early as the first rehearsals of *The Shadow of the Glen*, Synge had begun work on *The Well of the Saints*. He finally finished the play in July 1904, but it was not produced until the following February, and in the meantime he had become embroiled in the problems of converting the theatre company from an amateur group playing in halls into a semi-professional limited society with its own theatre, a gift to Yeats and his ideals from the Englishwoman Annie Horniman. Caught between the narrow nationalist fervour of some of the actors and his own determination to present the play as he saw it, Synge spent more time with the company and took further responsibility for casting and rehearsing. He

[13] W. G. Fay and Catherine Carswell, *The Fays of the Abbey Theatre* (London: Rich and Cowan, 1935), 138–9.

had already been attacked by the players when several of the company, led by Maud Gonne, had ostentatiously walked out of the first performance of *The Shadow of the Glen*. Now more were objecting. Willie Fay complained of the consistent bad humour of the characters in *The Well of the Saints*, but Synge explained that he wanted to write 'like a monochrome painting, all in shades of one colour'.[14] To Frank Fay he wrote about a further complaint:

Tell Miss G[arvey].—or whoever it may be—that what I write of Irish country life I know to be true and I most emphatically will not change a syllable of it because A. B. or C. may think they know better than I do. . . . You understand my position: I am *quite ready* to avoid hurting people's feelings needlessly, but I will *not* falsify what I believe to be true for anybody. If one began that where would one end? I would rather drop play-writing altogether.

He provided brief notes for the company and, still dissatisfied, later experimented with the dialogue in his own copy of the play. When the play was revived in the spring of 1908 he revised the third act.[15]

Both audience and players also had difficulty with Synge's use of irony and the sudden sweep from the near-tragic to farce he had already introduced in *The Shadow of the Glen*. Now, in his first three-act work, he developed further the contrapuntal style which would become his trade-mark. But the deliberate play on dark and light, vision and revision, the contrast between the lyricism of blind Martin and Mary and the grotesquerie of their relationship with those who have their sight, are not easy for the audience. We are encouraged to laugh at that which normally incites pity, while at the same time we are seduced into acknowledging certain truths of human nature which do not always coincide with institutional authority. We are, in fact, constantly thrown off balance in our emotional responses to what we see before us, while being drawn in both by the charm of Synge's language and such atmospheric devices as the silence which surrounds the beginning of each act. We are literally forced to lean in and listen.

The riots provoked by *The Playboy of the Western World* on its first production in January 1907 most clearly emphasize this enforced attention and bewildering conflict of responses. Once again the

---

[14] Ibid. 167–8.
[15] See Nicholas Grene's edition of *The Well of the Saints* (Washington, DC: Catholic University of America Press, 1982) for a description of the Abbey Theatre prompt-book incorporating some of these changes.

playwright refused to allow emotions to blur the precision of his painfully acquired technique. The plot is based on a story current in Aran and strengthened by the notorious case of James Lynchehaun who, like the Aran refugee, had been harboured by peasants even though convicted of a brutal murder.[16] But far more of the flavour of the action and brilliance of language come from Synge's delight in County Kerry, which he visited annually from 1904. The earliest drafts of the play date from this time, but he was still frantically revising when rehearsals began. In October 1906 he wrote to Yeats:

My play, though in its last agony, is not finished and I cannot promise it for any definite day. It is more than likely that when I read it to you and Fay . . . there will be little things to alter that have escaped me. And with my stuff it takes time to get even half a page of new dialogue fully into key with what goes before it. The play, I think, will be one of the longest we have done, and in places extremely difficult.

When they did receive the finished play both Directors and cast expressed anxiety over the strong language. However, no one could have been prepared for the uproar, now almost legendary, that the first production of *The Playboy* created.[17] The opening-night audience, already made uneasy by disturbing rumours circulating about the play, erupted at the word 'shifts', the line being made even more explosive by Willie Fay's substitution of 'Mayo girls' for 'chosen females' in Christy's 'what'd I care if you brought me a drift of chosen females standing in their shifts itself'. On the second night an angry audience forced Lady Gregory to call in the police, and the actors were reduced to performing in dumb show. The following day, when Yeats returned from lecturing in Scotland, the three Directors decided as a matter of policy to continue the performances for the rest of the week, under police protection, until Synge's play was given its fair hearing. By the end of the week the players had earned their first uninterrupted performance, and on the following Monday Yeats invited those interested to a public debate on 'the freedom of the theatre'.

It is clear from the early drafts and many scenarios that Synge had some doubts as to the players' capacity to provide the deliberately

---

[16] Synge quotes the Aran version in *The Aran Islands* and Yeats also describes hearing it when he and Arthur Symons visited Aran in 1896, in his *Autobiographies* and his essay 'J. M. Synge and the Ireland of his Time'. See James Carney, *The Playboy and the Yellow Lady* (Dublin: Poolbeg Press, 1986), for the story of Lynchehaun.

[17] See James Kilroy (ed.), *The 'Playboy' Riots* (Dublin: Dolmen, 1971).

mannered production his concept of the play demanded. However, the violence of the attacks against him and his play upset him more than he was perhaps willing to admit. He denied the realism of the play, although Willie Fay's acting and production and further cutting by his colleagues tended to emphasize the realistic style of performance. He even went so far as to say in an interview that his play was 'a comedy, an extravaganza made to amuse'. He later retracted this in part by publishing a letter in the *Irish Times* claiming that there were 'several sides to "The Playboy" '. Privately he was more explicit. To a Scottish friend he wrote: 'As to the point you raise as to a possible want of contrast in the moral attitude of my people, I am doubtful myself. I feel the want, and yet my instinct when I am working is always towards keeping my characters bound together as far as possible in one mood.'

In response to a criticism forwarded by his American patron John Quinn he was even more emphatic:

He is quite right that early work, like 'Riders to the Sea', has a certain quality that more mature work is without. People who prefer the early quality are quite free to do so. When he blames the 'coarseness', however, I don't think he sees that the romantic note and a Rabelaisian note are working to a climax through a great part of the play, and that the Rabelaisian note, the 'gross' note, if you will, *must* have its climax no matter who may be shocked.

And to a young aspiring playwright he wrote, 'you see—what it seems so impossible to get our Dublin people to see, obvious as it is—that the wildness and, if you will, vices of the Irish peasantry are due, like their extraordinary good points of all kinds, to the *richness* of their nature—a thing that is priceless beyond words'.

In the more than a thousand typescript pages of *The Playboy* extant we can trace the deliberate development of this complex patterning. The title alone kept changing as Synge's concept of the play deepened, from 'The Murderer (a Farce)', then 'Murder Will Out', 'The Fool of the Family', 'The Fool of Farnham', to 'Christy Mahon', and, finally, 'The Playboy of the Western World', with all its accompanying ambiguities of meaning. Similarly, not only did the characterization of Christy expand, but that of the Widow Quin, who did not appear at all in the earliest drafts of the play, gradually developed out of Sally Quin, originally one of the village girls, when Synge discovered he needed a foil to Christy and a transition into Old Mahon's appearance. Apparently he then decided to develop the Widow as a foil to Pegeen also, becoming so interested in her that at one time she threatened to overturn the delicate balance between the two young lovers on the one hand, and the relationship between Christy and Old Mahon on the other. Finally he ruthlessly cut out entire scenes with the Widow Quin.[18] It is hardly surprising that the company and the audience found the complexities of the play bewildering.

But again, in his insistence on including the harshness and complexity of emotions in his plays, Synge was being true to his vision of life. There is a revealing passage in an early autobiographical fragment which casts some light on his methods of characterization as well as on his apparent diffidence over the extreme audience reaction to his work:

I studied the arabs of the streets . . . I remember coming out of St Patrick's, Sunday after Sunday, strained almost to torture by the music, and walking out through the slums of Harold's Cross as the lamps were being lit. Hordes of wild children used to play round the cathedral of St Patrick and I remember there was something appalling—a proximity of emotions as conflicting as the perversions of the Black Mass—in coming out suddenly from the white harmonies of the Passion according to St. Matthew among this blasphemy of childhood. . . . I often stood for hours in a shadow to watch their manoeuvres and extraordinarily passionate quarrels . . .

If we find in Bach an agreeable vibration of some portion of the brain and in the study of these children the vibration of another portion a little inferior—the attitude of science—we loose [sic] in the music our transcendent admiration, and in the slums the ecstasy of pity and with it the thin relish of delightful sympathy with the wildness of evil which all feel but few acknowledge even to themselves.[19]

It could well be that the uproar over *The Playboy of the Western World* influenced Synge's decision to publish *The Tinker's Wedding* later that year, after six complete drafts in as many years. But the Directors still hesitated to produce it at the Abbey, fearing a further uproar over the treatment of the priest and, perhaps, the frankness of Mary Byrne. What could be read with equanimity in Douglas Hyde's translations of Irish folk writing was a different matter when presented visually in a theatre, especially one as intimate as the Abbey. Despite Synge's placatory introduction to the text, the play would not be professionally produced in Ireland until 1963.

---

[18] See the notes and Appendix to *Plays Book II* for some of the passages Synge finally deleted.

[19] *J. M. Synge: Prose*, 6.

However, by this time Synge was already at work on *Deirdre of the Sorrows*, although slowed down by the Hodgkin's disease which was to kill him less than two years later. To John Quinn he enlarged on the difficulties of a new medium:

I don't know whether I told you that I am trying a three-act prose 'Deirdre', to change my hand. I am not sure yet whether I shall be able to make a satisfactory play out of it. These saga people, when one comes to deal with them, seem very remote; one does not know what they thought or what they are or where they went to sleep, so one is apt to fall into rhetoric. In any case, I find it an interesting experiment, full of new difficulties, and I shall be the better, I think, for the change.

Daily letters to Molly Allgood record his struggles with the new play. In December 1906, while still working frantically on *The Playboy* in which she was to play Pegeen, he had written: 'My next play must be quite different from the P. Boy. I want to do something quiet and stately and restrained and I want you to act in it.' Almost a year later he was still making major revisions to the scenario and just completing the first rough draft of the play. Further illness intervened, however, and when Synge entered hospital for the last time he was still altering the action, strengthening various motifs, and reworking the characterization. He died on 24 March 1909; on the back of a fragment of Deirdre's keen over the grave of Naisi are scribbled the words: 'Unfinish[ed] play of "Deirdre", can be sent if desired to Mr W. B. Yeats.'

It would be a mistake to assume, then, that the play as it now stands is any more than half finished, either in mood or characterization. Synge was fairly well satisfied with the third act, and thought the first act 'worth keeping', although certain specific alterations were required. His notebooks during the final months of revisions show many changes as he sought to strengthen Owen's role in an effort to balance the 'poetic' with the 'Rabelaisian' and to provide a spectrum of responses to love and the passage of time.[20] According to Yeats, Synge several times during his final illness asked that his fellow directors should 'finish' the play, bringing Owen into the action of the first act and giving him more business in the second. During the summer of 1909 Yeats, Lady Gregory, and Molly Allgood worked on the manuscript, trying to determine some order and form from the

[20] The relationship between Synge's aesthetic theory and his range of characterization is discussed in Ann Saddlemyer, '*Deirdre of the Sorrows*: "Literature First . . . Drama Afterwards" ', *J. M. Synge Centenary Papers 1971* (Dublin: Dolmen, 1972).

thousand typescript pages. But finally they decided to produce the play without any additional material or alterations, and the same assemblage of manuscripts was used for its first publication. The present edition takes into account additional notebook material belonging to Synge's last revisions of this play.

John Millington Synge's creative life was brief, but it resulted in some of the finest examples in the twentieth century of both tragedy and comedy, and anticipated the experiments of later playwrights (and even the later Yeats) with form, language, style, and theatrical practice. As one of the early founders of the Abbey Theatre, his role in theatre history is assured. As a playwright of astonishing originality and sensitivity, his works continue to challenge and refresh.

NOTE ON THE TEXTS

The copy text used for all plays is that of *J. M. Synge: Plays*, ed. Ann Saddlemyer (Oxford University Press, 1968), which was based on an examination of every available draft of each play, as well as scenarios, worksheets, and notebooks. A more recent edition by Nicholas Grene of *The Well of the Saints* (Washington, DC: Catholic University of America Press, 1982) offers variants based on a prompt-book and typescript versions of several scenes which were subsequently discovered in the Abbey Theatre. I have referred to this edition in the Explanatory Notes where it differs from the copy text.

Other works which offer valuable glosses on the texts are T. R. Henn, *Plays and Poems of J. M. Synge* (London: Methuen, 1963), Declan Kiberd, *Synge and the Irish Language* (London: Macmillan, 1979), and Alan Bliss, 'A Synge Glossary', in *Sunshine and the Moon's Delight*, ed. S. B. Bushrui (Gerrards Cross: Colin Smythe, 1972), 297–316.

SELECT BIBLIOGRAPHY

The works of J. M. Synge, containing much new manuscript material, were published in four volumes by Oxford University Press: *Poems* (ed. Robin Skelton, 1962), *Prose* (ed. Alan Price, 1966), and *Plays 1 and 2* (ed. Ann Saddlemyer, 1968), which published for the first time *When the Moon Has Set*, worksheets, and scenarios. A new edition of these four volumes, with minor revisions to the volumes of plays, was published by Colin Smythe Ltd. in 1982. (In the notes, this edition is referred to as *Works* with the appropriate volume number.) *The Collected Letters of J. M. Synge*, edited by Ann Saddlemyer, were published in two volumes in 1983 and 1984, also by Oxford University Press. The new material made accessible by these publications has somewhat superseded the standard biography by D. H. Greene and E. M. Stephens, *J. M. Synge, 1871–1909* (New York: Macmillan, 1959; rev. edn. 1989), as has the edition by Andrew Carpenter of the material in E. M. Stephens's unpublished biography not incorporated by David Greene, entitled *My Uncle John: Edward Stephens's Life of J. M. Synge* (London: Oxford University Press, 1974).

Of the earlier critical studies, Maurice Bourgeois's *John Millington Synge and the Irish Theatre* (London: Constable, 1913) and Una Ellis Fermor's *The Irish Dramatic Movement* (London: Methuen, 1939) are still valuable for their attempts to place Synge's work in a larger context, while T. R. Henn's edition of *J. M. Synge: The Complete Plays* (London: Eyre Methuen, 1963) offers many insights into Synge's Anglo-Irish background and travels in Wicklow and the west.

The many studies published once the manuscript material was made available include works by all three editors—Alan Price, *Synge and Anglo-Irish Drama* (London: Methuen, 1961); Ann Saddlemyer, ' "A Share in the Dignity of the World": J. M. Synge's Aesthetic Theory', in *The World of W. B. Yeats*, ed. Robin Skelton and Ann Saddlemyer (Dublin: Dolmen, and Seattle: University of Washington Press, 1965) and *J. M. Synge and Modern Comedy* (Dublin: Dolmen, 1968); Robin Skelton, *J. M. Synge and his World* (London: Thames and Hudson, 1971) and *The Writings of J. M. Synge* (London: Thames and Hudson, 1971). Three editions in particular should be noted for their use of the Synge manuscripts: Nicholas Grene's *The Well of the Saints* (Washington, DC: Catholic University of America

Press, 1982); Malcolm Kelsall's *The Playboy of the Western World* (London: Earnest Benn, 1975); Mary King's two-act version of *When the Moon Has Set* in *Long Room* [Trinity College, Dublin], 24–5 (1982). Donna Gerstenberger offered a scholarly evaluation for Twayne's English Authors Series, *John Millington Synge* (New York: Twayne, 1964; rev. edn. 1990), and Denis Johnston provided a refreshing overview in the Columbia Essays on Modern Writers series, *John Millington Synge* (New York: Columbia University Press, 1965). However, the most innovative and original full-length studies in recent years have come from younger scholars: Nicholas Grene, *Synge: A Critical Study of the Plays* (London: Macmillan, 1975); Toni O'Brien Johnson, *Synge: The Medieval and the Grotesque* (Gerrards Cross: Colin Smythe, 1982); Declan Kiberd, *Synge and the Irish Language* (London: Macmillan, 1979; Mary C. King, *The Drama of J. M. Synge* (London: Fourth Estate, 1985); Weldon Thornton, *J. M. Synge and the Western Mind* (Gerrards Cross: Colin Smythe, 1979).

The centenary of Synge's birth produced two collections of essays by scholars from around the world: *Synge Centenary Essays*, ed. Maurice Harmon (Dublin: Dolmen, 1971) and *Sunshine and the Moon's Delight*, ed. S. B. Bushrui (Gerrards Cross: Colin Smythe, 1972), both of which include chapters by Alan J. Bliss on Synge's use of the Irish language. Ronald Ayling (ed.), *J. M. Synge: Four Plays* (London and Basingstoke: Macmillan, 1992), is a selection of critical essays on *Riders to the Sea*, *The Well of the Saints*, *The Playboy of the Western World*, and *Deirdre of the Sorrows*. Casebooks on individual plays include David R. Clark (ed.), *John Millington Synge: Riders to the Sea* (Columbus: Charles E. Merrill, 1970) and Thomas R. Whitaker (ed.), *The Playboy of the Western World: A Collection of Critical Essays* (Englewood Cliffs, NJ: Prentice-Hall, 1969). For a thorough review of more recent books and articles published on Synge, see in particular Weldon Thornton's contributions to *Anglo-Irish Literature: A Review of Research* and *Recent Research on Anglo-Irish Writers: A Supplement*, both edited by Richard J. Finneran, and published by the Modern Language Association of America in 1976 and 1983 respectively. Edward A. Kopper, Jr. has edited *A J. M. Synge Literary Companion* (Westport, Conn.: Greenwood Press, 1988), which, in addition to new assessments of all of Synge's works, offers a bibliography and suggestions as to the direction future scholarship might take.

Further valuable material on Synge's sources can be found in James Carney's *The Playboy and the Yellow Lady* (Dublin: Poolbeg Press,

1986); Lady Gregory, *Cuchulain of Muirthemne* (Gerrards Cross: Colin Smythe, 1970); and Douglas Hyde, *The Love Songs of Connacht* (London: Dublin, 1893). For background on the Irish dramatic movement and Synge's role in it, see Lady Gregory's *Our Irish Theatre* (London: Putnam's, 1913); Ann Saddlemyer (ed.), *Theatre Business: The Correspondence of the First Abbey Theatre Directors* (Gerrards Cross: Colin Smythe, 1982); the first four volumes of *The Modern Irish Drama*, compiled by Robert Hogan, James Kilroy, and associates (Dublin: Dolmen, 1975–9); and James Kilroy (ed.), *The 'Playboy' Riots* (Dublin: Dolmen, 1971).

A CHRONOLOGY OF J. M. SYNGE

1871   16 April, born, youngest child of John Hatch and Kathleen (Traill) Synge, at 2 Newtown Villas, Rathfarnham, Dublin; his father dies of smallpox a year later.

1881–8   After four years of irregular attendance at private schools because of illness, receives tutoring at home.

1889   Enrols in Trinity College, Dublin, in February and in the Royal Irish Academy of Music in November.

1891   Joins student orchestra at the Academy; plays in first concert; studies German.

1892   Awarded scholarship and medal in counterpoint at the Academy; takes first place in examinations in Hebrew and Irish at Trinity.

1893   After a summer in County Wicklow with his mother, goes to Germany to study violin and piano.

1894   Begins to write his first play (uncompleted) and turns from study of music to literature; spends summer in County Wicklow.

1895   Enrols at the Sorbonne in courses in French language and literature; returns to County Wicklow for the summer.

1896   Spends three months studying art and literature in Italy; after summer in Wicklow returns to Paris to study at the Sorbonne; on 21 December meets W. B. Yeats.

1897   Summer in Wicklow; operation on swollen gland in December (first indication of Hodgkin's disease, as yet undiagnosed).

1898   To Paris and the Sorbonne, studying Irish and Homeric civilizations under d'Arbois de Jubainville. From 10 May to 25 June visits Aran Islands for first time, followed by first visit to Coole before summer in Wicklow; in November he rents the room which will be his permanent address in Paris until 1903 and begins studying Breton; publishes the first of his articles on Aran.

1899   Visits Quimper, Brittany, in April before returning to Dublin, where he attends the Irish Literary Theatre production of Yeats's *The Countess Cathleen* before spending the summer in Wicklow; after three-and-a-half weeks on Inishmaan, returns to Paris in November.

1900   After summer in Wicklow, spends a month on Inishmaan, returning to Paris in November.

1901   After summer in Wicklow, spends a week at Coole with Lady Gregory and Yeats, then to Aran for a month, returning to Dublin to attend the Irish Literary Theatre production of Yeats and Moore's *Diarmuid and Grania* and Hyde's *Casadh an tSugain*; returns to Paris via London with MS of *The Aran Islands*.

1902   Studies Old Irish at the Sorbonne and begins writing verse plays; writes *Riders to the Sea*, *The Shadow of the Glen*, and the first draft of *The Tinker's Wedding* while in Wicklow before spending three weeks on Inishere, his last visit to Aran; in Dublin in December sees W. G. Fay's company perform for the first time.

1903 Spends January to mid-March in London, before crossing to Paris (where he spends time with James Joyce) to give up his room; back in Dublin completes *When the Moon Has Set* and spends three weeks in September in County Kerry. In October *Riders to the Sea* is published and *In the Shadow of the Glen* produced by W. G. Fay's Irish National Theatre Society.

1904 In February *Riders to the Sea* is produced by the Irish National Theatre Society and both one-act plays are taken to London in March; in July spends two weeks at Coole helping Lady Gregory with her play *Kincora* before travelling in County Kerry and North Mayo; *The Shadow of the Glen* published in December.

1905 *The Well of the Saints* produced and published in February; in June tours the Congested Districts of the west of Ireland with Jack Yeats, publishing twelve articles for the *Manchester Guardian*; spends six weeks in West Kerry and the Blasket Islands in August to mid-September; on 22 September is elected one of the directors of the Irish National Theatre Ltd.

1906 Performances of Max Meyerfeld's translation of *The Well of the Saints* in Berlin in January and Karel Musek's translation of *The Shadow of the Glen* in Prague in February; travels with company on tours in Ireland and England; visits County Kerry for three weeks in August and September.

1907 Publication and performance of *The Playboy of the Western World* in January with unruly audiences for a week: *The Aran Islands* is published in April; his engagement to Molly Allgood, who played Pegeen Mike, is officially recognized and they holiday in Wicklow in July; operation to remove swollen glands on his neck in September; asthma attack cuts short his last visit to Kerry; *The Tinker's Wedding* published in December but considered 'too dangerous' for production at the Abbey Theatre.

1908 While making preparations for his marriage he directs Lady Gregory's translations of Sudermann's *Teja* and Molière's *The Rogueries of Scapin* before undergoing an abdominal operation on 5 May; is not told of discovery of inoperable tumour; while in Germany convalescing and visiting old friends in October his mother dies.

1909 Dies on 24 March, three weeks before his thirty-eighth birthday; *Poems and Translations* published in June.

1910 *Deirdre of the Sorrows*, in a script assembled by Molly, Lady Gregory, and Yeats, produced in January with Molly as Deirdre, and published in July; *The Works of John M. Synge*, in four volumes, published in November.

RIDERS TO THE SEA

A Play in One Act

(1900–1905)

PERSONS

MAURYA, an old woman
BARTLEY, her son
CATHLEEN, her daughter
NORA, a younger daughter
MEN AND WOMEN

SCENE

An Island off the West of Ireland°

FIRST PRODUCTION
(Dublin, 25 February 1904)

Maurya	Honor Lavelle
Bartley	W. G. Fay
Cathleen	Sara Allgood
Nora	Emma Vernon
Men and Women	P. J. Kelly, Seamus O'Sullivan, George Roberts, Maire Nic Shiubhlaigh, Maire Ni Gharbhaigh, and Doreen Gunning

Cottage kitchen, with nets, oil-skins, spinning wheel, some new boards standing by the wall, etc. Cathleen, a girl of about twenty, finishes kneading cake, and puts it down in the pot-oven°by the fire; then wipes her hands, and begins to spin at the wheel. Nora, a young girl, puts her head in at the door

NORA [*in a low voice*] Where is she?

CATHLEEN She's lying down, God help her, and maybe sleeping, if she's able.

[*Nora comes in softly, and takes a bundle from under her shawl*]

CATHLEEN [*spinning the wheel rapidly*] What is it you have?

NORA The young priest is after bringing them. It's a shirt and a plain stocking were got off a drowned man in Donegal.° 5

[*Cathleen stops her wheel with a sudden movement, and leans out° to listen*]

NORA We're to find out if it's Michael's they are, some time herself will be down looking by the sea.

CATHLEEN How would they be Michael's, Nora. How would he go the length of that way to the far north? 10

NORA The young priest says he's known the like of it. 'If it's Michael's they are,' says he, 'you can tell herself he's got a clean burial by the grace of God, and if they're not his, let no one say a word about them, for she'll be getting her death,' says he, 'with crying and lamenting.' 15

[*The door which Nora half closed behind her is blown open by a gust of wind*]

CATHLEEN [*looking out anxiously*] Did you ask him would he stop Bartley going this day with the horses to the Galway fair?°

NORA 'I won't stop him,' says he, 'but let you not be afraid. Herself does be saying prayers half through the night, and the Almighty God won't leave her destitute,' says he, 'with no son living.' 20

CATHLEEN Is the sea bad by the white rocks, Nora?

NORA Middling bad, God help us. There's a great roaring in the west, and it's worse it'll be getting when the tide's turned to the wind.°
[*She goes over to the table with the bundle*] Shall I open it now?

CATHLEEN Maybe she'd wake up on us, and come in before we'd 25 done [*coming to the table*] It's a long time we'll be, and the two of us crying.

NORA [*goes to the inner door and listens*] She's moving about on the bed. She'll be coming in a minute.

CATHLEEN Give me the ladder, and I'll put them up in the turf-loft,° 30
the way° she won't know of them at all, and maybe when the tide turns she'll be going down to see would he be floating from the east.
[*They put the ladder against the gable of the chimney; Cathleen goes up a few steps and hides the bundle in the turf-loft. Maurya comes from the inner room*]

MAURYA [*looking up at Cathleen and speaking querulously*] Isn't it turf enough you have for this day and evening?

CATHLEEN There's a cake baking at the fire for a short space 35
[*throwing down the turf*], and Bartley will want it when the tide turns if he goes to Connemara.
[*Nora picks up the turf and puts it round the pot-oven*]

MAURYA [*sitting down on a stool at the fire*] He won't go this day with the wind rising from the south and west. He won't go this day, for the young priest will stop him surely. 40

NORA He'll not stop him, mother, and I heard Eamon Simon and Stephen Pheety and Colum Shawn saying he would go.

MAURYA Where is he itself?

NORA He went down to see would there be another boat sailing in the week, and I'm thinking it won't be long till he's here now, 45
for the tide's turning at the green head,° and the hooker's tacking from the east.°

CATHLEEN I hear some one passing the big stones.

NORA [*looking out*] He's coming now, and he in a hurry.

BARTLEY [*comes in and looks round the room; speaking sadly and quietly*] 50
Where is the bit of new rope, Cathleen, was bought in Connemara?

CATHLEEN [*coming down*] Give it to him, Nora; it's on a nail by the white boards. I hung it up this morning, for the pig with the black feet was eating it.°

NORA [*giving him a rope*] Is that it, Bartley? 55

MAURYA [*as before*] You'd do right to leave that rope, Bartley, hanging by the boards. [*Bartley takes the rope*] It will be wanting in this place, I'm telling you, if Michael is washed up tomorrow morning, or the next morning, or any morning in the week, for it's a deep grave we'll make him by the grace of God. 60

BARTLEY [*beginning to work with the rope*] I've no halter the way I can ride down on the mare, and I must go now quickly. This is the one boat going for two weeks or beyond it, and the fair will be a good fair for horses I heard them saying below.

MAURYA It's a hard thing they'll be saying below if the body is 65
washed up and there's no man in it to make the coffin, and I after
giving a big price for the finest white boards you'd find in
Connemara.° [*She looks round at the boards*]

BARTLEY How would it be washed up, and we after looking each day
for nine days, and a strong wind blowing a while back from the 70
west and south?

MAURYA If it isn't found itself, that wind is raising the sea, and there
was a star up against the moon, and it rising in the night. If it was
a hundred horses, or a thousand horses you had itself, what is the
price of a thousand horses against a son where there is one son 75
only?

BARTLEY [*working at the halter, to Cathleen*] Let you go down each
day, and see the sheep aren't jumping in on the rye, and if the
jobber° comes you can sell the pig with the black feet if there is a
good price going. 80

MAURYA How would the like of her get a good price for a pig?

BARTLEY [*to Cathleen*] If the west wind holds with the last bit of the
moon let you and Nora get up weed enough for another cock for
the kelp.° It's hard set we'll be from this day with no one in it but
one man to work. 85

MAURYA It's hard set we'll be surely the day you're drown'd with
the rest. What way will I live and the girls with me, and I an old
woman looking for the grave?

[*Bartley lays down the halter, takes off his old coat, and puts on
a newer one of the same flannel*]

BARTLEY [*to Nora*] Is she coming to the pier?

NORA [*looking out*] She's passing the green head and letting fall her 90
sails.

BARTLEY [*getting his purse and tobacco*] I'll have half an hour to go
down, and you'll see me coming again in two days, or in three
days, or maybe in four days if the wind is bad.

MAURYA [*turning round to the fire, and putting her shawl over her head*] 95
Isn't it a hard and cruel man won't hear a word from an old
woman, and she holding him from the sea?

CATHLEEN It's the life of a young man to be going on the sea, and
who would listen to an old woman with one thing and she saying
it over? 100

BARTLEY [*taking the halter*] I must go now quickly. I'll ride down on
the red mare, and the grey pony'll run behind me. . . . The
blessing of God on you. [*He goes out*]

MAURYA [*crying out as he is in the door way*] He's gone now, God spare us, and we'll not see him again. He's gone now, and when the black night is falling I'll have no son left me in the world.

CATHLEEN Why wouldn't you give him your blessing and he looking round in the door? Isn't it sorrow enough is on every one in this house without your sending him out with an unlucky word behind him, and a hard word in his ear?°
[*Maurya takes up the tongs and begins raking the fire aimlessly without looking round*]

NORA [*turning towards her*] You're taking away the turf from the cake.

CATHLEEN [*crying out*] The Son of God forgive us, Nora, we're after forgetting his bit of bread. [*She comes over to the fire*]

NORA And it's destroyed° he'll be going till dark night, and he after eating nothing since the sun went up.

CATHLEEN [*turning the cake out of the oven*] It's destroyed he'll be, surely. There's no sense left on any person in a house where an old woman will be talking forever.
[*Maurya sways herself on her stool*]

CATHLEEN [*cutting off some of the bread and rolling it in a cloth, to Maurya*] Let you go down now to the spring well and give him this and he passing. You'll see him then and the dark word will be broken, and you can say 'God speed you', the way he'll be easy in his mind.

MAURYA [*taking the bread*] Will I be in it as soon as himself?

CATHLEEN If you go now quickly.

MAURYA [*standing up unsteadily*] It's hard set I am to walk.

CATHLEEN [*looking at her anxiously*] Give her the stick, Nora, or maybe she'll slip on the big stones.

NORA What stick?

CATHLEEN The stick Michael brought from Connemara.

MAURYA [*taking a stick Nora gives her*] In the big world° the old people do be leaving things after them for their sons and children, but in this place it is the young men do be leaving things behind for them that do be old. [*She goes out slowly*]
[*Nora goes over to the ladder*]

CATHLEEN Wait, Nora, maybe she'd turn back quickly. She's that sorry, God help her, you wouldn't know the thing she'd do.°

NORA Is she gone round by the bush?

CATHLEEN [*looking out*] She's gone now. Throw it down quickly, for the Lord knows when she'll be out of it again.

NORA [*getting the bundle from the loft*] The young priest said he'd be passing tomorrow,° and we might go down and speak to him below if it's Michael's they are surely.

CATHLEEN [*taking the bundle from Nora*] Did he say what way they were found? 145

NORA [*coming down*] 'There were two men,' says he, 'and they rowing round with poteen° before the cocks crowed, and the oar of one of them caught the body, and they passing the black cliffs of the north.'

CATHLEEN [*trying to open the bundle*] Give me a knife, Nora, the 150 string's perished with the salt water, and there's a black knot on it you wouldn't loosen in a week.°

NORA [*giving her a knife*] I've heard tell it was a long way to Donegal.

CATHLEEN [*cutting the string*] It is surely. There was a man in here a while ago—the man sold us that knife—and he said if you set off 155 walking from the rocks beyond, it would be in seven days you'd be in Donegal.

NORA And what time would a man take, and he floating?

[*Cathleen opens the bundle and takes out a bit of a shirt and a stocking. They look at them eagerly*]

CATHLEEN [*in a low voice*] The Lord spare us, Nora! Isn't it a queer hard thing° to say if it's his they are surely? 160

NORA I'll get his shirt off the hook the way we can put the one flannel on the other. [*She looks through some clothes hanging in the corner*] It's not with them, Cathleen, and where will it be?

CATHLEEN I'm thinking Bartley put it on him in the morning, for his own shirt was heavy with the salt in it. [*Pointing to the corner*] 165 There's a bit of a sleeve was of the same stuff. Give me that and it will do.

[*Nora brings it to her and they compare the flannel*]

CATHLEEN It's the same stuff, Nora; but if it is itself aren't there great rolls of it in the shops of Galway, and isn't it many another man may have a shirt of it as well as Michael himself? 170

NORA [*who has taken up the stocking and counted the stitches, crying out*] It's Michael, Cathleen, it's Michael; God spare his soul, and what will herself say when she hears this story, and Bartley on the sea?

CATHLEEN [*taking the stocking*] It's a plain stocking.

NORA It's the second one of the third pair I knitted, and I put up 175 three score stitches, and I dropped four of them.

CATHLEEN [*counts the stitches*] It's that number is in it. [*Crying out*] Ah, Nora, isn't it a bitter thing to think of him floating that way

to the far north, and no one to keen° him but the black hags° that
do be flying on the sea?   180

NORA [*swinging herself round and throwing out her arms on the clothes*]
And isn't it a pitiful thing when there is nothing left of a man who
was a great rower and fisher, but a bit of an old shirt and a plain
stocking?

CATHLEEN [*after an instant*] Tell me is herself coming, Nora? I hear   185
a little sound on the path.

NORA [*looking out*] She is, Cathleen. She's coming up to the door.

CATHLEEN Put these things away before she'll come in. Maybe it's
easier she'll be after giving her blessing to Bartley, and we won't
let on we've heard anything the time he's on the sea.   190

NORA [*helping Cathleen to close the bundle*] We'll put them here in the
corner. [*They put them into a hole in the chimney corner. Cathleen
goes back to the spinning-wheel*]

NORA Will she see it was crying I was?

CATHLEEN Keep your back to the door the way the light'll not be on   195
you.

> [*Nora sits down at the chimney corner, with her back to the door.
> Maurya comes in very slowly, without looking at the girls, and
> goes over to her stool at the other side of the fire. The cloth with
> the bread is still in her hand. The girls look at each other, and
> Nora points to the bundle of bread*]

CATHLEEN [*after spinning for a moment*] You didn't give him his bit
of bread?

> [*Maurya begins to keen softly, without turning round*]

CATHLEEN Did you see him riding down?

> [*Maurya goes on keening*]

CATHLEEN [*a little impatiently*] God forgive you; isn't it a better   200
thing to raise your voice and tell what you seen, than to be making
lamentation for a thing that's done? Did you see Bartley, I'm
saying to you.

MAURYA [*with a weak voice*] My heart's broken from this day.

CATHLEEN [*as before*] Did you see Bartley?   205

MAURYA I seen the fearfullest thing.

CATHLEEN [*leaves her wheel and looks out*] God forgive you; he's
riding the mare now over the green head, and the grey pony
behind him.

MAURYA [*starts, so that her shawl falls back from her head and shows   210
her white tossed hair. With a frightened voice*] The grey pony behind
him . . .

CATHLEEN [*coming to the fire*] What is it ails you, at all?

MAURYA [*speaking very slowly*] I've seen the fearfullest thing any
person has seen, since the day Bride Dara seen the dead man with   215
the child in his arms.°

CATHLEEN and NORA Uah. [*They crouch down in front of the old
woman at the fire*]

NORA Tell us what it is you seen.

MAURYA I went down to the spring well, and I stood there saying a   220
prayer to myself. Then Bartley came along, and he riding on the
red mare with the grey pony behind him [*she puts up her hands,
as if to hide something from her eyes*] The Son of God spare us,
Nora!

CATHLEEN What is it you seen?   225

MAURYA I seen Michael himself.

CATHLEEN [*speaking softly*] You did not, mother; it wasn't Michael
you seen, for his body is after being found in the far north, and
he's got a clean burial by the grace of God.

MAURYA [*a little defiantly*] I'm after seeing him this day, and he   230
riding and galloping. Bartley came first on the red mare; and I tried
to say 'God speed you,' but something choked the words in my
throat. He went by quickly; and 'the blessing of God on you,' says
he, and I could say nothing. I looked up then, and I crying, at the
grey pony, and there was Michael upon it°—with fine clothes on   235
him, and new shoes on his feet.°

CATHLEEN [*begins to keen*] It's destroyed we are from this day. It's
destroyed, surely.°

NORA Didn't the young priest say the Almighty God won't leave her
destitute with no son living?   240

MAURYA [*in a low voice, but clearly*] It's little the like of him knows
of the sea. . . . Bartley will be lost now, and let you call in Eamon
and make me a good coffin out of the white boards, for I won't live
after them. I've had a husband, and a husband's father, and six
sons in this house—six fine men, though it was a hard birth I had   245
with every one of them and they coming to the world—and some
of them were found and some of them were not found, but they're
gone now the lot of them. . . . There were Stephen, and Shawn,
were lost in the great wind, and found after in the Bay of Gregory
of the Golden Mouth,° and carried up the two of them on one   250
plank, and in by that door.

[*She pauses for a moment; the girls start as if they heard
something through the door that is half open behind them*]

9

NORA [*in a whisper*] Did you hear that, Cathleen? Did you hear a noise in the north-east?

CATHLEEN [*in a whisper*] There's some one after crying out by the seashore.   255

MAURYA [*continues without hearing anything*] There was Sheamus and his father, and his own father again, were lost in a dark night, and not a stick or sign was seen of them when the sun went up. There was Patch after was drowned out of a curagh° that turned over. I was sitting here with Bartley, and he a baby, lying on my   260 two knees, and I seen two women, and three women, and four women coming in, and they crossing themselves, and not saying a word. I looked out then, and there were men coming after them, and they holding a thing in the half of a red sail, and water dripping out of it—it was a dry day, Nora—and leaving a track to   265 the door.

> [*She pauses again with her hand stretched out towards the door. It opens softly and old women begin to come in, crossing themselves on the threshold, and kneeling down in front of the stage with red petticoats over their heads*°]

MAURYA [*half in a dream, to Cathleen*] Is it Patch, or Michael, or what is it at all?

CATHLEEN Michael is after being found in the far north, and when he is found there how could he be here in this place?   270

MAURYA There does be a power of young men floating round in the sea, and what way would they know if it was Michael they had, or another man like him, for when a man is nine days in the sea, and the wind blowing, it's hard set his own mother would be to say what man was in it.   275

CATHLEEN It's Michael, God spare him, for they're after sending us a bit of his clothes from the far north.

> [*She reaches out and hands Maurya the clothes that belonged to Michael. Maurya stands up slowly, and takes them in her hands. Nora looks out*]

NORA They're carrying a thing among them and there's water dripping out of it and leaving a track by the big stones.

CATHLEEN [*in a whisper to the women who have come in*] Is it Bartley   280 it is?

ONE OF THE WOMEN It is surely, God rest his soul.

> [*Two younger women come in and pull out the table. Then men carry in the body of Bartley, laid on a plank, with a bit of a sail over it, and lay it on the table*]

CATHLEEN [*to the women, as they are doing so*] What way was he drowned?

ONE OF THE WOMEN The grey pony knocked him over into the sea, 285
and he was washed out where there is a great surf on the white rocks.

> [*Maurya has gone over and knelt down at the head of the table. The women are keening softly and swaying themselves with a slow movement. Cathleen and Nora kneel at the other end of the table. The men kneel near the door*]

MAURYA [*raising her head and speaking as if she did not see the people around her*] They're all gone now, and there isn't anything more the sea can do to me. . . . I'll have no call now to° be up crying 290
and praying when the wind breaks from the south, and you can hear the surf is in the east, and the surf is in the west, making a great stir with the two noises, and they hitting one on the other. I'll have no call now to be going down and getting Holy Water in the dark nights after Samhain,° and I won't care what way the sea 295
is when the other women will be keening. [*To Nora*] Give me the Holy Water, Nora, there's a small sup° still on the dresser. [*Nora gives it to her. Maurya drops Michael's clothes across Bartley's feet, and sprinkles the Holy Water over him*]. . . . It isn't that I haven't prayed for you, Bartley, to the Almighty God. It isn't that I 300
haven't said prayers in the dark night till you wouldn't know what I'd be saying; but it's a great rest I'll have now, and it's time surely. It's a great rest I'll have now, and great sleeping in the long nights after Samhain, if it's only a bit of wet flour we do have to eat, and maybe a fish that would be stinking. [*She kneels down again, crossing* 305
herself, and saying prayers under her breath]

CATHLEEN [*to an old man kneeling near her*] Maybe yourself and Eamon would make a coffin when the sun rises. We have fine white boards herself bought, God help her, thinking Michael would be found, and I have a new cake° you can eat while you'll 310
be working.

THE OLD MAN [*looking at the boards*] Are there nails with them?

CATHLEEN There are not, Colum; we didn't think of the nails.

ANOTHER MAN It's a great wonder she wouldn't think of the nails, and all the coffins she's seen made already. 315

CATHLEEN It's getting old she is, and broken.

> [*Maurya stands up again very slowly and spreads out the pieces of Michael's clothes beside the body, sprinkling them with the last of the Holy Water*]

NORA [*in a whisper to Cathleen*] She's quiet now and easy; but the day Michael was drowned you could hear her crying out from this to the spring well. It's fonder she was of Michael, and would any one have thought that? 320

CATHLEEN [*slowly and clearly*] An old woman will soon be tired with anything she will do, and isn't it nine days herself is after crying, and keening, and making great sorrow in the house?

MAURYA [*puts the empty cup mouth downwards on the table, and lays her hands together on Bartley's feet*°] They're all together this time, 325 and the end is come. May the Almighty God have mercy on Bartley's soul, and on Michael's soul, and on the souls of Sheamus and Patch, and Stephen and Shawn [*bending her head*]. . . . and may He have mercy on my soul, Nora, and on the soul of everyone is left living in the world. [*She pauses, and the keen rises a little more* 330 *loudly from the women, then sinks away. Continuing*] Michael has a clean burial in the far north, by the grace of the Almighty God. Bartley will have a fine coffin out of the white boards, and a deep grave surely. . . . What more can we want than that? . . . No man at all can be living for ever, and we must be satisfied.° 335

[*She kneels down again and the curtain falls slowly*]

THE END

THE SHADOW OF THE GLEN

A Play in One Act

(1902–1905)

PERSONS

DAN BURKE, farmer and herd ‾
NORA BURKE, his wife°
MICHAEL DARA, a young herd°
A TRAMP

SCENE

*The last cottage at the head of a
long glen in County Wicklow*

FIRST PRODUCTION
(Dublin, 8 October 1903)

Dan Burke	George Roberts
Nora Burke	Maire Nic Shiubhlaigh
Michael Dara	P. J. Kelly
A Tramp	W. G. Fay

Cottage kitchen; turf fire on the right; a bed near it against the wall with a body lying on it covered with a sheet. A door is at the other end of the room, with a low table near it, and stools, or wooden chairs. There are a couple of glasses on the table, and a bottle of whiskey, as if for a wake, with two cups, a tea-pot, and a home-made cake. There is another small door near the bed. Nora Burke is moving about the room, settling a few things and lighting candles on the table, looking now and then at the bed with an uneasy look. Someone knocks softly at the door on the left. She takes up a stocking with money from the table° and puts it in her pocket. Then she opens the door

TRAMP [*outside*] Good evening to you, lady of the house.°

NORA Good evening kindly, stranger, it's a wild night, God help you, to be out in the rain falling.

TRAMP It is surely, and I walking to Brittas from the Aughrim fair.°   5

NORA Is it walking on your feet, stranger?

TRAMP On my two feet, lady of the house, and when I saw the light below I thought maybe if you'd a sup of new milk and a quiet decent corner where a man could sleep.... [*He looks in past her and sees the body on the bed*] The Lord have mercy on us all!   10

NORA It doesn't matter any way, stranger, come in out of the rain.

TRAMP [*coming in slowly and going towards the bed*] Is it departed he is?

NORA It is, stranger. He's after dying on me, God forgive him, and there I am now with a hundred sheep beyond on the hills, and no   15
turf drawn for the winter.°

TRAMP [*looking closely at the body*] It's a queer look° is on him for a man that's dead.

NORA [*half-humorously*] He was always queer, stranger, and I suppose them that's queer and they living men will be queer bodies after.   20

TRAMP Isn't it a great wonder you're letting him lie there, and he not tidied, or laid out itself?°

NORA [*coming to the bed*] I was afeard, stranger, for he put a black curse on me this morning if I'd touch his body the time he'd die sudden, or let anyone touch it except his sister only, and it's ten   25
miles away she lives, in the big glen over the hill.

TRAMP [*looking at her and nodding slowly*] It's a queer story he wouldn't let his own wife touch him, and he dying quiet in his bed.

NORA He was an old man, and an odd man, stranger, and it's always up on the hills he was, thinking thoughts in the dark mist. [*She pulls back a bit more of the sheet*] Lay your hand on him now, and tell me if it's cold he is surely.

TRAMP Is it getting the curse on me you'd be, woman of the house? I wouldn't lay my hand on him for the Lough Nahanagan° and it filled with gold.

NORA [*looking uneasily at the body*] Maybe cold would be no sign of death with the like of him,° for he was always cold, every day since I knew him,—and every night, stranger—[*she covers up his face and comes away from the bed*]; but I'm thinking it's dead he is surely, for he's complaining a while back of a pain in his heart, and this morning, the time he was going off to Brittas for three days or four, he was taken with a sharp turn. Then he went into his bed and he was saying it was destroyed he was, the time the shadow was going up through the glen, and when the sun set on the bog beyond he made a great lep, and let a great cry out of him, and stiffened himself out the like of a dead sheep.

TRAMP [*crosses himself*] God rest his soul.

NORA [*pouring him out a glass of whiskey*] Maybe that would do you better than the milk of the sweetest cow in County Wicklow.

TRAMP The Almighty God reward you,° and may it be to your good health. [*He drinks*]

NORA [*giving him a pipe and tobacco from the table*] I've no pipes saving his own, stranger, but they're sweet pipes to smoke.

TRAMP Thank you kindly, lady of the house.

NORA Sit down now, stranger, and be taking your rest.

TRAMP [*filling a pipe and looking about the room*] I've walked a great way through the world, lady of the house, and seen great wonders, but I never seen a wake till this day with fine spirits, and good tobacco, and the best of pipes, and no one to taste them but a woman only.°

NORA Didn't you hear me say it was only after dying on me he was when the sun went down, and how would I go out into the glen and tell the neighbours and I a lone woman with no house near me?

TRAMP [*drinking*] There's no offence, lady of the house?

NORA No offence in life, stranger. How would the like of you passing in the dark night know the lonesome way I was with no house near me at all?

16

TRAMP [*sitting down*] I knew rightly. [*He lights his pipe so that there is a sharp light beneath his haggard face*] And I was thinking, and I coming in through the door, that it's many a lone woman would be afeard of the like of me in the dark night, in a place wouldn't be as lonesome as this place, where there aren't two living souls would see the little light you have shining from the glass.

NORA [*slowly*] I'm thinking many would be afeard, but I never knew what way I'd be afeard of beggar or bishop or any man of you at all. [*She looks towards the window and lowers her voice*] It's other things than the like of you, stranger, would make a person afeard.

TRAMP [*looking round with a half-shudder*] It is surely, God help us all!

NORA [*looking at him for a moment with curiosity*] You're saying that, stranger, as if you were easy afeard.

TRAMP [*speaking mournfully*] Is it myself, lady of the house, that does be walking round in the long nights, and crossing the hills when the fog is on them, the time a little stick would seem as big as your arm, and a rabbit as big as a bay horse, and a stack of turf as big as a towering church in the city of Dublin? If myself was easily afeard, I'm telling you, it's long ago I'd have been locked into the Richmond Asylum,° or maybe have run up into the back hills with nothing on me but an old shirt, and been eaten with crows the like of Patch Darcy—the Lord have mercy on him—in the year that's gone.

NORA [*with interest*] You knew Darcy?

TRAMP Wasn't I the last one heard his living voice in the whole world?

NORA There were great stories of what was heard at that time, but would anyone believe the things they do be saying in the glen?

TRAMP It was no lie, lady of the house . . . I was passing below on a dark night the like of this night, and the sheep were lying under the ditch and every one of them coughing, and choking, like an old man, with the great rain and the fog . . . Then I heard a thing talking—queer talk, you wouldn't believe at all, and you out of your dreams,—and 'Merciful God,' says I, 'if I begin hearing the like of that voice out of the thick mist, I'm destroyed surely.' Then I run, and I run, and I run, till I was below in Rathvanna.° I got drunk that night, I got drunk in the morning, and drunk the day after,—I was coming from the races beyond—and the third day they found Darcy . . . Then I knew it was himself I was after hearing, and I wasn't afeard any more.

NORA [*speaking sorrowfully and slowly*] God spare Darcy, he'd always look in here and he passing up or passing down, and it's very 110 lonesome I was after him a long while [*she looks over at the bed and lowers her voice, speaking very clearly*], and then I got happy again—if it's ever happy we are, stranger—for I got used to being lonesome. [*A short pause; then she stands up*] Was there anyone on the last bit of the road, stranger, and you coming from Aughrim? 115

TRAMP There was a young man with a drift of mountain ewes, and he running after them this way and that.

NORA [*with a half-smile*] Far down, stranger?

TRAMP A piece only.°

[*She fills the kettle and puts it on the fire*]

NORA Maybe, if you're not easy afeard, you'd stay here a short while 120 alone with himself?°

TRAMP I would surely. A man that's dead can do no hurt.

NORA [*speaking with a sort of constraint*] I'm going a little back to the west, stranger, for himself would go there one night and another, and whistle at that place, and then the young man you're after 125 seeing—a kind of a farmer has come up from the sea to live in a cottage beyond—would walk round to see if there was a thing we'd have to be done, and I'm wanting him this night, the way he can go down into the glen when the sun goes up and tell the people that himself is dead. 130

TRAMP [*looking at the body in the sheet*] It's myself will go for him, lady of the house, and let you not be destroying yourself with the great rain.

NORA You wouldn't find your way, stranger, for there's a small path only, and it running up between two sluigs where an ass and cart 135 would be drowned. [*She puts a shawl over her head*] Let you be making yourself easy, and saying a prayer for his soul, and it's not long I'll be coming again.

TRAMP [*moving uneasily*] Maybe if you'd a piece of a grey thread and a sharp needle—there's great safety in a needle,° lady of the 140 house—I'd be putting a little stitch here and there in my old coat, the time I'll be praying for his soul, and it going up naked to the saints of God.

NORA [*takes a needle and thread from the front of her dress and gives it to him*] There's the needle, stranger, and I'm thinking you won't 145 be lonesome, and you used to the back hills, for isn't a dead man itself more company than to be sitting alone, and hearing the winds crying, and you not knowing on what thing your mind would stay?

TRAMP [*slowly*] It's true, surely, and the Lord have mercy on us all! 150

> [*Nora goes out. The Tramp begins stitching one of the tags in his coat, saying the 'De Profundis' under his breath.*° *In an instant the sheet is drawn slowly down, and Dan Burke looks out. The Tramp moves uneasily, then looks up, and springs to his feet with a movement of terror*]

DAN [*with a hoarse voice*] Don't be afeard, stranger; a man that's dead can do no hurt.

TRAMP [*trembling*] I meant no harm, your honour;° and won't you leave me easy to be saying a little prayer for your soul?

> [*A long whistle is heard outside*]

DAN [*listening, sitting up in his bed and speaking fiercely*] Ah, the devil 155 mend her° . . . Do you hear that, stranger? Did ever you hear another woman could whistle the like of that with two fingers in her mouth? [*He looks at the table hurriedly*] I'm destroyed with the drouth, and let you bring me a drop quickly before herself will come back. 160

TRAMP [*doubtfully*] Is it not dead you are?

DAN How would I be dead, and I as dry as a baked bone, stranger?

TRAMP [*pouring out the whiskey*] What will herself say if she smells the stuff on you, for I'm thinking it's not for nothing you're letting on° to be dead? 165

DAN It is not, stranger, but she won't be coming near me at all, and it's not long now I'll be letting on, for I've a cramp in my back, and my hip's asleep on me, and there's been the devil's own fly itching my nose. . . . It's near dead I was wanting to sneeze, and you blathering about the rain, and Darcy [*bitterly*]—the devil choke 170 him—and the towering church. [*Crying out impatiently*] Give me that whiskey. Would you have herself come back before I taste a drop at all? [*Tramp gives him the glass and he drinks*] . . . Go over now to that cupboard, and bring me a black stick° you'll see in the west corner by the wall. 175

TRAMP [*taking a stick from the cupboard*] Is it that?

DAN It is, stranger; it's a long time I'm keeping that stick, for I've a bad wife in the house.

TRAMP [*with a queer look*] Is it herself, master of the house, and she a grand woman to talk?° 180

DAN It's herself, surely, it's a bad wife she is—a bad wife for an old man, and I'm getting old, God help me, though I've an arm to me still. [*He takes the stick in his hand*] Let you wait now a short while, and it's a great sight you'll see in this room in two hours or three. [*He stops to listen*] Is that somebody above? 185

TRAMP [*listening*] There's a voice speaking on the path.

DAN Put that stick here in the bed, and smooth the sheet the way it was lying. [*He covers himself up hastily*] Be falling to sleep now and don't let on you know anything, or I'll be having your life. I wouldn't have told you at all but it's destroyed with the drouth I 190 was.

TRAMP [*covering his head*] Have no fear, master of the house. What is it I know of the like of you that I'd be saying a word or putting out my hand to stay you at all? [*He goes back to the fire, sits down on a stool with his back to the bed and goes on stitching his coat*] 195

DAN [*under the sheet, querulously*] Stranger.

TRAMP [*quickly*] Whisht, whisht. Be quiet I'm telling you, they're coming now at the door.

[*Nora comes in with Michael Dara, a tall, innocent young man, behind her*]

NORA I wasn't long at all, stranger, for I met himself on the path.

TRAMP You were middling long, lady of the house. 200

NORA There was no sign from himself?

TRAMP No sign at all, lady of the house.

NORA [*to Michael*] Go over now and pull down the sheet, and look on himself, Michael Dara, and you'll see it's the truth I'm telling you. 205

MICHAEL I will not, Nora, I do be afeard of the dead.

[*He sits down on a stool next the table facing The Tramp. Nora puts the kettle on a lower hook of the pot-hooks, and piles turf under it*]

NORA [*turning to Tramp*] Will you drink a sup of tea with myself and the young man, stranger, or [*speaking more persuasively*] will you go into the little room and stretch yourself a short while on the bed. I'm thinking it's destroyed you are walking the length of that 210 way in the great rain.

TRAMP Is it go away and leave you, and you having a wake, lady of the house? I will not surely. [*He takes a drink from his glass which he has beside him*] And it's none of your tea I'm asking either. [*He goes on stitching*] 215

[*Nora makes the tea*]

MICHAEL [*after looking at The Tramp rather scornfully for a moment*] That's a poor coat you have, God help you, and I'm thinking it's a poor tailor you are with it.

TRAMP [*looks up at him for a moment*] If it's a poor tailor I am, I'm
thinking it's a poor herd does be running back and forward after　220
a little handful of ewes the way I seen yourself running this day,
young fellow, and you coming from the fair.

NORA [*comes back to the table. To Michael in a low voice*] Let you not
mind him at all, Michael Dara. He has a drop taken, and it's soon
he'll be falling asleep.　225

MICHAEL It's no lie he's telling, I was destroyed surely . . . They
were that wilful they were running off into one man's bit of oats,
and another man's bit of hay, and tumbling into the red bogs till
it's more like a pack of old goats than sheep they were . . .
Mountain ewes is a queer breed, Nora Burke, and I'm not used to　230
them at all.

NORA [*settling the tea things*] There's no one can drive a mountain ewe
but the men do be reared in the Glen Malure, I've heard them say,
and above by Rathvanna, and the Glen Imaal,° men the like of Patch
Darcy, God spare his soul, who would walk through five hundred　235
sheep and miss one of them, and he not reckoning them at all.°

MICHAEL [*uneasily*] Is it the man went queer in his head the year
that's gone?

NORA It is surely.

TRAMP [*plaintively*] That was a great man, young fellow, a great man　240
I'm telling you. There was never a lamb from his own ewes he
wouldn't know before it was marked, and he'd run from this to the
city of Dublin, and never catch for his breath.

NORA [*turning round quickly*] He was a great man surely, stranger,
and isn't it a grand thing when you hear a living man saying a good　245
word of a dead man, and he mad dying?

TRAMP It's the truth I'm saying, God spare his soul.
[*He puts the needle under the collar of his coat, and settles
himself to sleep in the chimney-corner. Nora sits down at the
table: their backs are turned to the bed*]

MICHAEL [*looking at her with a queer look*] I heard tell this day, Nora
Burke, that it was on the path below Patch Darcy would be passing
up and passing down, and I heard them say he'd never pass it night　250
or morning without speaking with yourself.

NORA [*in a low voice*] It was no lie you heard, Michael Dara.

MICHAEL [*as before*] I'm thinking it's a power of men you're after
knowing if it's in a lonesome place you live itself.

NORA [*slowly, giving him his tea*] It's in a lonesome place you do have　255
to be talking with someone, and looking for someone, in the evening

of the day, and if it's a power of men I'm after knowing they were fine men, for I was a hard child to please, and a hard girl to please [*she looks at him a little sternly*], and it's a hard woman I am to please this day, Michael Dara, and it's no lie, I'm telling you.   260

MICHAEL [*looking over to see that The Tramp is asleep and then, pointing to the dead man*] Was it a hard woman to please you were when you took himself for your man?

NORA What way would I live and I an old woman if I didn't marry a man with a bit of a farm, and cows on it, and sheep on the back   265 hills?°

MICHAEL [*considering*] That's true, Nora, and maybe it's no fool you were, for there's good grazing on it, if it is a lonesome place, and I'm thinking it's a good sum he's left behind.

NORA [*taking the stocking with money from her pocket, and putting it on*   270 *the table*] I do be thinking in the long nights it was a big fool I was that time, Michael Dara, for what good is a bit of a farm with cows on it, and sheep on the back hills, when you do be sitting, looking out from a door the like of that door, and seeing nothing but the mists rolling down the bog, and the mists again, and they   275 rolling up the bog, and hearing nothing but the wind crying out in the bits of broken trees were left from the great storm, and the streams roaring with the rain?

MICHAEL [*looking at her uneasily*] What is it ails you this night, Nora Burke? I've heard tell it's the like of that talk you do hear from   280 men, and they after being a great while on the back hills.

NORA [*putting out the money on the table*] It's a bad night, and a wild night, Michael Dara, and isn't it a great while I am at the foot of the back hills, sitting up here boiling food for himself, and food for the brood sow, and baking a cake when the night falls? [*She*   285 *puts up the money, listlessly, in little piles on the table*] Isn't it a long while I am sitting here in the winter, and the summer, and the fine spring, with the young growing behind me and the old passing, saying to myself one time, to look on Mary Brien who wasn't that height [*holding out her hand*], and I a fine girl growing up, and   290 there she is now with two children, and another coming on her in three months or four [*she pauses*].

MICHAEL [*moving over three of the piles*] That's three pounds we have now, Nora Burke.

NORA [*continuing in the same voice*] And saying to myself another   295 time, to look on Peggy Cavanagh, who had the lightest hand at milking a cow that wouldn't be easy, or turning a cake,° and there she is now walking round on the roads, or sitting in a dirty old house, with no teeth in her mouth, and no sense, and no more hair than you'd see on a bit of a hill and they after burning the furze from it. [*She pauses again*] 300

MICHAEL That's five pounds and ten notes, a good sum, surely! . . . It's not that way you'll be talking when you marry a young man, Nora Burke, and they were saying in the fair my lambs were the best lambs, and I got a grand price, for I'm no fool now at making 305 a bargain when my lambs are good.

NORA What was it you got?

MICHAEL Twenty pound for the lot, Nora Burke . . . We'd do right to wait now till himself will be quiet a while in the Seven Churches,° and then you'll marry me in the chapel of Rathvanna, 310 and I'll bring the sheep up on the bit of a hill you have on the back mountain, and we won't have anything we'd be afeard to let our minds on when the mist is down.

NORA [*pouring him out some whiskey*] Why would I marry you, Mike Dara? You'll be getting old, and I'll be getting old, and in a little 315 while, I'm telling you, you'll be sitting up in your bed—the way himself was sitting—with a shake in your face, and your teeth falling, and the white hair sticking out round you like an old bush where sheep do be leaping a gap.

[*Dan Burke sits up noiselessly from under the sheet, with his hand to his face. His white hair is sticking out round his head*]

NORA [*goes on slowly without hearing him*] It's a pitiful thing to be 320 getting old, but it's a queer thing surely . . . It's a queer thing to see an old man sitting up there in his bed, with no teeth in him, and a rough word in his mouth, and his chin the way it would take the bark from the edge of an oak board you'd have building a door . . . God forgive me, Michael Dara, we'll all be getting old, but it's 325 a queer thing surely.

MICHAEL It's too lonesome you are from living a long time with an old man, Nora, and you're talking again like a herd that would be coming down from the thick mist [*he puts his arm round her*], but it's a fine life you'll have now with a young man, a fine life surely . . . 330

[*Dan sneezes violently. Michael tries to get to the door, but before he can do so, Dan jumps out of the bed in queer white clothes, with the stick in his hand, and goes over and puts his back against it*]

MICHAEL The Son of God deliver us . . . [*Crosses himself, and goes backward across the room*]

23

DAN [*holding up his hand at him*] Now you'll not marry her the time I'm rotting below in the Seven Churches, and you'll see the thing I'll give you will follow you on the back mountains when the   335
wind is high.

MICHAEL [*to Nora*] Get me out of it, Nora, for the love of God. He always did what you bid him, and I'm thinking he would do it now.

NORA [*looking at The Tramp*] Is it dead he is or living?

DAN [*turning towards her*] It's little you care if it's dead or living I   340
am, but there'll be an end now of your fine times, and all the talk you have of young men and old men, and of the mist coming up or going down. [*He opens the door*] You'll walk out now from that door, Nora Burke, and it's not tomorrow, or the next day, or any day of your life, that you'll put in your foot through it again.   345

TRAMP [*standing up*] It's a hard thing you're saying, for an old man, master of the house, and what would the like of her do if you put her out on the roads?

DAN Let her walk round the like of Peggy Cavanagh below, and be begging money at the cross roads, or selling songs to the men. [*To*   350
Nora] Walk out now, Nora Burke, and it's soon you'll be getting old with that life, I'm telling you; it's soon your teeth'll be falling and your head'll be the like of a bush where sheep do be leaping a gap.

   [*He pauses; she looks round at Michael*]

MICHAEL [*timidly*] There's a fine Union below in Rathdrum.   355

DAN The like of her would never go there° ... It's lonesome roads she'll be going, and hiding herself away till the end will come, and they find her stretched like a dead sheep with the frost on her, or the big spiders, maybe, and they putting their webs on her, in the butt of a ditch.   360

NORA [*angrily*] What way will yourself be that day, Daniel Burke? What way will you be that day and you lying down a long while in your grave? For it's bad you are living, and it's bad you'll be when you're dead. [*She looks at him a moment fiercely, then half turns away and speaks plaintively again*] Yet, if it is itself, Daniel   365
Burke, who can help it at all, and let you be getting up into your bed, and not be taking your death with the wind blowing on you, and the rain with it, and you half in your skin.°

DAN It's proud and happy you'd be if I was getting my death the day I was shut of yourself. [*Pointing to the door*] Let you walk out   370
through that door, I'm telling you, and let you not be passing this way if it's hungry you are, or wanting a bed.

24

TRAMP [*pointing to Michael*] Maybe himself would take her.

NORA What would he do with me now?

TRAMP Give you the half of a dry bed, and good food in your mouth. 375

DAN Is it a fool you think him, stranger, or is it a fool you were born yourself? Let her walk out of that door, and let you go along with her, stranger—if it's raining itself—for it's too much talk you have surely.

TRAMP [*going over to Nora*] We'll be going now, lady of the 380 house—the rain is falling but the air is kind, and maybe it'll be a grand morning by the grace of God.

NORA What good is a grand morning when I'm destroyed surely, and I going out to get my death walking the roads?

TRAMP You'll not be getting your death with myself, lady of the 385 house, and I knowing all the ways a man can put food in his mouth. . . . We'll be going now, I'm telling you, and the time you'll be feeling the cold and the frost, and the great rain, and the sun again, and the south wind blowing in the glens, you'll not be sitting up on a wet ditch the way you're after sitting in this place, 390 making yourself old with looking on each day and it passing you by. You'll be saying one time, 'It's a grand evening by the grace of God,' and another time, 'It's a wild night, God help us, but it'll pass surely.' You'll be saying—

DAN [*goes over to them crying out impatiently*] Go out of that door, I'm 395 telling you, and do your blathering below in the glen.

[*Nora gathers a few things into her shawl*]

TRAMP [*at the door*] Come along with me now, lady of the house, and it's not my blather you'll be hearing only, but you'll be hearing the herons crying out over the black lakes,° and you'll be hearing the grouse, and the owls with them, and the larks and the big 400 thrushes when the days are warm, and it's not from the like of them you'll be hearing a talk of getting old like Peggy Cavanagh, and losing the hair off you, and the light of your eyes, but it's fine songs you'll be hearing when the sun goes up, and there'll be no old fellow wheezing the like of a sick sheep close to your ear. 405

NORA I'm thinking it's myself will be wheezing that time with lying down under the Heavens when the night is cold, but you've a fine bit of talk, stranger, and it's with yourself I'll go. [*She goes towards the door, then turns to Dan*] You think it's a grand thing you're after doing with your letting on to be dead, but what is it at all? What 410 way would a woman live in a lonesome place the like of this place, and she not making a talk with the men passing? And what way will yourself live from this day, with none to care you? What is it you'll have now but a black life, Daniel Burke, and it's not long, I'm telling you, till you'll be lying again under that sheet, and you dead surely. 415

[*She goes out with The Tramp. Michael is slinking after them, but Dan stops him*]

DAN Sit down now and take a little taste of the stuff, Michael Dara, there's a great drouth on me, and the night is young.

MICHAEL [*coming back to the table*] And it's very dry I am surely, with the fear of death you put on me, and I after driving mountain 420 ewes since the turn of the day.°

DAN [*throwing away his stick*] I was thinking to strike you, Michael Dara, but you're a quiet man, God help you, and I don't mind you at all. [*He pours out two glasses of whiskey, and gives one to Michael*]

DAN Your good health, Michael Dara. 425

MICHAEL God reward you, Daniel Burke, and may you have a long life and a quiet life, and good health with it. [*They drink*]

CURTAIN

THE TINKER'S WEDDING

A Comedy in Two Acts

(1902–1907)

PREFACE

The drama is made serious—in the French sense° of the word—not
by the degree in which it is taken up with problems that are serious
in themselves, but by the degree in which it gives the nourishment,
not very easy to define, on which our imaginations live. We should
not go to the theatre as we go to a chemist's, or a dram-shop, but as   5
we go to a dinner, where the food we need is taken with pleasure and
excitement. This was nearly always so in Spain and England and
France when the drama was at its richest—the infancy and decay of
the drama tend to be didactic—but in these days the playhouse is too
often stocked with the drugs of many seedy problems, or with the   10
absinthe or vermouth of the last musical comedy.

The drama, like the symphony, does not teach or prove anything.
Analysts with their problems, and teachers with their systems, are
soon as old-fashioned as the pharmacopoeia of Galen,°—look at Ibsen
and the Germans°—but the best plays of Ben Jonson and Molière can   15
no more go out of fashion than the blackberries on the hedges.

Of the things which nourish the imagination humour is one of the
most needful, and it is dangerous to limit or destroy it. Baudelaire
calls laughter the greatest sign of the Satanic element in man;° and
where a country loses its humour, as some towns in Ireland are doing,   20
there will be morbidity of mind, as Baudelaire's mind was morbid.

In the greater part of Ireland, however, the whole people, from the
tinkers to the clergy, have still a life, and view of life, that are rich
and genial and humorous. I do not think that these country people,
who have so much humour themselves, will mind being laughed at   25
without malice, as the people in every country have been laughed
at in their own comedies.

J. M. S.

December 2nd, 1907.

Note—'The Tinker's Wedding' was first written a few years ago,
about the time I was working at 'Riders to the Sea', and 'In the   30
Shadow of the Glen'. I have re-written it since.°

J. M. S.

Act 1

After nightfall. A fire of sticks is burning near the ditch° a little to the right. Michael is working beside it. In the background, on the left, a sort of tent and ragged clothes drying on the hedge. On the right a chapel-gate

SARAH CASEY [*coming in on right, eagerly*] We'll see his reverence° this place, Michael Byrne, and he passing backward° to his house tonight.

MICHAEL [*grimly*] That'll be a sacred and a sainted joy!

SARAH [*sharply*] It'll be small joy for yourself if you aren't ready with 5
my wedding ring. [*She goes over to him*] Is it near done this time, or what way is it at all?

MICHAEL A poor way only, Sarah Casey, for it's the divil's job° making a ring, and you'll be having my hands destroyed in a short while the way I'll not be able to make a tin can at all maybe at the 10
dawn of day.

SARAH [*sitting down beside him and throwing sticks on the fire*] If it's the divil's job, let you mind it, and leave your speeches that would choke a fool.

MICHAEL [*slowly and glumly*] And it's you'll go talking of fools,° 15
Sarah Casey, when no man did ever hear a lying story even of your like° unto this mortal day. You to be going beside me a great while, and rearing a lot of them,° and then to be setting off with your talk of getting married, and your driving me to it, and I not asking it at all. 20

[*Sarah turns her back to him and arranges something in the ditch*]

MICHAEL [*angrily*] Can't you speak a word when I'm asking what is it ails you since the moon did change?

SARAH [*musingly*] I'm thinking there isn't anything ails me, Michael Byrne; but the spring-time is a queer time, and it's queer thoughts maybe I do think at whiles.° 25

MICHAEL It's hard set you'd be to think queerer than welcome,° Sarah Casey; but what will you gain dragging me to the priest this night, I'm saying, when it's new thoughts you'll be thinking at the dawn of day?

SARAH [*teasingly*] It's at the dawn of day I do be thinking I'd have 30
a right to be going off to the rich tinkers do be travelling

from Tibradden to the Tara Hill;° for it'd be a fine life to be driving with young Jaunting Jim, where there wouldn't be any big hills to break the back of you,° with walking up and walking down.

MICHAEL [*with dismay*] It's the like of that you do be thinking!

SARAH The like of that, Michael Byrne, when there is a bit of sun in it, and a kind air, and a great smell coming from the thorn trees is above your head.

MICHAEL [*looks at her for a moment with horror, and then hands her the ring*] Will that fit you now?

SARAH [*trying it on*] It's making it tight you are, and the edges sharp on the tin.

MICHAEL [*looking at it carefully*] It's the fat of your own finger, Sarah Casey; and isn't it a mad thing I'm saying again that you'd be asking marriage of me, or making a talk of going away from me, and you thriving and getting your good health by the grace of the Almighty God?

SARAH [*giving it back to him*] Fix it now, and it'll do, if you're wary° you don't squeeze it again.

MICHAEL [*moodily, working again*] It's easy saying be wary; there's many things easy said, Sarah Casey, you'd wonder a fool even would be saying at all. [*He starts violently*] The divil mend you,° I'm scalded again!

SARAH [*scornfully*] If you are, it's a clumsy man you are this night, Michael Byrne [*raising her voice*]; and let you make haste now, or herself will be coming with the porter.°

MICHAEL [*defiantly, raising his voice*] Let me make haste? I'll be making haste maybe to hit you a great clout; for I'm thinking it's the like of that you want. I'm thinking on the day I got you above at Rathvanna,° and the way you began crying out and we coming down off the hill, crying out and saying, 'I'll go back to my ma,' and I'm thinking on the way I came behind you that time, and hit you a great clout in the lug,° and how quiet and easy it was you came along with me from that hour to this present day.

SARAH [*standing up and throwing all her sticks into the fire*] And a big fool I was too, maybe; but we'll be seeing Jaunting Jim tomorrow in Ballinaclash,° and he after getting a great price for his white foal in the horse-fair of Wicklow, the way it'll be a great sight to see him squandering his share of gold, and he with a grand eye for a fine horse, and a grand eye for a woman.

MICHAEL [*working again with impatience*] The divil do him good with the two of them.

SARAH [*kicking up the ashes with her foot*] Ah, he's a great lad, I'm telling you, and it's proud and happy I'll be to see him, and he the first one called me the Beauty of Ballinacree,° a fine name for a woman.

MICHAEL [*with contempt*] It's the like of that name they do be putting on the horses they have below racing in Arklow.° It's easy pleased you are, Sarah Casey, easy pleased with a big word, or the liar speaks it.

SARAH Liar!

MICHAEL Liar, surely.

SARAH [*indignantly*] Liar, is it? Didn't you ever hear tell of the peelers followed me ten miles along the Glen Malure,° and they talking love to me in the dark night, or of the children you'll meet coming from school and they saying one to the other, 'It's this day we seen Sarah Casey, the Beauty of Ballinacree, a great sight surely.'

MICHAEL God help the lot of them!

SARAH It's yourself you'll be calling God to help, in two weeks or three, when you'll be waking up in the dark night and thinking you see me coming with the sun on me, and I driving a high cart° with Jaunting Jim going behind. It's lonesome and cold you'll be feeling the ditch where you'll be lying down that night, I'm telling you, and you hearing the old woman making a great noise in her sleep, and the bats squeaking in the trees.

MICHAEL Whisht. I hear some one coming the road.

SARAH [*looking out right*] It's some one coming forward from the doctor's door.

MICHAEL It's often his reverence does be in there playing cards, or drinking a sup, or singing songs, until the dawn of day.

SARAH It's a big boast of a man° with a long step on him and a trumpeting voice. It's his reverence surely; and if you have the ring done, it's a great bargain we'll make now and he after drinking his glass.

MICHAEL [*going to her and giving her the ring*] There's your ring, Sarah Casey; but I'm thinking he'll walk by and not stop to speak with the like of us at all.

SARAH [*tidying herself, in great excitement*] Let you be sitting here and keeping a great blaze, the way he can look on my face; and let you seem to be working, for it's great love the like of him have to talk of work.

MICHAEL [*moodily, sitting down and beginning to work at a tin can*] Great love surely.

SARAH [*eagerly*] Make a great blaze now, Michael Byrne.

[*The Priest comes in on right; she comes forward in front of him*]

SARAH [*in a very plausible voice*] Good evening, your reverence. It's a grand fine night, by the grace of God.

PRIEST The Lord have mercy on us! What kind of a living woman is it that you are at all?   120

SARAH It's Sarah Casey I am, your reverence, the Beauty of Ballinacree, and it's Michael Byrne is below in the ditch.

PRIEST A holy pair, surely! Let you get out of my way. [*He tries to pass by*]

SARAH [*keeping in front of him*] We are wanting a little word with   125
your reverence.

PRIEST I haven't a halfpenny at all. Leave the road I'm saying.

SARAH It isn't a halfpenny we're asking, holy father; but we were thinking maybe we'd have a right to be getting married; and we were thinking it's yourself would marry us for not a halfpenny at   130
all; for you're a kind man, your reverence, a kind man with the poor.

PRIEST [*with astonishment*] Is it marry you for nothing at all?

SARAH It is, your reverence; and we were thinking maybe you'd give us a little small bit of silver to pay for the ring.   135

PRIEST [*loudly*] Let you hold your tongue; let you be quiet, Sarah Casey. I've no silver at all for the like of you; and if you want to be married, let you pay your pound. I'd do it for a pound only, and that's making it a sight cheaper° than I'd make it for one of my own pairs is living here in the place.   140

SARAH Where would the like of us get a pound, your reverence?

PRIEST Wouldn't you easy get it with your selling asses, and making cans, and your stealing east and west in Wicklow and Wexford and the county Meath? [*He tries to pass her*] Let you leave the road, and not be plaguing me more.   145

SARAH [*pleadingly, taking money from her pocket*] Wouldn't you have a little mercy on us, your reverence? [*Holding out money*] Wouldn't you marry us for a half a sovereign,° and it a nice shiny one with a view on it of the living king's mamma?

PRIEST If it's ten shillings you have, let you get ten more the same   150
way, and I'll marry you then.

SARAH [*whining*] It's two years we are getting that bit, your reverence, with our pence and our halfpence and an odd threepenny bit; and if you don't marry us now, himself and the old woman, who has a great drouth, will be drinking it tomorrow in the fair [*she puts*   155

34

her apron to her eyes, half sobbing], and then I won't be married any
time, and I'll be saying till I'm an old woman: 'It's a cruel and a
wicked thing to be bred poor.'

PRIEST [*turning up towards the fire*] Let you not be crying, Sarah
Casey. It's a queer woman you are to be crying at the like of that,   160
and you your whole life walking the roads.

SARAH [*sobbing*] It's two years we are getting the gold, your reverence, and now you won't marry us for that bit, and we hard-
working poor people do be making cans in the dark night, and
blinding our eyes with the black smoke from the bits of twigs we   165
do be burning.

[*An old woman is heard singing tipsily on the left*]

PRIEST [*looking at the can Michael is making*] When will you have that
can done, Michael Byrne?

MICHAEL In a short space only, your reverence, for I'm putting the
last dab of solder on the rim.   170

PRIEST Let you get a crown along with the ten shillings and the
gallon can, Sarah Casey, and I will wed you so.

MARY [*suddenly shouting behind, tipsily*] Larry was a fine lad,° I'm
saying; Larry was a fine lad, Sarah Casey—

MICHAEL Whisht, now, the two of you. There's my mother coming,   175
and she'd have us destroyed° if she heard the like of that talk the
time she's been drinking her fill.

MARY [*comes in singing*]—
      And when we asked him what way he'd die,
        And he hanging unrepented,   180
     'Begob,'° says Larry, 'that's all in my eye,
        By the clergy first-invented.'

SARAH Give me the jug now, or you'll have it spilt in the ditch.

MARY [*holding the jug with both her hands, in a stilted voice*] Let you
leave me easy, Sarah Casey. I won't spill it, I'm saying. God help   185
you; are you thinking it's frothing full to the brim it is at this hour
of the night, and I after carrying it in my two hands a long step
from Jemmy Neill's?

MICHAEL [*anxiously*] Is there a sup left at all?

SARAH [*looking into the jug*] A little small sup only I'm thinking.   190

MARY [*sees the priest, and holds out jug towards him*] God save your
reverence. I'm after bringing down a smart drop;° and let you
drink it up now, for it's a middling drouthy man you are at all
times,° God forgive you, and this night is cruel dry.° [*She tries to
go towards him. Sarah holds her back*]   195

PRIEST [*waving her away*] Let you not be falling to the flames. Keep off, I'm saying.

MARY [*persuasively*] Let you not be shy of us, your reverence. Aren't we all sinners, God help us! Drink a sup now, I'm telling you; and we won't let on a word about it till the Judgment Day. [*She takes up a tin mug, pours some porter into it, and gives it to him*] 200

MARY [*singing, and holding the jug in her hand*]—
        A lonesome ditch in Ballygan
        The day you're beating a tenpenny can;
        A lonesome bank in Ballyduff   205
        The time . . . [*She breaks off*]

It's a bad, wicked song, Sarah Casey; and let you put me down now in the ditch, and I won't sing it till himself will be gone; for it's bad enough he is, I'm thinking, without ourselves making him worse.   210

SARAH [*putting her down, to the Priest, half laughing*] Don't mind her at all, your reverence. She's no shame the time she's a drop taken; and if it was the Holy Father from Rome was in it, she'd give him a little sup out of her mug, and say the same as she'd say to yourself.   215

MARY [*to the Priest*] Let you drink it up, holy father. Let you drink it up, I'm saying, and not be letting on you wouldn't do the like of it, and you with a stack of pint bottles above, reaching the sky.

PRIEST [*with resignation*] Well, here's to your good health, and God forgive us all. [*He drinks*]   220

MARY That's right now, your reverence, and the blessing of God be on you. Isn't it a grand thing to see you sitting down, with no pride in you, and drinking a sup with the like of us, and we the poorest, wretched, starving creatures you'd see any place on the earth?

PRIEST If it's starving you are itself, I'm thinking it's well for the like 225 of you that do be drinking when there's drouth on you, and lying down to sleep when your legs are stiff. [*He sighs gloomily*] What would you do if it was the like of myself you were, saying Mass with your mouth dry, and running east and west for a sick call maybe, and hearing the rural people again and they saying their 230 sins?

MARY [*with compassion*] It's destroyed you must be hearing the sins of the rural people on a fine spring.

PRIEST [*with despondency*] It's a hard life I'm telling you, a hard life, Mary Byrne; and there's the bishop coming in the morning, and 235 he an old man, would have you destroyed if he seen a thing at all.

MARY [*with great sympathy*] It'd break my heart to hear you talking and sighing the like of that, your reverence. [*She pats him on the knee*] Let you rouse up, now, if it's a poor, single man you are itself, and I'll be singing you songs unto the dawn of day.   240

PRIEST [*interrupting her*] What is it I want with your songs when it'd be better for the like of you, that'll soon die, to be down on your two knees saying prayers to the Almighty God?

MARY If it's prayers I want, you'd have a right to say one yourself, holy father; for we don't have them at all, and I've heard tell a   245
power of times it's that you're for. Say one now, your reverence; for I've heard a power of queer things and I walking the world, but there's one thing I never heard any time, and that's a real priest saying a prayer.

PRIEST The Lord protect us!   250

MARY It's no lie, holy father. I often heard the rural people making a queer noise and they going to rest; but who'd mind the like of them? And I'm thinking it should be great game to hear a scholar, the like of you, speaking Latin to the saints above.°

PRIEST [*scandalized*] Stop your talking, Mary Byrne; you're an old   255
flagrant heathen, and I'll stay no more with the lot of you. [*He rises*]

MARY [*catching hold of him*] Stop till you say a prayer, your reverence; stop till you say a little prayer, I'm telling you, and I'll give you my blessing and the last sup from the jug.   260

PRIEST [*breaking away*] Leave me go, Mary Byrne; for I never met your like for hard abominations the score and two years I'm living in the place.

MARY [*innocently*] Is that the truth?

PRIEST It is, then, and God have mercy on your soul.   265

   [*The Priest goes towards the left, and Sarah follows him*]

SARAH [*in a low voice*] And what time will you do the thing I'm asking, holy father? for I'm thinking you'll do it surely, and not have me growing into an old wicked heathen like herself.

MARY [*calling out shrilly*] Let you be walking back here, Sarah Casey, and not be talking whisper-talk with the like of him in the face of   270
the Almighty God.

SARAH [*to the Priest*] Do you hear her now, your reverence? Isn't it true, surely, she's an old, flagrant heathen, would destroy the world?

PRIEST [*to Sarah, moving off*] Well, I'll be coming down early to the   275
chapel, and let you come to me a while after you see me passing,

and bring the bit of gold along with you, and the tin can. I'll marry
you for them two, though it's a pitiful small sum; for I wouldn't
be easy in my soul if I left you growing into an old, wicked heathen
the like of her.   280

SARAH [*following him out*] The blessing of the Almighty God be on
you, holy father, and that He may reward and watch you from this
present day.

MARY [*nudging Michael*] Did you see that, Michael Byrne?
Didn't you hear me telling you she's flighty° a while back since the   285
change of the moon? With her fussing for marriage, and she
making whisper-talk with one man or another man along by the
road.

MICHAEL Whisht now, or she'll knock the head of you the time she
comes back.   290

MARY Ah, it's a bad, wicked way the world is this night, if there's a
fine air in it itself. You'd never have seen me, and I a young
woman, making whisper-talk with the like of him, and he the
fearfullest old fellow you'd see any place walking the world.
     [*Sarah comes back quickly*]

MARY [*calling out to her*] What is it you're after whispering above   295
with himself?

SARAH [*exultingly*] Lie down, and leave us in peace. [*She whispers
with Michael*]

MARY [*poking out her pipe with a straw, sings*]—
     She'd whisper with one, and she'd whisper with two—   300
[*She breaks off coughing*] My singing voice is gone for this night,
Sarah Casey. [*She lights her pipe*] But if it's flighty you are itself,
you're a grand handsome woman, the glory of tinkers, the pride of
Wicklow, the Beauty of Ballinacree. I wouldn't have you lying
down and you lonesome to sleep this night in a dark ditch when   305
the spring is coming in the trees; so let you sit down there by the
big bough, and I'll be telling you the finest story you'd hear any
place from Dundalk° to Ballinacree, with great queens in it,
making themselves matches from the start to the end, and they
with shiny silks on them the length of the day, and white shifts for   310
the night.

MICHAEL [*standing up with the tin can in his hand*] Let you go asleep,
and not have us destroyed.

MARY [*lying back sleepily*] Don't mind him, Sarah Casey. Sit down
now, and I'll be telling you a story would be fit to tell a woman   315
the like of you in the spring-time of the year.

38

SARAH [*taking the can from Michael, and tying it up in a piece of sacking*] That'll not be rusting now in the dews of night. I'll put it up in the ditch the way it will be handy in the morning; and now we've that done, Michael Byrne, I'll go along with you and welcome for Tim Flaherty's hens. [*She puts the can in the ditch*] 320

MARY [*sleepily*] I've a grand story of the great queens of Ireland with white necks on them the like of Sarah Casey, and fine arms would hit you a slap the way Sarah Casey would hit you.

SARAH [*beckoning on the left*] Come along now, Michael, while she's falling asleep. 325

> [*He goes towards left. Mary sees that they are going, starts up suddenly, and turns over on her hands and knees*]

MARY [*piteously*] Where is it you're going? Let you walk back here, and not be leaving me lonesome when the night is fine.

SARAH Don't be waking the world with your talk when we're going up through the back wood to get two of Tim Flaherty's hens are roosting in the ash-tree above at the well. 330

MARY And it's leaving me lone you are? Come back here, Sarah Casey. Come back here, I'm saying; or if it's off you must go, leave me the two little coppers° you have, the way I can walk up in a short while, and get another pint for my sleep. 335

SARAH It's too much you have taken. Let you stretch yourself out° and take a long sleep; for isn't that the best thing any woman can do, and she an old drinking heathen like yourself.

> [*She and Michael go out left*]

MARY [*standing up slowly*] It's gone they are, and I with my feet that weak under me you'd knock me down with a rush, and my head with a noise in it the like of what you'd hear in a stream and it running between two rocks and rain falling. [*She goes over to the ditch where the can is tied in sacking, and takes it down*] What good am I this night, God help me? What good are the grand stories I have when it's few would listen to an old woman, few but a girl maybe would be in great fear the time her hour was come,° or a little child wouldn't be sleeping with the hunger on a cold night? [*She takes the can from the sacking, and fits in three empty bottles and straw in its place, and ties them up*] Maybe the two of them have a good right to be walking out the little short while they'd be young; but if they have itself, they'll not keep Mary Byrne from her full pint when the night's fine, and there's a dry moon in the sky. [*She takes up the can, and puts the package back in the ditch*] Jemmy Neill's a decent lad; and he'll give me a good drop for the can; and 340 345 350

maybe if I keep near the peelers tomorrow for the first bit of the   355
fair, herself won't strike me at all; and if she does itself, what's a
little stroke on your head beside sitting lonesome on a fine night,
hearing the dogs barking, and the bats squeaking, and you saying
over, it's a short while only till you die. [*She goes out singing 'The
night before Larry was stretched'*]   360

CURTAIN

Act 2

The same. Early morning. Sarah is washing her face in an old bucket; then plaits her hair. Michael is tidying himself also. Mary Byrne is asleep against the ditch

SARAH [*to Michael, with pleased excitement*] Go over, now, to the bundle beyond, and you'll find a kind of a red handkerchief to put upon your neck, and a green one for myself.

MICHAEL [*getting them*] You're after spending° more money on the like of them. Well, it's a power we're losing this time, and we not gaining a thing at all. [*With the handkerchiefs*] Is it them two? 5

SARAH It is, Michael. [*She takes one of them*] Let you tackle° that one round under your chin; and let you not forget to take your hat from your head when we go up into the church. I asked Biddy Flynn below, that's after marrying her second man, and she told me it's the like of that they do. 10

[*Mary yawns, and turns over in her sleep*]

SARAH [*with anxiety*] There she is waking up on us, and I thinking we'd have the job done before she'd know of it at all.

MICHAEL She'll be crying out now, and making game of us, and saying it's fools we are surely. 15

SARAH I'll send her to her sleep again, or get her out of it one way or another; for it'd be a bad case to have a divil's scholar the like of her turning the priest against us maybe with her godless talk.

MARY [*waking up, and looking at them with curiosity, blandly*] That's 20 fine things you have on you, Sarah Casey; and it's a great stir you're making this day, washing your face. I'm that used to the hammer, I wouldn't hear it at all, but washing is a rare thing, and you're after waking me up, and I having a great sleep in the sun. [*She looks around cautiously at the bundle in which she has hidden the* 25 *bottles*]

SARAH [*coaxingly*] Let you stretch out again for a sleep, Mary Byrne, for it'll be a middling time yet before we go to the fair.

MARY [*with suspicion*] That's a sweet tongue you have, Sarah Casey; but if sleep's a grand thing, it's a grand thing to be waking up a 30 day the like of this, when there's a warm sun in it, and a kind air, and you'll hear the cuckoos singing and crying out on the top of the hills.

SARAH   If it's that gay you are, you'd have a right to walk down and
see would you get a few halfpence from the rich men do be driving   35
early to the fair.

MARY   When rich men do be driving early, it's queer tempers they
have, the Lord forgive them; the way it's little but bad words and
swearing out you'd get from them all.

SARAH   [*losing her temper and breaking out fiercely*] Then if you'll   40
neither beg nor sleep, let you walk off from this place where you're
not wanted, and not have us waiting for you maybe at the turn of
day.°

MARY   [*rather uneasy, turning to Michael*] God help our spirits,
Michael; there she is again rousing cranky from the break of dawn.   45
Oh! isn't she a terror since the moon did change [*she gets up
slowly*]? and I'd best be going forward to sell the gallon can. [*She
goes over and takes up the bundle*]

SARAH   [*crying out angrily*] Leave that down, Mary Byrne. Oh! aren't
you the scorn of women to think that you'd have that drouth and   50
roguery on you that you'd go drinking the can and the dew not
dried from the grass?

MARY   [*in a feigned tone of pacification, with the bundle still in her hand*]
It's not a drouth but a heartburn I have this day, Sarah Casey, so
I'm going down to cool my gullet at the blessed well; and I'll sell   55
the can to the parson's daughter below, a harmless poor creature
would fill your hand with shillings for a brace of lies.

SARAH   Leave down the tin can, Mary Byrne, for I hear the drouth
upon your tongue today.

MARY   There's not a drink-house from this place to the fair, Sarah   60
Casey; the way you'll find me below with the full price, and not a
farthing gone. [*She turns to go off left*]

SARAH   [*jumping up, and picking up the hammer threateningly*] Put
down that can, I'm saying.

MARY   [*looking at her for a moment in terror, and putting down the bundle   65
in the ditch*] Is it raving mad you're going, Sarah Casey, and you
the pride of women to destroy the world?

SARAH   [*going up to her, and giving her a push off left*] I'll show you if
it's raving mad I am. Go on from this place, I'm saying, and be
wary now.   70

MARY   [*turning back after her*] If I go, I'll be telling old and young
you're a weathered heathen savage, Sarah Casey, the one did put
down a head of the parson's cabbage to boil in the pot with your
clothes° [*the priest comes in behind her on the left, and listens*], and

quenched the flaming candles on the throne of God the time your   75
shadow fell within the pillars of the chapel door.

>   [*Sarah turns on her, and she springs round nearly into the
>   Priest's arms. When she sees him, she claps her shawl over her
>   mouth, and goes up towards the ditch, laughing to herself*]

PRIEST [*going to Sarah, half terrified at the language that he has heard*]
Well, aren't you a fearful lot? I'm thinking it's only humbug you
were making at the fall of night, and you won't need me at all.

SARAH [*with anger still in her voice*] Humbug is it! would you be   80
turning back upon your spoken promise in the face of God!

PRIEST [*dubiously*] I'm thinking you were never christened, Sarah
Casey; and it would be a queer job to go dealing Christian
sacraments unto the like of you. [*Persuasively, feeling in his pocket*]
So it would be best, maybe, I'd give you a shilling for to drink my   85
health, and let you walk on, and not trouble me at all.

SARAH That's your talking, is it? If you don't stand to your spoken
word, holy father, I'll make my own complaint to the mitred
bishop in the face of all.

PRIEST You'd do that!   90

SARAH I would surely, holy father, if I walked to the city of Dublin
with blood and blisters on my naked feet.

PRIEST [*uneasily scratching his ear*] I wish this day was done, Sarah
Casey; for I'm thinking it's a risky thing getting mixed in any
matters with the like of you.   95

SARAH Be hasty then, and you'll have us done with before you'd
think at all.

PRIEST [*giving in*] Well, maybe it's right you are, and let you come
up to the chapel when you see me looking from the door. [*He goes
up into the chapel*]   100

SARAH [*calling after him*] We will, and God preserve you, holy father.

MARY [*coming down to them, speaking with amazement and consterna-
tion, but without anger*] Going to the chapel! It's at marriage you're
fooling again, maybe? [*Sarah turns her back on her*] It was for that
you were washing your face, and you after sending me for porter   105
at the fall of night the way I'd drink a good half from the jug?
[*Going round in front of Sarah*] Is it at marriage you're fooling
again?

SARAH [*triumphantly*] It is, Mary Byrne. I'll be married now in a
short while; and from this day there will no one have a right to   110
call me a dirty name and I selling cans in Wicklow or Wexford or
the city of Dublin itself.

MARY [*turning to Michael*] And it's yourself is wedding her, Michael Byrne?

MICHAEL [*gloomily*] It is, God spare us.   115

MARY [*looks at Sarah for a moment, and then bursts out into a laugh of derision*] Well, she's a tight,° hardy girl, and it's no lie; but I never knew till this day it was a black born fool° I had for a son. You'll breed asses, I've heard them say, and poaching dogs, and horses'd go licking the wind,° but it's a hard thing, God help me, to breed   120 sense in a son.

MICHAEL [*gloomily*] If I didn't marry her, she'd be walking off to Jaunting Jim maybe at the fall of night; and it's well yourself knows there isn't the like of her for getting money and selling songs to the men.   125

MARY And you're thinking it's paying gold to his reverence would make a woman stop when she's a mind to go?

SARAH [*angrily*] Let you not be destroying us with your talk when I've as good a right to a decent marriage as any speckled° female does be sleeping in the black hovels above, would choke a mule.°   130

MARY [*soothingly*] It's as good a right you have surely, Sarah Casey, but what good will it do? Is it putting that ring on your finger will keep you from getting an aged woman and losing the fine face you have, or be easing your pains, when it's the grand ladies do be married in silk dresses, with rings of gold, that do pass any woman   135 with their share of torment in the hour of birth, and do be paying the doctors in the city of Dublin a great price at that time, the like of what you'd pay for a good ass and a cart? [*She sits down*]

SARAH [*puzzled*] Is that the truth?

MARY [*pleased with the point she has made*] Wouldn't any know it's   140 the truth? Ah, it's few short years you are yet in the world, Sarah Casey, and it's little or nothing at all maybe you know about it.

SARAH [*vehement but uneasy*] What is it yourself knows of the fine ladies when they wouldn't let the like of you go near to them at all?   145

MARY If you do be drinking a little sup in one town and another town, it's soon you get great knowledge and a great sight into the world. You'll see men there, and women there, sitting up on the ends of barrels in the dark night, and they making great talk would soon have the like of you, Sarah Casey, as wise as a March hare.   150

MICHAEL [*to Sarah*] That's the truth she's saying, and maybe if you've sense in you at all, you'd have a right still to leave your fooling, and not be wasting our gold.

SARAH [*decisively*] If it's wise or fool I am, I've made a good bargain and I'll stand to it now.   155

MARY What is it he's making you give?

MICHAEL The ten shillings in gold, and the tin can is above tied in the sack.

MARY [*looking at the bundle with surprise and dread*] The bit of gold and the tin can, is it?   160

MICHAEL The half a sovereign, and the gallon can.

MARY [*scrambling to her feet quickly*] Well, I think I'll be walking off the road to the fair the way you won't be destroying me going too fast on the hills. [*She goes a few steps towards the left, then turns and speaks to Sarah very persuasively*] Let you not take the can from the   165 sack, Sarah Casey; for the people is coming above would be making game of you, and pointing their fingers if they seen you do the like of that. Let you leave it safe in the bag, I'm saying, Sarah darling. It's that way will be best. [*She goes towards left, and pauses for a moment, looking about her with embarrassment*]   170

MICHAEL [*in a low voice*] What ails her at all?

SARAH [*anxiously*] It's real wicked she does be when you hear her speaking as easy as that.

MARY [*to herself*] I'd be safer in the chapel, I'm thinking; for if she caught me after on the road, maybe she would kill me then. [*She   175 comes hobbling back towards the right*]

SARAH Where is it you're going? It isn't that way we'll be walking to the fair.

MARY I'm going up into the chapel to give you my blessing and hear the priest saying his prayers. It's a lonesome road is running below   180 to Greenane,° and a woman would never know the things might happen her and she walking single in a lonesome place.

[*As she reaches the chapel-gate, the Priest comes to it in his surplice*]

PRIEST [*crying out*] Come along now. Is it the whole day you'd keep me here saying my prayers, and I getting my death with not a bit in my stomach, and my breakfast in ruins, and the Lord Bishop   185 maybe driving on the road today?

SARAH We're coming now, holy father.

PRIEST Give me the bit of gold into my hand.

SARAH It's here, holy father.

[*She gives it to him. Michael takes the bundle from the ditch and brings it over, standing a little behind Sarah. He feels the bundle, and looks at Mary with a meaning look*]

PRIEST [*looking at the gold*] It's a good one I'm thinking wherever   190
you got it. And where is the can?

SARAH [*taking the bundle*] We have it here in a bit of clean sack, your
reverence. We tied it up in the inside of that to keep it from
rusting in the dews of night, and let you not open it now or you'll
have the people making game of us and telling the story on us, east   195
and west to the butt of the hills.

PRIEST [*taking the bundle*] Give it here into my hand, Sarah Casey.
What is it any person would think of a tinker making a can? [*He
begins opening the bundle*]

SARAH It's a fine can, your reverence, for if it's poor simple people   200
we are, it's fine cans we can make, and himself, God help him, is
a great man surely at the trade.

[*Priest opens the bundle; the three empty bottles fall out*]

SARAH Glory to the saints of joy!

PRIEST Did ever any man see the like of that? To think you'd be
putting deceit on me, and telling lies to me, and I going to marry   205
you for a little sum wouldn't marry a child.

SARAH [*crestfallen and astonished*] It's the divil did it, your reverence,
and I wouldn't tell you a lie. [*Raising her hands*] May the Lord
Almighty strike me dead if the divil isn't after hooshing the tin can
from the bag.   210

PRIEST [*vehemently*] Go along now, and don't be swearing your lies.
Go along now, and let you not be thinking I'm big fool enough to
believe the like of that, when it's after selling it you are or making
a swap for drink of it, maybe, in the darkness of the night.

MARY [*in a peacemaking voice, putting her hand on the Priest's left arm*]   215
She wouldn't do the like of that, your reverence, when she hasn't
a decent standing drouth on her at all; and she's setting great store
on her marriage the way you'd have a right to be taking her easy,
and not minding the can. What differ° would an empty can make
with a fine, rich, hardy man the like of you?   220

SARAH [*imploringly*] Marry us, your reverence, for the ten shillings
in gold, and we'll make you a grand can in the evening—a can
would be fit to carry water for the holy man of God. Marry us now
and I'll be saying fine prayers for you, morning and night, if it'd
be raining itself, and it'd be in two black pools I'd be setting my   225
knees.

PRIEST [*loudly*] It's a wicked, thieving, lying, scheming lot you are,
the pack of you. Let you walk off now and take every stinking rag
you have there from the ditch.

MARY [*putting her shawl over her head*] Marry her, your reverence, 230
for the love of God, for there'll be queer doings below if you send
her off the like of that and she swearing crazy on the road.

SARAH [*angrily*] It's the truth she's saying; for it's herself, I'm
thinking, is after swapping the tin can for a pint, the time she was
raging mad with the drouth, and ourselves above walking the hill. 235

MARY [*crying out with indignation*] Have you no shame, Sarah Casey,
to tell lies unto a holy man?

SARAH [*to Mary, working herself into a rage*] It's making game of me
you'd be, and putting a fool's head on me in the face of the world;
but if you were thinking to be mighty cute° walking off, or going 240
up to hide in the church, I've got you this time, and you'll not run
from me now. [*She seizes up one of the bottles*]

MARY [*hiding behind the Priest*] Keep her off, your reverence, keep
her off for the love of the Almighty God. What at all would the
Lord Bishop say if he found me here lying with my head broken 245
across, or the two of yous maybe digging a bloody grave for me at
the door of the church?

PRIEST [*waving Sarah off*] Go along, Sarah Casey. Would you be
doing murder at my feet? Go along from me now, and wasn't I a
big fool to have to do with you when it's nothing but distraction 250
and torment I get from the kindness of my heart?

SARAH [*shouting*] I've bet° a power of strong lads east and west
through the world, and are you thinking I'd turn back from a
priest? Leave the road now, or maybe I would strike yourself.

PRIEST You would not, Sarah Casey. I've no fear for the lot of you; 255
but let you walk off I'm saying, and not be coming where you've
no business, and screeching tumult and murder at the doorway of
the church.

SARAH I'll not go a step till I have her head broke, or till I'm wed
with himself. If you want to get shut of us, let you marry us now, 260
for I'm thinking the ten shillings in gold is a good price for the
like of you, and you near burst with the fat.

PRIEST I wouldn't have you coming in on me and soiling my church;
for there's nothing at all, I'm thinking, would keep the like of you
from hell. [*He throws down the ten shillings on the ground*] Gather 265
up your gold now, and begone from my sight, for if ever I set an
eye on you again you'll hear me telling the peelers who it was stole
the black ass belonging to Philly O'Cullen, and whose hay it is the
grey ass does be eating.

SARAH You'd do that? 270

PRIEST I would, surely.

SARAH If you do, you'll be getting all the tinkers from Wicklow and
Wexford, and the County Meath, to put up block tin in the place
of glass to shield your windows where you do be looking out and
blinking at the girls.° It's hard set you'll be that time, I'm telling   275
you, to fill the depth of your belly the long days of Lent; for we
wouldn't leave a laying pullet in your yard at all.

PRIEST [*losing his temper finally*] Go on, now, or I'll send the Lords
of Justice° a dated story of your villainies—burning, stealing,
robbing, raping to this mortal day. Go on now, I'm saying, if you'd   280
run from Kilmainham or the rope itself.°

MICHAEL [*taking off his coat*] Is it run from the like of you, holy
father? Go up to your own shanty, or I'll beat you with the ass's
reins till the world would hear you roaring from this place to the
coast of Clare.   285

PRIEST Is it lift your hand upon myself when the Lord would blight
your members if you'd touch me now? Go on from this. [*He gives
him a shove*]

MICHAEL Blight me is it? Take it then, your reverence, and God help
you so.° [*He runs at him with the reins*]   290

PRIEST [*runs up to ditch, crying out*] There are the peelers passing by
the grace of God—hey, below!

MARY [*clapping her hand over his mouth*] Knock him down on the
road; they didn't hear him at all.
[*Michael pulls him down*]

SARAH Gag his jaws.   295

MARY Stuff the sacking in his teeth.
[*They gag him with the sack that had the can in it*]

SARAH Tie the bag around his head,° and if the peelers come, we'll
put him headfirst in the boghole is beyond the ditch.
[*They tie him up in some sacking*]

MICHAEL [*to Mary*] Keep him quiet, and the rags tight on him for
fear he'd screech. [*He goes back to their camp*] Hurry with the   300
things, Sarah Casey. The peelers aren't coming this way, and
maybe we'll get off from them now.
[*They bundle the things together in wild haste, the Priest
wriggling and struggling about on the ground, with old Mary
trying to keep him quiet*]

MARY [*patting his head*] Be quiet, your reverence. What is it ails you,
with your wrigglings now? Is it choking maybe? [*She puts her hand
under the sack, and feels his mouth, patting him on the back*] It's only   305

letting on you are, holy father, for your nose is blowing back and forward as easy as an east wind on an April day. [*In a soothing voice*] There now, holy father, let you stay easy, I'm telling you, and learn a little sense and patience, the way you'll not be so airy° again going to rob poor sinners of their scraps of gold. [*He gets quieter*] That's a good boy you are now, your reverence, and let you not be uneasy, for we wouldn't hurt you at all. It's sick and sorry we are to tease you; but what did you want meddling with the like of us, when it's a long time we are going our own ways—father and son, and his son after him, or mother and daughter, and her own daughter again—and it's little need we ever had of going up into a church and swearing—I'm told there's swearing with it°—a word no man would believe, or with drawing rings on our fingers, would be cutting our skins maybe when we'd be taking the ass from the shafts, and pulling the straps the time they'd be slippy with going around beneath the heavens in rains falling.

MICHAEL [*who has finished bundling up the things, comes over with Sarah*] We're fixed now; and I have a mind to run him in a bog-hole the way he'll not be tattling to the peelers of our games today.

SARAH You'd have a right too, I'm thinking.

MARY [*soothingly*] Let you not be rough with him, Sarah Casey, and he after drinking his sup of porter with us at the fall of night. Maybe he'd swear a mighty oath he wouldn't harm us, and then we'd safer loose him; for if we went to drown him, they'd maybe hang the batch of us, man and child and woman, and the ass itself.

MICHAEL What would he care for an oath?

MARY Don't you know his like do live in terror of the wrath of God? [*Putting her mouth to the Priest's ear in the sacking*] Would you swear an oath, holy father, to leave us in our freedom, and not talk at all? [*Priest nods in sacking*] Didn't I tell you? Look at the poor fellow nodding his head off in the bias of the sacks.° Strip them off from him, and he'll be easy now.

MICHAEL [*as if speaking to a horse*] Hold up, holy father.
        [*He pulls the sacking off, and shows the Priest with his hair on end. They free his mouth*]

MARY Hold him till he swears.

PRIEST [*in a faint voice*] I swear surely. If you let me go in peace, I'll not inform against you or say a thing at all, and may God forgive me for giving heed unto your like today.

49

SARAH [*puts the ring on his finger*] There's the ring, holy father, to   345
keep you minding of your oath until the end of time; for my heart's
scalded with your fooling; and it'll be a long day till I go making
talk of marriage or the like of that.

MARY [*complacently, standing up slowly*] She's vexed now, your
reverence; and let you not mind her at all, for she's right surely,   350
and it's little need we ever had of the like of you to get us our bit
to eat, and our bit to drink, and our time of love when we were
young men and women, and were fine to look at.

MICHAEL Hurry on now. He's a great man to have kept us from
fooling° our gold; and we'll have a great time drinking that bit with   355
the trampers on the green of Clash.°

   [*They gather up their things. The Priest stands up*]

PRIEST [*lifting up his hand*] I've sworn not to call the hand of man
upon your crimes today; but I haven't sworn I wouldn't call the
fire of heaven from the hand of the Almighty God. [*He begins
saying a Latin malediction in a loud ecclesiastical voice*]   360

MARY There's an old villain.

ALL [*together*] Run, run. Run for your lives.

   [*They rush out, leaving the Priest master of the situation*]

   CURTAIN

THE WELL OF THE SAINTS

A Play in Three Acts

(1903–1908)

PREFACE TO THE FIRST EDITION OF
THE WELL OF THE SAINTS

by W. B. YEATS

MR SYNGE AND HIS PLAYS

Six years ago° I was staying in a students' hotel in the Latin Quarter, and somebody, whose name I cannot recollect, introduced me to an Irishman, who, even poorer than myself, had taken a room at the top of the house. It was J. M. Synge, and I, who thought I knew the name of every Irishman who was working at literature, had never heard of 5 him. He was a graduate of Trinity College, Dublin, too, and Trinity College does not, as a rule, produce artistic minds. He told me that he had been living in France and Germany, reading French and German literature, and that he wished to become a writer. He had, however, nothing to show but one or two poems and impressionistic 10 essays, full of that kind of morbidity that has its root in too much brooding over methods of expression, and ways of looking upon life, which come, not out of life, but out of literature, images reflected from mirror to mirror. He had wandered among people whose life is as picturesque as the Middle Ages, playing his fiddle to Italian 15 sailors,° and listening to stories in Bavarian woods, but life had cast no light into his writings. He had learned Irish years ago, but had begun to forget it, for the only language that interested him was that conventional language of modern poetry which has begun to make us all weary. I was very weary of it, for I had finished *The Secret Rose*, 20 and felt how it had separated my imagination from life, sending my Red Hanrahan, who should have trodden the same roads with myself, into some undiscoverable country.° I said: 'Give up Paris. You will never create anything by reading Racine,° and Arthur Symons° will always be a better critic of French literature. Go to the Aran Islands. 25 Live there as if you were one of the people themselves; express a life that has never found expression.' I had just come from Aran, and my imagination was full of those grey islands where men must reap with knives because of the stones.

He went to Aran and became a part of its life, living upon salt fish 30 and eggs, talking Irish for the most part, but listening also to the beautiful English which has grown up in Irish-speaking districts, and takes its vocabulary from the time of Malory° and of the translators of the Bible, but its idiom and its vivid metaphor from Irish. When Mr Synge began to write in this language, Lady Gregory had already used it finely in her translations of Dr Hyde's lyrics° and plays, or of old Irish literature, but she had listened with different ears. He made his own selection of word and phrase, choosing what would express his own personality. Above all, he made word and phrase dance to a very strange rhythm, which will always, till his plays have created their own tradition, be difficult to actors who have not learned it from his lips. It is essential, for it perfectly fits the drifting emotion, the dreaminess, the vague yet measureless desire, for which he would create a dramatic form. It blurs definition, clear edges, everything that comes from the will, it turns imagination from all that is of the present, like a gold background in a religious picture, and it strengthens in every emotion whatever comes to it from far off, from brooding memory and dangerous hope. When he brought *The Shadow of the Glen*, his first play, to the Irish National Theatre Society, the players were puzzled by the rhythm,° but gradually they became certain that his Woman of the Glen, as melancholy as a curlew, driven to distraction by her own sensitiveness, her own fineness, could not speak with any other tongue, that all his people would change their life if the rhythm changed. Perhaps no Irish countryman had ever that exact rhythm in his voice, but certainly if Mr Synge had been born a countryman, he would have spoken like that. It makes the people of his imagination a little disembodied; it gives them a kind of innocence even in their anger and their cursing. It is part of its maker's attitude towards the world, for while it makes the clash of wills among his persons indirect and dreamy, it helps him to see the subject-matter of his art with wise, clear-seeing, unreflecting eyes; to preserve the integrity of art in an age of reasons and purposes. Whether he write of old beggars by the roadside, lamenting over the misery and ugliness of life, or of an old Aran woman mourning her drowned sons, or of a young wife married to an old husband, he has no wish to change anything, to reform anything; all these people pass by as before an open window, murmuring strange, exciting words.

If one has not fine construction, one has not drama, but if one has not beautiful or powerful and individual speech, one has not literature, or, at any rate, one has not great literature. Rabelais, Villon, Shakespeare, William Blake,° would have known one another by their speech. Some of them knew how to construct a story, but all of them had abundant, resonant, beautiful, laughing, living speech. It is only

the writers of our modern dramatic movement, our scientific dramat- 75
ists, our naturalists of the stage, who have thought it possible to be
like the greatest, and yet to cast aside even the poor persiflage of the
comedians, and to write in the impersonal language that has come, not
out of individual life, nor out of life at all, but out of necessities of
commerce, of Parliament, of Board Schools, of hurried journeys by rail.

If there are such things as decaying art and decaying institutions, 80
their decay must begin when the element they receive into their care
from the life of every man in the world begins to rot. Literature
decays when it no longer makes more beautiful, or more vivid, the
language which unites it to all life, and when one finds the criticism of the student, and the purpose of the reformer, and the logic 85
of the man of science, where there should have been the reveries of
the common heart, ennobled into some raving Lear or unabashed Don
Quixote. One must not forget that the death of language, the
substitution of phrases as nearly impersonal as algebra for words and
rhythms varying from man to man, is but a part of the tyranny of 90
impersonal things. I have been reading through a bundle of German
plays, and have found everywhere a desire, not to express hopes and
alarms common to every man that ever came into the world, but
politics or social passion, a veiled or open propaganda. Now it is
duelling that has need of reproof; now it is the ideas of an actress, 95
returning from the free life of the stage, that must be contrasted with
the prejudice of an old-fashioned town; now it is the hostility of
Christianity and Paganism in our own day that is to find an obscure
symbol in a bell thrown from its tower by spirits of the wood. I
compare the work of these dramatists with the greater plays of their 100
Scandinavian master,° and remember that even he, who has made so
many clear-drawn characters, has made us no abundant character, no
man of genius in whom we could believe, and that in him also,
even when it is Emperor and Galilean that are face to face, even the
most momentous figures are subordinate to some tendency, to some 105
movement, to some inanimate energy, or to some process of thought
whose very logic has changed it into mechanism—always to 'something other than human life'.

We must not measure a young talent, whether we praise or blame,
with that of men who are among the greatest of our time, but we may 110
say of any talent, following out a definition, that it takes up the
tradition of great drama as it came from the hands of the Masters
who are acknowledged by all time, and turns away from a dramatic
movement which, though it has been served by fine talent, has been
imposed upon us by science, by artificial life, by a passing order. 115

54

When the individual life no longer delights in its own energy, when the body is not made strong and beautiful by the activities of daily life, when men have no delight in decorating the body, one may be certain that one lives in a passing order, amid the inventions of a fading vitality. If Homer were alive today, he would only resist, after 120 a deliberate struggle, the temptation to find his subject not in Helen's beauty, that every man has desired, nor in the wisdom and endurance of Odysseus that has been the desire of every woman that has come into the world, but in what somebody would describe, perhaps, as 'the inevitable contest', arising out of economic causes, between the 125 country-places and small towns on the one hand, and, upon the other, the great city of Troy, representing one knows not what 'tendency to centralisation'.

Mr Synge has in common with the great theatre of the world, with that of Greece and that of India, with the creator of Falstaff, with 130 Racine, a delight in language, a preoccupation with individual life. He resembles them also by a preoccupation with what is lasting and noble, that came to him, not, as I think, from books, but while he listened to old stories in the cottages, and contrasted what they remembered with reality. The only literature of the Irish country 135 people is their songs, full often of extravagant love, and their stories of kings and of kings' children. 'I will cry my fill, but not for God, but because Finn and the Fianna are not living,' says Oisin in the story.° Every writer, even every small writer, who has belonged to the great tradition, has had his dream of an impossibly noble life, and 140 the greater he is, the more does it seem to plunge him into some beautiful or bitter reverie. Some, and of these are all the earliest poets of the world, gave it direct expression; others mingle it so subtly with reality that it is a day's work to disentangle it; others bring it near by showing us whatever is most its contrary. Mr Synge, indeed, sets 145 before us ugly, deformed or sinful people, but his people, moved by no practical ambition, are driven by a dream of that impossible life. That we may feel how intensely his Woman of the Glen dreams of days that shall be entirely alive, she that is 'a hard woman to please' must spend her days between a sour-faced old husband, a man who 150 goes mad upon the hills, a craven lad and a drunken tramp; and those two blind people of *The Well of the Saints* are so transformed by the dream that they choose blindness rather than reality. He tells us of realities, but he knows that art has never taken more than its symbols from anything that the eye can see or the hand measure. 155

It is the preoccupation of his characters with their dream that gives his plays their drifting movement, their emotional subtlety. In most of the dramatic writing of our time, and this is one of the reasons why our dramatists do not find the need for a better speech, one finds a simple motive lifted, as it were, into the full light of the stage. The 160 ordinary student of drama will not find anywhere in *The Well of the Saints* that excitement of the will in the presence of attainable advantages, which he is accustomed to think the natural stuff of drama, and if he see it played he will wonder why act is knitted to act so loosely, why it is all like a decoration on a flat surface, why there 165 is so much leisure in the dialogue, even in the midst of passion. If he see *The Shadow of the Glen*, he will ask, Why does this woman go out of her house? Is it because she cannot help herself, or is she content to go? Why is it not all made clearer? And yet, like everybody when caught up into great events, she does many things without being quite 170 certain why she does them. She hardly understands at moments why her action has a certain form, more clearly than why her body is tall or short, fair or brown. She feels an emotion that she does not understand. She is driven by desires that need for their expression, not 'I admire this man,' or 'I must go, whether I will or no,' but words 175 full of suggestion, rhythms of voice, movements that escape analysis. In addition to all this, she has something that she shares with none but the children of one man's imagination. She is intoxicated by a dream which is hardly understood by herself, but possesses her like something half remembered on a sudden wakening. 180

While I write, we are rehearsing *The Well of the Saints*, and are painting for it decorative scenery, mountains in one or two flat colours and without detail, ash-trees and red salleys with something of recurring pattern in their woven boughs. For though the people of the play use no phrase they could not use in daily life, we know that 185 we are seeking to express what no eye has ever seen.

W. B. YEATS

ABBEY THEATRE
January 27, 1905

56

PERSONS

MARTIN DOUL,° a weather-beaten, blind beggar
MARY DOUL, his wife, a weather-beaten, ugly
  woman, blind also, nearly fifty
TIMMY, a middle-aged, almost elderly, but
  vigorous smith
MOLLY BYRNE, a fine-looking girl with fair hair
BRIDE, another handsome girl
MAT SIMON
THE SAINT,° a wandering Friar
OTHER GIRLS AND MEN

SCENE

*Some lonely mountainous district in the east of Ireland,°
one or more centuries ago*

*The first act is in the autumn; the second towards the
end of winter; and the third at the beginning of spring.*

FIRST PRODUCTION
(Dublin, 4 February 1905)

Martin Doul	W. G. Fay
Mary Doul	Emma Vernon
Timmy, a smith	George Roberts
Molly Byrne	Sara Allgood
Bride	Maire Nic Shiubhlaigh
Mat Simon	P. Mac Shiubhlaigh
A Wandering Friar	F. J. Fay

Act 1

Roadside with big stones, etc. on the right; low loose wall at back with gap near centre; at left, ruined doorway of church with bushes beside it. Martin Doul and Mary Doul grope in on left and pass over to stones on right, where they sit

MARY DOUL What place arc we now, Martin Doul?

MARTIN DOUL Passing the gap.

MARY DOUL [*raising her head*] The length of that! Well, the sun's coming warm this day if it's late autumn itself.

MARTIN DOUL [*putting out his hands in sun*] What way wouldn't it be warm and it getting high up in the south? You were that length° plaiting your yellow hair° you have the morning lost on us, and the people are after passing to the fair of Clash.°

MARY DOUL It isn't going to the fair, the time they do be driving their cattle and they with a litter of pigs maybe squealing in their carts, they'd give us a thing at all. [*She sits down*] It's well you know that, but you must be talking.

MARTIN DOUL [*sitting down beside her and beginning to shred rushes she gives him°*] If I didn't talk I'd be destroyed in a short while listening to the clack you do be making, for you've a queer cracked voice, the Lord have mercy on you, if it's fine to look on you are itself.

MARY DOUL Who wouldn't have a cracked voice sitting out all the year in the rain falling? It's a bad life for the voice, Martin Doul, though I've heard tell there isn't anything like the wet south wind does be blowing upon us, for keeping a white beautiful skin––the like of my skin––on your neck and on your brows, and there isn't anything at all like a fine skin for putting splendour on a woman.

MARTIN DOUL [*teasingly, but with good-humour*] I do be thinking odd times° we don't know rightly what way you have your splendour, or asking myself, maybe, if you have it at all, for the time I was a young lad, and had fine sight, it was the ones with sweet voices were the best in face.

MARY DOUL Let you not be making the like of that talk when you've heard Timmy the smith, and Mat Simon, and Patch Ruadh,° and a power besides saying fine things of my face, and you know rightly it was 'the beautiful dark° woman', they did call me in Ballina-tone.°

5

10

15

20

25

30

MARTIN DOUL [*as before*] If it was itself° I heard Molly Byrne saying
at the fall of night it was little more than a fright you were.   35

MARY DOUL [*sharply*] She was jealous, God forgive her, because
Timmy the smith was after praising my hair—

MARTIN DOUL [*with mock irony*] Jealous!

MARY DOUL Ay, jealous, Martin Doul, and if she wasn't itself, the
young and silly do be always making game of them that's dark, and   40
they'd think it a fine thing if they had us deceived, the way we
wouldn't know we were so fine-looking at all. [*She puts her hand to
her face with a complacent gesture and smoothes her hair back with her
hands*]

MARTIN DOUL [*a little plaintively*] I do be thinking in the long nights   45
it'd be a grand thing if we could see ourselves for one hour, or a
minute itself, the way we'd know surely we were the finest man,
and the finest woman,° of the seven counties of the east . . .°
[*bitterly*] and then the seeing rabble below might be destroying
their souls telling bad lies, and we'd never heed a thing they'd say.   50

MARY DOUL If you weren't a big fool you wouldn't heed them this
hour Martin Doul, for they're a bad lot those that have their sight,
and they do have great joy, the time they do be seeing a grand
thing, to let on they don't see it at all, and to be telling fools' lies,
the like of what Molly Byrne was telling to yourself.   55

MARTIN DOUL If it's lies she does be telling she's a sweet beautiful
voice you'd never tire to be hearing, if it was only the pig she'd be
calling, or crying out in the long grass, maybe, after her hens. . . .
[*Speaking pensively*] It should be a fine soft, rounded woman, I'm
thinking, would have a voice the like of that.   60

MARY DOUL [*sharply again, scandalized*] Let you not be minding if
it's flat or rounded she is, for she's a flighty, foolish woman you'll
hear when you're off a long way, and she making a great noise and
laughing at the well.

MARTIN DOUL Isn't laughing a nice thing the time a woman's   65
young?

MARY DOUL [*bitterly*] A nice thing is it? A nice thing to hear a
woman making a loud braying laugh the like of that? Ah, she's a
great one for drawing the men, and you'll hear Timmy himself,
the time he does be sitting in his forge, getting mighty fussy if   70
she'll come walking from Grianan, the way you'll hear his breath
going, and he wringing his hands.

MARTIN DOUL [*slightly piqued*] I've heard him say a power of times,
it's nothing at all she is when you see her at the side of you, and

yet I never heard any man's breath getting uneasy the time he'd   75
be looking on yourself.

MARY DOUL I'm not the like of the girls do be running round on the
roads, swinging their legs, and they with their necks out looking
on the men . . . Ah, there's a power of villainy walking the world,
Martin Doul, among them that do be gadding around, with their   80
gaping eyes, and their sweet words, and they with no sense in them
at all.

MARTIN DOUL [*sadly*] It's the truth, maybe, and yet I'm told it's a
grand thing to see a young girl walking the road.

MARY DOUL You'd be as bad as the rest of them if you had your   85
sight, and I did well surely, not to marry a seeing man—it's scores
would have had me and welcome—for the seeing is a queer lot,
and you'd never know the thing they'd do.

   [*A moment's pause*]

MARTIN DOUL [*listening*] There's someone coming on the road.

MARY DOUL Let you put the pith away out of their sight, or they'll   90
be picking it out with the spying eyes they have, and saying it's
rich we are, and not sparing us a thing at all.

   [*They bundle away the rushes. Timmy the Smith comes in on
left*]

MARTIN DOUL [*with a begging voice*] Leave a bit of silver for blind
Martin, your honour. Leave a bit of silver, or a penny copper itself,
and we'll be praying the Lord to bless you and you going the way.   95

TIMMY [*stopping before them*] And you letting on a while back you
knew my step! [*He sits down*]

MARTIN DOUL [*with his natural voice*] I know it when Molly Byrne's
walking in front, or when she's two perches,° maybe, lagging
behind, but it's few times I've heard you walking up the like of   100
that, as if you'd met a thing wasn't right° and you coming on the
road.

TIMMY [*hot and breathless, wiping his face*] You've good ears, God
bless you, if you're a liar itself, for I'm after walking up in great
haste from hearing wonders in the fair.   105

MARTIN [*rather contemptuously*] You're always hearing queer wonderful things, and the lot of them nothing at all, but I'm thinking, this
time, it's a strange thing surely, you'd be walking up before the
turn of day, and not waiting below to look on them lepping, or
dancing, or playing shows° on the green of Clash.   110

TIMMY [*huffed*] I was coming to tell you it's in this place there'd be
a bigger wonder done in a short while [*Martin Doul stops working*

and looks at him], than was ever done on the green of Clash, or the width of Leinster itself, but you're thinking, maybe, you're too cute a little fellow to be minding me at all.°   115

MARTIN DOUL [*amused but incredulous*] There'll be wonders in this place is it?

TIMMY Here at the crossing of the roads.

MARTIN DOUL I never heard tell of anything to happen in this place since the night they killed the old fellow going home with his gold,   120 the Lord have mercy on him, and threw down his corpse into the bog. Let them not be doing the like of that this night, for it's ourselves have a right to the crossing roads, and we don't want any of your bad tricks, or your wonders either, for it's wonder enough we are ourselves.°   125

TIMMY If I'd a mind I'd be telling you of a real wonder this day, and the way you'll be having a great joy, maybe, you're not thinking on at all.

MARTIN DOUL [*interested*] Are they putting up a still° behind in the rocks? It'd be a grand thing if I'd a sup handy the way I wouldn't   130 be destroying myself groping up across the bogs in the rain falling.

TIMMY [*still moodily*] It's not a still they're bringing or the like of it either.

MARY DOUL [*persuasively, to Timmy*] Maybe they're hanging a thief, above at the bit of a tree? I'm told it's a great sight to see a man   135 hanging by his neck, but what joy would that be to ourselves, and we not seeing it at all?

TIMMY [*more pleasantly*] They're hanging no one this day, Mary Doul, and yet with the help of God, you'll see a power hanged before you die.   140

MARY DOUL Well you've queer humbugging talk.° . . . What way would I see a power hanged, and I a dark woman since the seventh year of my age?

TIMMY Did ever you hear tell of a place across a bit of the sea, where there is an island, and the grave of the four beautiful saints?°   145

MARY DOUL I've heard people have walked round from the west and they speaking of that.

TIMMY [*impressively*] There's a green ferny well, I'm told, behind of that place, and if you put a drop of the water out of it, on the eyes of a blind man, you'll make him see as well as any person is   150 walking the world.

MARTIN DOUL [*with excitement*] Is that the truth, Timmy? I'm thinking you're telling a lie.

TIMMY [*gruffly*] That's the truth, Martin Doul, and you may believe it now, for you're after believing a power of things weren't as likely   155
at all.

MARY DOUL Maybe we could send a young lad to bring us the water. I could wash a naggin° bottle in the morning, and I'm thinking Patch Ruadh would go for it, if we gave him a good drink, and the bit of money we have hid in the thatch.°   160

TIMMY It'd be no good to be sending a sinful man the like of ourselves, for I'm told the holiness of the water does be getting soiled with the villainy of your heart, the time you'd be carrying it, and you looking round on the girls, maybe, or drinking a small sup at a still.   165

MARTIN DOUL [*with disappointment*] It'd be a long terrible way to be walking ourselves, and I'm thinking that's a wonder will bring small joy to us at all.

TIMMY [*turning on him impatiently*] What is it you want with your walking? It's as deaf as blind you're growing if you're not after   170
hearing me say it's in this place the wonder would be done.

MARTIN DOUL [*with a flash of anger*] If it is can't you open the big slobbering mouth you have and say what way it'll be done, and not be making blather till the fall of night.

TIMMY [*jumping up*] I'll be going on now [*Mary Doul rises*], and not   175
wasting time talking civil talk with the like of you.

MARY DOUL [*standing up, disguising her impatience*] Let you come here to me, Timmy, and not be minding him at all. [*Timmy stops, and she gropes up to him and takes him by the coat*] . . . You're not huffy with myself, and let you tell me the whole story and don't   180
be fooling me more . . . Is it yourself has brought us the water?

TIMMY It is not, surely.

MARY DOUL Then tell us your wonder, Timmy . . . What person'll bring it at all?

TIMMY [*relenting*] It's a fine holy man will bring it, a saint of the   185
Almighty God.

MARY DOUL [*overawed*] A saint is it?

TIMMY Ay, a fine saint, who's going round through the churches of Ireland, with a long cloak on him, and naked feet, for he's brought a sup of the water slung at his side, and, with the like of him, any   190
little drop is enough to cure the dying, or to make the blind see as clear as the grey hawks do be high up, on a still day, sailing the sky.

MARTIN DOUL [*feeling for his stick*] What place is he, Timmy? I'll be walking to him now.

TIMMY Let you stay quiet, Martin. He's straying around saying   195
prayers at the churches and high crosses, between this place and
the hills, and he with a great crowd going behind—for it's fine
prayers he does be saying, and fasting with it, till he's as thin as
one of the empty rushes you have there on your knee—then he'll
be coming after to this place to cure the two of you, we're after   200
telling him the way you are, and to say his prayers in the church.

MARTIN DOUL [*turning suddenly to Mary Doul*] And we'll be seeing
ourselves this day. Oh, glory be to God, is it true surely?

MARY DOUL [*very pleased, to Timmy*] Maybe I'd have time to walk
down and get the big shawl I have below, for I do look my best,   205
I've heard them say, when I'm dressed up with that thing on my
head.

TIMMY You'd have time surely—

MARTIN DOUL [*listening*] Whisht now . . . I hear people again coming by the stream.   210

TIMMY [*looking out left, puzzled*] It's the young girls I left walking
after the saint. . . . They're coming now [*goes up to entrance*]
carrying things in their hands, and they walking as easy as you'd
see a child walk, who'd have a dozen eggs hid in her bib.

MARTIN DOUL [*listening*] That's Molly Byrne, I'm thinking.   215
[*Molly Byrne and Bride come on left and cross to Martin Doul,
carrying water-can, Saint's bell, and cloak*]

MOLLY [*volubly*] God bless you, Martin. I've holy water here from
the grave of the four saints of the west, will have you cured in a
short while and seeing like ourselves—

TIMMY [*crosses to Molly, interrupting her*] He's heard that, God help
you. But where at all is the saint, and what way is he after trusting   220
the holy water with the likes of you?

MOLLY BYRNE He was afeard to go a far way with the clouds is
coming beyond, so he's gone up now through the thick woods to
say a prayer at the crosses of Grianan, and he's coming on this road
to the church.   225

TIMMY [*still astonished*] And he's after leaving the holy water with
the two of you? It's a wonder, surely. [*Comes down left a little*]

MOLLY BYRNE The lads told him no person could carry them things
through the briars, and steep, slippy-feeling rocks he'll be climbing
above, so he looked round then, and gave the water, and his big   230
cloak, and his bell to the two of us, for young girls, says he, are
the cleanest holy people you'd see walking the world.
[*Mary Doul goes near seat*]

MARY DOUL [*sits down, laughing to herself*] Well, the saint's a simple fellow, and it's no lie.°

MARTIN DOUL [*leaning forward, holding out his hands*] Let you give 235 me the water in my hand, Molly Byrne, the way I'll know you have it surely.

MOLLY BYRNE [*giving it to him*] Wonders is° queer things, and maybe it'd cure you, and you holding it alone.

MARTIN DOUL [*looking round*] It does not, Molly. I'm not seeing at 240 all. [*He shakes the can*] There's a small sup only. Well, isn't it a great wonder the little trifling thing would bring seeing to the blind, and be showing us the big women and the young girls, and all the fine things is walking the world. [*He feels for Mary Doul and gives her the can*] 245

MARY DOUL [*shaking it*] Well, glory be to God—

MARTIN DOUL [*pointing to Bride*] And what is it herself has, making sounds in her hand?

BRIDE [*crossing to Martin Doul*] It's the saint's bell, you'll hear him ringing out the time he'll be going up some place, to be saying his 250 prayers.

[*Martin Doul holds out his hands; she gives it to him*]

MARTIN DOUL [*ringing it*] It's a sweet, beautiful sound.

MARY DOUL You'd know I'm thinking by the little silvery voice of it, a fasting holy man was after carrying it a great way at his side. 255

[*Bride crosses a little right behind Martin Doul*]

MOLLY BYRNE [*unfolding Saint's cloak*] Let you stand up now, Martin Doul, till I put his big cloak on you, the way we'd see how you'd look, and you a saint of the Almighty God.

MARTIN DOUL [*rises, comes forward centre, a little diffidently*] I've heard the priests a power of times making great talk and praises of 260 the beauty of the saints.

[*Molly Byrne slips cloak round him*]

TIMMY [*uneasily*] You'd have a right to be leaving him alone, Molly. What would the saint say if he seen you making game with his cloak?

MOLLY BYRNE [*recklessly*] How would he see us, and he saying 265 prayers in the wood? [*She turns Martin Doul round*] Isn't that a fine holy-looking saint, Timmy the smith? [*Laughing foolishly*] There's a grand handsome fellow, Mary Doul, and if you seen him now, you'd be as proud, I'm thinking, as the archangels below, fell out with the Almighty God.° 270

MARY DOUL [*with quiet confidence going to Martin Doul and feeling his cloak*] It's proud we'll be this day, surely.

[*Martin Doul is still ringing bell*]

MOLLY BYRNE [*to Martin Doul*] Would you think well to be all your life walking round the like of that Martin Doul, and you bell-ringing with the saints of God? 275

MARY DOUL [*turning on her, fiercely*] How would he be bell-ringing with the saints of God and he wedded with myself?

MARTIN DOUL It's the truth she's saying, and if bell-ringing is a fine life, yet I'm thinking, maybe, it's better I am wedded with the beautiful dark woman of Ballinatone. 280

MOLLY BYRNE [*scornfully*] You're thinking that, God help you, but it's little you know of her at all.°

MARTIN DOUL It's little surely, and I'm destroyed this day waiting to look upon her face.

TIMMY [*awkwardly*] It's well you know the way she is, for the like 285 of you do have great knowledge in the feeling of your hands.

MARTIN DOUL [*still feeling the cloak*] We do maybe. Yet it's little I know of faces, or of fine beautiful cloaks, for it's few cloaks I've had my hand to, and few faces [*plaintively*], for the young girls is mighty shy, Timmy the smith, and it isn't much they heed me, 290 though they do be saying I'm a handsome man.

MARY DOUL [*mockingly, with good-humour*] Isn't it a queer thing the voice he puts on him, when you hear him talking of the skinny young-looking girls, and he married with a woman he's heard called the wonder of the western world? 295

TIMMY [*pityingly*] The two of you will see a great wonder this day, and it's no lie.

MARTIN DOUL I've heard tell her yellow hair, and her white skin, and her big eyes are a wonder, surely—

BRIDE [*who has looked out left*] Here's the saint coming from the 300 selvage° of the wood . . . Strip the cloak from him, Molly, or he'll be seeing it now.

MOLLY BYRNE [*hastily to Bride*] Take the bell and put herself by the stones. [*To Martin Doul*] Will you hold your head up till I loosen the cloak. [*She pulls off the cloak and throws it over her arm. Then* 305 *she pushes Martin Doul over and stands him beside Mary Doul*] Stand there now, quiet, and let you not be saying a word.

[*She and Bride stand a little on their left, demurely, with bell, etc., in their hands*]

MARTIN DOUL [*nervously arranging his clothes*] Will he mind the way we are, and we not tidied or washed cleanly at all?

MOLLY BYRNE He'll not see what way you are. . . . He'd walk by the   310
finest woman in Ireland, I'm thinking, and not trouble to raise his
two eyes to look upon her face . . . Whisht!
  [*Saint comes on left, with crowd [including Mat Simon and
  Patch Ruadh*]]
SAINT Are these the two poor people?
TIMMY [*officiously*] They are, holy father, they do be always sitting
here at the crossing of the roads, asking a bit of copper° from them   315
that do pass, or stripping rushes for lights, and they not mournful
at all, but talking out straight with a full voice, and making game
with them that likes it.
SAINT [*to Martin Doul and Mary Doul*] It's a hard life you've had
not seeing sun or moon, or the holy priests itself praying to the   320
Lord, but it's the like of you who are brave in a bad time will make
a fine use of the gift of sight the Almighty God will bring to you
today. [*He takes his cloak and puts it about him*] It's on a bare
starving rock that there's the grave of the four beauties of God,
the way it's little wonder, I'm thinking, if it's with bare starving   325
people the water should be used. [*He takes the water and bell and
slings them round his shoulders*] So it's to the like of yourselves I do
be going, who are wrinkled and poor, a thing rich men would
hardly look at at all, but would throw a coin to or a crust of bread.
MARTIN DOUL [*moving uneasily*] When they look on herself who is   330
a fine woman—
TIMMY [*shaking him*] Whisht now, and be listening to the saint.
SAINT [*looks at them a moment, continues*] If it's raggy and dirty you
are itself, I'm saying, the Almighty God isn't at all like the rich
men of Ireland; and, with the power of the water I'm after bringing   335
in a little curagh into Cashla Bay,° he'll have pity on you, and put
sight into your eyes.
MARTIN DOUL [*taking off his hat*] I'm ready now, holy father—
SAINT [*taking him by the hand*] I'll cure you first, and then I'll come
for your wife. We'll go up now into the church, for I must say a   340
prayer to the Lord . . . [*To Mary Doul as he moves off*] And let you
be making your mind still and saying praises in your heart, for it's
a great wonderful thing when the power of the Lord of the world
is brought down upon your like.
PEOPLE [*pressing after him*] Come now till we watch.   345
BRIDE Come, Timmy.
SAINT [*waving them back*] Stay back where you are, for I'm not
wanting a big crowd making whispers in the church. Stay back
there, I'm saying, and you'd do well to be thinking on the way sin

has brought blindness to the world, and to be saying a prayer for   350
your own sakes against false prophets and heathens, and the words
of women and smiths,° and all knowledge that would soil the soul
or the body of a man.

> [*People shrink back. He goes into church. Mary Doul gropes half
> way towards the door and kneels near path. People form a group
> at right*]

TIMMY Isn't it a fine, beautiful voice he has, and he a fine, brave°
man if it wasn't for the fasting?   355

BRIDE Did you watch him moving his hands?

MOLLY BYRNE It'd be a fine thing if some one in this place could
pray the like of him, for I'm thinking the water from our own
blessed well would do rightly° if a man knew the way to be saying
prayers, and then there'd be no call to be bringing water from that   360
wild place, where, I'm told, there are no decent houses, or fine-
looking people at all.

BRIDE [*who is looking in at door from right*] Look at the great
trembling Martin has shaking him, and he on his knees.

TIMMY [*anxiously*] God help him. . . . What will he be doing when   365
he sees his wife this day? I'm thinking it was bad work we did
when we let on she was fine-looking, and not a wrinkled wizened
hag the way she is.

MAT SIMON Why would he be vexed, and we after giving him great
joy and pride, the time he was dark?   370

MOLLY BYRNE [*sitting down in Mary Doul's seat and tidying her hair*]
If it's vexed he is itself, he'll have other things now to think on as
well as his wife, and what does any man care for a wife, when it's
two weeks, or three, he is looking on her face?

MAT SIMON That's the truth now, Molly, and it's more joy dark   375
Martin got from the lies we told of that hag is kneeling by the path,
than your own man will get from you, day or night, and he living
at your side.

MOLLY BYRNE [*defiantly*] Let you not be talking, Mat Simon, for
it's not yourself will be my man, though you'd be crowing and   380
singing fine songs if you'd that hope in you at all.

TIMMY [*shocked, to Molly Byrne*] Let you not be raising your voice
when the saint's above at his prayers.

BRIDE [*crying out*] Whisht. . . . Whisht. . . . I'm thinking he's cured.

MARTIN DOUL [*crying out in the church*] Oh, glory be to God—   385

SAINT [*solemnly*] Laus patri sit et filio cum spiritu paraclito
　　　　　Qui suae dono gratiae miseratus est Hiberniae—°

MARTIN DOUL [*ecstatically*] Oh, glory be to God, I see now surely.
. . . I see the walls of the church, and the green bits of ferns in
them, and yourself, holy father, and the great width of the sky.   390
    [*He runs out half foolish with joy, and comes past Mary Doul
    as she scrambles to her feet, drawing a little away from her as
    he goes by*]
TIMMY [*to the others*] He doesn't know her at all.
    [*Saint comes out behind Martin Doul and leads Mary Doul into
    the church. Martin Doul comes on to the People. The Men
    are between him and the Girls. He verifies his position with his
    stick*]
MARTIN DOUL [*crying out joyfully*] That's Timmy, I know Timmy
by the black of his head.° . . . That's Mat Simon, I know Mat by
the length of his legs. . . . That should be Patch Ruadh, with the
gamey eyes in him,° and the fiery hair. [*He sees Molly Byrne on*   395
Mary Doul's seat, and his voice changes completely] Oh, it was no lie
they told me, Mary Doul. Oh, glory to God and the seven saints
I didn't die and not see you at all. The blessing of God on the
water, and the feet carried it round through the land. The blessing
of God on this day, and them that brought me the saint, for it's   400
grand hair you have [*she lowers her head, a little confused*], and soft
skin, and eyes would make the saints, if they were dark awhile and
seeing again, fall down out of the sky. [*He goes nearer to her*] Hold
up your head, Mary, the way I'll see it's richer I am than the great
kings of the east. Hold up your head, I'm saying, for it's soon   405
you'll be seeing me, and I not a bad one° at all. [*He touches her and
she starts up*]
MOLLY BYRNE Let you keep away from me, and not be soiling my
chin.
    [*People laugh loudly*]
MARTIN DOUL [*bewildered*] It's Molly's voice you have. . .   410
MOLLY BYRNE Why wouldn't I have my own voice? Do you think
I'm a ghost?
MARTIN DOUL Which of you all is herself? [*He goes up to Bride*] Is
it you is Mary Doul? I'm thinking you're more the like of what
they said. [*Peering at her*] For you've yellow hair, and white skin,   415
and it's the smell of my own turf is rising from your shawl. [*He
catches her shawl*]
BRIDE [*pulling away her shawl*] I'm not your wife, and let you get
out of my way.
    [*People laugh again*]

MARTIN DOUL [*with misgiving, to another girl*] Is it yourself it is?   420
You're not so fine looking, but I'm thinking you'd do, with the
grand nose you have, and your nice hands and your feet.

GIRL [*scornfully*] I never seen any person that took me for blind, and
a seeing woman, I'm thinking, would never wed the like of you.
    [*She turns away, and the People laugh once more, drawing back
    a little and leaving him on their left*]

PEOPLE [*jeeringly*] Try again, Martin, try again, you'll find her yet.   425

MARTIN DOUL [*passionately*] Where is it you have her hidden away?
Isn't it a black shame for a drove of pitiful beasts the like of you
to be making game of me, and putting a fool's head on me the
grand day of my life? Ah, you're thinking you're a fine lot, with
your giggling, weeping eyes,° a fine lot to be making game of   430
myself, and the woman I've heard called the great wonder of the
west. . . .
    [*During this speech, which he gives with his back towards the
    church, Mary Doul has come out with her sight cured, and come
    down towards the right with a silly simpering smile, till she is a
    little behind Martin Doul*]

MARY DOUL [*when he pauses*] Which of you is Martin Doul?

MARTIN DOUL [*wheeling round*] It's her voice surely. . . . [*They stare
at each other blankly*]   435

MOLLY BYRNE [*to Martin Doul*] Go up now and take her under the
chin and be speaking the way you spoke to myself. . . .

MARTIN DOUL [*in a low voice, with intensity*] If I speak now, I'll
speak hard to the two of you.° . . .

MOLLY BYRNE [*to Mary Doul*] You're not saying a word, Mary.   440
What is it you think of himself, with the fat legs on him, and the
little neck like a ram?

MARY DOUL I'm thinking it's a poor thing when the Lord God gives
you sight, and puts the like of that man in your way.

MARTIN DOUL It's on your two knees you should be thanking the   445
Lord God you're not looking on yourself, for if it was yourself
you seen, you'd be running round in a short while like the old
screeching madwoman is running round in the glen.

MARY DOUL [*beginning to realize herself*] If I'm not so fine as some
of them said, I have my hair, and my big eyes, and my white   450
skin—

MARTIN DOUL [*breaking out into a passionate cry*] Your hair, and your
big eyes, is it? . . . I'm telling you there isn't a wisp on any grey
mare° on the ridge of the world° isn't finer than the dirty twist on

your head. There isn't two eyes in any starving sow, isn't finer than   455
the eyes you were calling blue like the sea.

MARY DOUL [*interrupting him*] It's the devil cured you this day with
your talking of sows; it's the devil cured you this day, I'm saying,
and drove you crazy with lies.

MARTIN DOUL Isn't it yourself is after playing lies on me, ten years,   460
in the day, and in the night, but what is that to you° now the Lord
God has given eyes to me, the way I see you an old, wizendy hag,
was never fit to rear a child to me itself.°

MARY DOUL I wouldn't rear a crumpled whelp the like of you. It's
many a woman is married with finer than yourself should be   465
praising God if she's no child, and isn't loading the earth with
things would make the heavens lonesome above, and they scaring
the larks, and the crows, and the angels passing in the sky.

MARTIN DOUL Go on now to be seeking a lonesome place where the
earth can hide you away, go on now, I'm saying, or you'll be   470
having men and women with their knees bled,° and they screaming
to God for a holy water would darken their sight, for there's no
man but would liefer be blind a hundred years, or a thousand itself,
than to be looking on your like.

MARY DOUL [*raising her stick*] Maybe if I hit you a strong blow you'd   475
be blind again, and having what you want—

[*Saint is seen in church-door with his head bent in prayer*]

MARTIN DOUL [*raising his stick and driving Mary Doul back towards
left*] Let you keep off from me now if you wouldn't have me strike
out the little handful of brains you have about on the road.

[*He is going to strike her, but Timmy catches him by the arm*]

TIMMY Have you no shame to be making a great row and the saint   480
above saying his prayers?

MARTIN DOUL What is it I care for the like of him? [*Struggling to
free himself*] Let me hit her one good one for the love of the
Almighty God, and I'll be quiet after till I die.

TIMMY [*shaking him*] Will you whisht, I'm saying.   485

SAINT [*coming forward, centre*] Are their minds troubled with joy, or
is their sight uncertain the way it does often be the day a person
is restored?

TIMMY It's too certain their sight is, holy father, and they're after
making a great fight, because they're a pair of pitiful shows.   490

SAINT [*coming between them*] May the Lord who has given you sight
send a little sense into your heads, the way it won't be on your two
selves you'll be looking—on two pitiful sinners of the earth—but

on the splendour of the Spirit of God, you'll see an odd time shining out through the big hills, and steep streams falling to the   495 sea. For if it's on the like of that you do be thinking, you'll not be minding the faces of men, but you'll be saying prayers and great praises, till you'll be living the way the great saints do be living, with little but old sacks, and skin covering their bones. [*To Timmy*] Leave him go now,° you're seeing he's quiet again. [*Timmy frees*   500 *Martin Doul*] And let you [*Saint turns to Mary Doul*] not be raising your voice, a bad thing in a woman, but let the lot of you, who have seen the power of the Lord, be thinking on it in the dark night, and be saying to yourselves it's great pity, and love he has, for the poor, starving people of Ireland. [*He gathers his cloak about*   505 *him*] And now the Lord send blessing to you all, for I am going on to Annagolan,° where there is a deaf woman, and to Laragh° where there are two men without sense, and to Glenassil° where there are children, blind from their birth, and then I'm going to sleep this night in the bed of the holy Kevin,° and to be praising   510 God, and asking great blessing on you all. [*He bends his head*]

CURTAIN

Act 2

Village roadside, on left the door of a forge, with broken wheels, etc., lying about. A well near centre, with board above it, and room to pass behind it. Martin Doul is sitting near forge, cutting sticks

TIMMY [*heard hammering inside forge, then calls*] Let you make haste out there. . . . I'll be putting up new fires at the turn of day, and you haven't the half of them cut yet.

MARTIN DOUL [*gloomily*] It's destroyed I'll be whacking your old thorns° till the turn of day, and I with no food in my stomach would keep the life in a pig. [*He turns towards the door*] Let you come out here and cut them yourself if you want them cut, for there's an hour every day when a man has a right to his rest.

TIMMY [*coming out, with a hammer, impatiently*] Do you want me to be driving you off again to be walking the roads? There you are now, and I giving you your food, and a corner to sleep, and money with it, and to hear the talk of you, you'd think I was after beating you, or stealing your gold.

MARTIN DOUL You'd do it handy,° maybe, if I'd gold to steal.

TIMMY [*throws down hammer; picks up some of the sticks already cut, and throws them into door*] There's no fear° of your having gold, a lazy, basking fool the like of you.

MARTIN DOUL No fear, maybe, and I here with yourself, for it's more I got a while since, and I sitting blinded in Grianan, than I get in this place, working hard, and destroying myself, the length of the day.

TIMMY [*stopping with amazement*] Working hard? [*He goes over to him*] I'll teach you to work hard, Martin Doul. Strip off your coat now, and put a tuck in your sleeves, and cut the lot of them, while I'd rake the ashes from the forge,° or I'll not put up with you another hour itself.

MARTIN DOUL [*horrified*] Would you have me getting my death sitting out in the black wintery air with no coat on me at all?

TIMMY [*with authority*] Strip it off now, or walk down upon the road.

MARTIN DOUL [*bitterly*] Oh, God help me! [*He begins taking off his coat*] I've heard tell you stripped the sheet from your wife and you putting her down into the grave, and that there isn't the like of you for plucking your living ducks, the short days, and leaving

them running round in their skins, in the great rains and the cold.
[*He tucks up his sleeves*] Ah, I've heard a power of queer things° of   35
yourself, and there isn't one of them I'll not believe from this day,
and be telling to the boys.

TIMMY [*pulling over a big stick*] Let you cut that now, and give me
a rest from your talk, for I'm not heeding you at all.

MARTIN DOUL [*taking stick*] That's a hard terrible stick, Timmy, and   40
isn't it a poor thing° to be cutting strong timber the like of that,
when it's cold the bark is, and slippy with the frost of the air?

TIMMY [*gathering up another armful of sticks*] What way wouldn't it
be cold, and it freezing since the moon was changed? [*He goes into
forge*]   45

MARTIN DOUL [*querulously, as he cuts slowly*] What way, indeed,
Timmy? For it's a raw, beastly day we do have each day, till I do
be thinking it's well for the blind don't be seeing° the like of them
grey clouds driving on the hill, and don't be looking on people
with their noses red, the like of your nose, and their eyes weeping,   50
and watering, the like of your eyes, God help you, Timmy the
smith.

TIMMY [*seen blinking in doorway*] Is it turning now you are against
your sight?

MARTIN DOUL [*very miserably*] It's a hard thing° for a man to have   55
his sight, and he living near to the like of you [*he cuts a stick, and
throws it away*], or wed with a wife [*cuts a stick*], and I do be
thinking it should be° a hard thing for the Almighty God to be
looking on the world bad days, and on men the like of yourself
walking around on it, and they slipping each way in the muck.°   60

TIMMY [*with pot-hooks° which he taps on anvil*] You'd have a right to
be minding, Martin Doul, for it's a power the saint cured lose their
sight after a while—it's well you know Mary Doul's dimming
again—and I'm thinking the Lord if He hears you making that talk
will have little pity left for you at all.   65

MARTIN DOUL There's not a bit of fear of me losing my sight, and
if it's a dark day itself it's too well I see every wicked wrinkle you
have round by your eye.

TIMMY [*looking at him sharply*] Dark day is it? The day's not dark
since the clouds broke in the east.   70

MARTIN DOUL Let you not be tormenting yourself trying to make
me afeard.° You told me a power of bad lies the time I was blind,
and it's right now for you° to stop, and be taking your rest [*Mary
Doul comes in unnoticed on right with a sack filled with green stuff on*

her arm], for it's little ease or quiet any person would get if the big 75
fools of Ireland weren't weary at times. [*He looks up and sees Mary
Doul*] Oh, glory be to God, she's coming again. [*He begins to work
busily with his back to her*]

TIMMY [*amused, to Mary Doul, as she is going by without looking at
them*] Look on him now, Mary Doul. You'd be a great one for 80
keeping him steady at his work, for he's after idling, and blathering, to this hour from the dawn of day.

MARY DOUL [*stiffly*] Of what is it you're speaking, Timmy the smith?

TIMMY [*laughing*] Of himself, surely. Look on him there, and he with
the shirt on him ripping from his back. You'd have a right to come 85
round this night, I'm thinking, and put a stitch into his clothes,
for it's long enough you are not speaking one to the other.

MARY DOUL Let the two of you not torment me at all. [*She goes out
left, with her head in the air*]

MARTIN DOUL [*stops work and looks after her*] Well, isn't it a 90
queer thing she can't keep herself two days without looking on my
face?

TIMMY [*jeeringly*] Looking on your face is it? And she after going
by° with her head turned the way you'd see a sainted lady going
where there'd be drunken people in the side ditch singing to 95
themselves.° [*Martin Doul gets up and goes to corner of forge, and
looks out left*] Come back here and don't mind her at all. Come
back here, I'm saying, you've no call to be spying behind her since
she went off, and left you, in place of breaking her heart, trying to
keep you in the decency of clothes and food. 100

MARTIN DOUL [*crying out indignantly*] You know rightly, Timmy, it
was myself drove her away.

TIMMY That's a lie you're telling, yet it's little I care which one of
you was driving the other, and let you walk back here I'm saying
to your work. 105

MARTIN DOUL [*turning round*] I'm coming, surely. [*He stops and
looks out right, going a step or two towards centre*]

TIMMY On what is it you're gaping, Martin Doul?

MARTIN DOUL There's a person walking above . . . It's Molly Byrne
I'm thinking, coming down with her can. 110

TIMMY If she is itself let you not be idling this day, or minding her
at all, and let you hurry with them sticks, for I'll want you in a
short while to be blowing in the forge. [*He throws down pot-hooks*]

MARTIN DOUL [*crying out*] Is it roasting me now, you'd be? [*He turns
back and sees pot-hooks; he takes them up*] Pot-hooks? Is it over 115

them you've been inside sneezing and sweating since the dawn of day?

TIMMY [*resting himself on anvil, with satisfaction*] I'm making a power of things you do have when you're settling with a wife, Martin Doul, for I heard tell last night the saint'll be passing again in a short while, and I'd have him wed Molly with myself. . . . He'd do it, I've heard them say, for not a penny at all.

MARTIN DOUL [*lays down hooks and looks at him steadily*] Molly'll be saying great praises now to the Almighty God and he giving her a fine stout hardy man the like of you.

TIMMY [*uneasily*] And why wouldn't she, if she's a fine woman itself?

MARTIN DOUL [*looking up right*] Why wouldn't she indeed, Timmy? . . . . The Almighty God's made a fine match in the two of you, for if you went marrying a woman was the like of yourself you'd be having the fearfullest little children, I'm thinking, was ever seen in the world.

TIMMY [*seriously offended*] God forgive you, if you're an ugly man to be looking at, I'm thinking your tongue's worse than your view.

MARTIN DOUL [*hurt also*] Isn't it destroyed with the cold I am, and if I'm ugly itself I never seen any one the like of you for dreepiness° this day, Timmy the smith, and I'm thinking now herself's coming above you'd have a right to step up into your old shanty, and give a rub to your face, and not be sitting there with your bleary eyes, and your big nose, the like of an old scarecrow stuck down upon the road.

TIMMY [*looking up the road uneasily*] She's no call° to mind what way I look, and I after building a house with four rooms in it above on the hill. [*He stands up*] But it's a queer thing the way yourself and Mary Doul are after setting every person in this place, and up beyond to Rathvanna,° talking of nothing, and thinking of nothing, but the way they do be looking in the face. [*Going towards forge*] It's the devil's work you're after doing with your talk of fine looks, and I'd do right, maybe, to step in, and wash the blackness from my eyes.

> [*He goes into forge. Martin Doul rubs his face furtively with the tail of his coat. Molly Byrne comes on right with a water-can, and begins to fill it at the well*]

MARTIN DOUL God save you, Molly Byrne.

MOLLY BYRNE [*indifferently*] God save you.

MARTIN DOUL That's a dark, gloomy day, and the Lord have mercy on us all.

MOLLY BYRNE Middling dark. . . .

MARTIN DOUL It's a power of dirty days, and dark mornings, and 155 shabby-looking fellows [*he makes a gesture over his shoulder*] we do have to be looking on when we have our sight, God help us, but there's one fine thing we have, to be looking on a grand, white, handsome girl, the like of you . . . and every time I set my eyes on you, I do be blessing the saints, and the holy water, and the power 160 of the Lord Almighty in the heavens above.

MOLLY BYRNE I've heard the priests say it isn't looking on a young girl would teach many to be saying their prayers. [*Baling water into her can with a cup*]

MARTIN DOUL It isn't many have been the way I was, hearing your 165 voice speaking, and not seeing you at all.

MOLLY BYRNE That should have been a queer time for an old wicked, coaxing° fool to be sitting there with your eyes shut, and not seeing a sight of girl or woman passing the road.

MARTIN DOUL If it was a queer time itself, it was great joy and pride 170 I had, the time I'd hear your voice speaking and you passing to Grianan [*beginning to speak with plaintive intensity*], for it's of many a fine thing your voice would put a poor dark fellow in mind, and the day I'd hear it, it's of little else at all I would be thinking.

MOLLY BYRNE I'll tell your wife if you talk to me the like of that. 175 . . . You've heard, maybe, she's below picking nettles for the widow O'Flinn, who took great pity on her when she seen the two of you fighting, and yourself putting shame on her at the crossing of the roads.

MARTIN DOUL [*impatiently*] Is there no living person can speak a 180 score of words to me, or say 'God speed you', itself, without putting me in mind of the old woman, or that day either at Grianan?

MOLLY BYRNE [*with malice*] I was thinking it should be a fine thing to put you in mind of the day you called the grand day of your 185 life.

MARTIN DOUL Grand day, is it? [*Plaintively again, throwing aside his work, and leaning towards her*] Or a bad black day when I was roused up and found I was the like of the little children do be listening to the stories of an old woman, and do be dreaming after 190 in the dark night that it's in grand houses of gold they are, with speckled° horses to ride, and do be waking again, in a short while, and they destroyed with the cold, and the thatch dripping maybe, and the starved ass braying in the yard?

MOLLY BYRNE [*working indifferently*] You've great romancing this 195
day, Martin Doul. Was it up at the still you were at the fall of
night?

MARTIN DOUL [*stands up, comes towards her, but stands at far—right—
side of well*] It was not, Molly Byrne, but lying down in a little
rickety shed. . . . Lying down across a sop of straw, and I thinking 200
I was seeing you walk, and hearing the sound of your step on a dry
road, and hearing you again, and you laughing and making great
talk in a high room with dry timber lining the roof.° For it's a fine
sound your voice has that time, and it's better I am, I'm thinking,
lying down, the way a blind man does be lying, than to be sitting 205
here in the grey light, taking hard words of Timmy the smith.

MOLLY BYRNE [*looking at him with interest*] It's queer talk you have
if it's a little, old, shabby stump of a man you are itself.

MARTIN DOUL I'm not so old as you do hear them say.

MOLLY BYRNE You're old, I'm thinking, to be talking that talk with 210
a girl.

MARTIN DOUL [*despondingly*] It's not a lie you're telling maybe, for
it's long years I'm after losing from the world, feeling love, and
talking love, with the old woman, and I fooled the whole while
with the lies of Timmy the smith. 215

MOLLY BYRNE [*half invitingly*] It's a fine way you're wanting to pay
Timmy the smith. . . . And it's not his *lies* you're making love to
this day, Martin Doul.

MARTIN DOUL It is not, Molly, but with the good looks of yourself
[*passing behind her and coming near her left*], for if it's old I am 220
maybe I've heard tell there are lands beyond in Cahir Iveraghig
and the Reeks of Cork° with warm sun in them, and fine light in
the sky. [*Bending towards her*] And light's a grand thing for a man
ever was blind, or a woman, with a fine neck, and a skin on her
the like of you, the way we'd have a right to go off this day till 225
we'd have a fine life passing abroad through them towns of the
south, and we telling stories, maybe, or singing songs at the fairs.

MOLLY BYRNE [*turning round half amused, and looking him over from
head to foot*] Well isn't it a queer thing when your own wife's after
leaving you because you're a pitiful show you'd talk the like of that 230
to me?

MARTIN [*drawing back a little, hurt, but indignant*] It's a queer thing
maybe for all things is queer in the world. [*In a low voice with
peculiar emphasis*] But there's one thing I'm telling you, if she
walked off away from me, it wasn't because of seeing me, and I no 235

78

more than I am, but because I was looking on her with my two eyes, and she getting up, and eating her food, and combing her hair, and lying down for her sleep.

MOLLY [*interested, off her guard*] Wouldn't any married man you'd have be doing the like of that? 240

MARTIN DOUL [*seizing the moment that he has her attention*] I'm thinking by the mercy of God it's few sees anything but them is blind for a space. [*With excitement*] It's few sees the old women rotting for the grave, and it's few sees the like of yourself [*he bends over her*], though it's shining you are, like a high lamp, would drag 245 in the ships out of the sea.

MOLLY BYRNE [*shrinking away from him*] Keep off from me, Martin Doul.

MARTIN DOUL [*quickly, with low, furious intensity. He puts his hand on her shoulder and shakes her*] You'd do right, I'm saying, not to 250 marry a man is after looking out a long while on the bad days of the world,° for what way would the like of him have fit eyes to look on yourself, when you rise up in the morning and come out of the little door you have above in the lane, the time it'd be a fine thing if a man would be seeing, and losing his sight, the way he'd 255 have your two eyes facing him, and he going the roads, and shining above him, and he looking in the sky, and springing up from the earth, the time he'd lower his head, in place of the muck that seeing men do meet all roads spread on the world.

MOLLY BYRNE [*who has listened half-mesmerized, starting away*] It's 260 the like of that talk you'd hear from a man would be losing his mind.

MARTIN DOUL [*going after her, passing to her right*] It'd be little wonder if a man near the like of you would be losing his mind. Put down your can now, and come along with myself, for I'm seeing you this day, seeing you, maybe, the way no man has seen 265 you in the world. [*He takes her by the arm and tries to pull her away softly to the right*] Let you come on now, I'm saying, to the lands of Iveragh and the Reeks of Cork, where you won't set down the width of your two feet and not be crushing fine flowers, and making sweet smells in the air... 270

MOLLY BYRNE [*laying down can; trying to free herself*] Leave me go, Martin Doul. ... Leave me go, I'm saying!

MARTIN DOUL Come along now, let you come on the little path through the trees.

MOLLY BYRNE [*crying out towards forge*] Timmy. ... Timmy the 275 smith. ... [*Timmy comes out of forge, and Martin Doul lets her go.*

Molly Byrne, excited and breathless, pointing to Martin Doul] Did ever you hear that them that loses their sight loses their sense along with it, Timmy the smith?

TIMMY [*suspicious, but uncertain*] He's no sense, surely, and he'll be having himself driven off this day from where he's good sleeping, and feeding, and wages for his work.

MOLLY BYRNE [*as before*] He's a bigger fool than that, Timmy. Look on him now, and tell me if that isn't a grand fellow to think he's only to open his mouth to have a fine woman, the like of me, running along by his heels.

[*Martin Doul recoils towards centre, with his hand to his eyes; Mary Doul is seen on left coming forward softly*]

TIMMY [*with blank amazement*] Oh, the blind is wicked people, and it's no lie. But he'll walk off this day and not be troubling us more. [*He walks back left and picks up Martin Doul's coat and stick; some things fall out of coat pocket, which he gathers up again*]

MARTIN DOUL [*turns round, sees Mary Doul, whispers to Molly Byrne with imploring agony*] Let you not put shame on me, Molly, before herself and the smith. Let you not put shame on me and I after saying fine words to you, and dreaming . . . dreams . . . in the night. [*He hesitates, and looks round the sky*] Is it a storm of thunder is coming, or the last end of the world? [*He staggers towards Mary Doul, tripping slightly over tin can*] The heavens is closing, I'm thinking, with darkness and great trouble passing in the sky. [*He reaches Mary Doul, and seizes her with both his hands—with a frantic cry*] Is it the darkness of thunder is coming, Mary Doul? Do you see me clearly with your eyes?

MARY DOUL [*snatches her arm away, and hits him with empty sack across the face*] I see you a sight° too clearly, and lèt you keep off from me now.

MOLLY BYRNE [*clapping her hands*] That's right, Mary. That's the way to treat the like of him is after standing there at my feet and asking me to go off with him, till I'd grow an old wretched road woman° the like of yourself.

MARY DOUL [*defiantly*] When the skin shrinks on your chin, Molly Byrne, there won't be the like of you for a shrunk hag in the four quarters of Ireland. . . . It's a fine pair you'd be, surely!

[*Martin Doul is standing at back right centre, with his back to the audience*]

TIMMY [*coming over to Mary Doul*] Is it no shame you have to let on she'd ever be the like of you?

MARY DOUL It's them that's fat and flabby do be wrinkled young, and that whitish yellowy hair she has does be soon turning the like of° a handful of thin grass you'd see rotting, where the wet lies, at the north of a sty. [*Turning to go out on right*] Ah, isn't it a grand thing for the like of your make to be setting fools mad a short while, and then to be turning a thing will drive off the little children from your feet.

315

320

[*She goes out. Martin Doul has come forward again, mastering himself, but uncertain*]

TIMMY Oh, God protect us, Molly, from the words of the blind. [*He throws down Martin Doul's coat and stick*] There's your old rubbish now, Martin Doul, and let you take it up, for it's all you have, and walk off through the world, and if ever I meet you coming again, if it's seeing or blind you are itself, I'll bring out the big hammer and hit you a welt° with it will leave you easy till the judgement day.

325

MARTIN DOUL [*rousing himself with an effort*] What call have you to talk the like of that with myself?

TIMMY [*pointing to Molly Byrne*] It's well you know what call I have. It's well you know a decent girl, I'm thinking to wed, has no right to have her heart scalded with hearing talk—and queer, bad talk, I'm thinking—from a raggy-looking fool the like of you.

330

MARTIN DOUL [*raising his voice*] It's making game of you she is,° for what seeing girl would marry with yourself? Look on him, Molly, look on him, I'm saying, for I'm seeing him still, and let you raise your voice,° for the time is come, and bid him go up into his forge and be sitting there by himself, sneezing, and sweating, and he beating pot-hooks till the judgement day. [*He seizes her arm again*]

335

MOLLY BYRNE Keep him off from me, Timmy!

340

TIMMY [*pushing Martin Doul aside*] Would you have me strike you, Martin Doul? Go along now after your wife, who's a fit match for you, and leave Molly with myself.

MARTIN DOUL [*despairingly*] Won't you raise your voice, Molly, and lay hell's long curse on his tongue?

345

MOLLY BYRNE [*on Timmy's left*] I'll be telling him it's destroyed I am with the sight of you and the sound of your voice. Go off now after your wife, and if she beats you again, let you go after the tinker girls is above running the hills, or down among the sluts of the town, and you'll learn one day, maybe, the way a man should speak with a well-reared civil girl the like of me. [*She takes Timmy by the arm*] Come up now into the forge till he'll be gone down a

350

81

bit on the road, for it's near afeard I am of the wild look he has come in his eyes.

[*She goes into the forge. Timmy stops in the doorway*]

TIMMY   Let me not find you out here again, Martin Doul. [*He bares   355
his arm*] It's well you know Timmy the smith has great strength in his arm, and it's a power of things it has broken a sight harder than the old bone of your skull. [*He goes into the forge and pulls the door after him*]

MARTIN DOUL [*stands a moment with his hand to his eyes*] And that's   360
the last thing I'm to set my sight on in the life of the world, the villainy of a woman and the bloody strength of a man. Oh, God, pity a poor blind fellow the way I am this day with no strength in me to do hurt to them at all. [*He begins groping about for a moment, then stops*] Yet if I've no strength in me I've a voice left for my   365
prayers, and may God blight them this day, and my own soul the same hour with them, the way I'll see them after, Molly Byrne and Timmy the smith, the two of them on a high bed, and they screeching in hell. . . . It'll be a grand thing that time to look on the two of them; and they twisting and roaring out, and twisting   370
and roaring again, one day and the next day, and each day always and ever. It's not blind I'll be that time, and it won't be hell to me I'm thinking, but the like of Heaven itself, and it's fine care I'll be taking the Lord Almighty doesn't know.° [*He turns to grope out*]

CURTAIN

Act 3

Same as in first Act, but gap in centre has been filled with briars, or branches of some sort. Mary Doul, blind again, gropes her way in on left, and sits as before. She has a few rushes with her. It is an early spring day

MARY DOUL [*mournfully*] Ah, God help me . . . God help me, the blackness wasn't so black at all the other time as it is this time, and it's destroyed I'll be now, and hard set° to get my living working alone, when it's few are passing and the winds are cold. [*She begins shredding rushes*] I'm thinking short days will be long days to me   5
from this time, and I sitting here, not seeing a blink,° or hearing a word, and no thought in my mind but long prayers that Martin Doul'll get his reward in a short while for the villainy of his heart. It's great jokes the people'll be making now, I'm thinking, and they passing me by, pointing their fingers, maybe, and asking what   10
place is himself,° the way it's no quiet or decency I'll have from this day till I'm an old woman with long white hair and it twisting from my brow. [*She fumbles with her hair, and then seems to hear something. Listens for a moment*] There's a queer slouching step coming on the road. . . . God help me, he's coming surely.   15

> [*She stays perfectly quiet. Martin Doul gropes in on right, blind also*]

MARTIN DOUL [*gloomily*] The devil mend° Mary Doul for putting lies on me, and letting on she was grand. The devil mend the old saint for letting me see it was lies. [*He sits down near her*] The devil mend Timmy the smith for killing me with hard work, and keeping me with an empty windy stomach in me, in the day and   20
in the night. Ten thousand devils mend the soul of Molly Byrne [*Mary Doul nods her head with approval*] and the bad wicked souls is hidden in all the women of the world. [*He rocks himself, with his hand over his face*] It's lonesome I'll be from this day, and if living people is a bad lot, yet Mary Doul herself, and she a dirty,   25
wrinkled-looking hag, was better maybe to be sitting along with than no one at all. I'll be getting my death now, I'm thinking, sitting alone in the cold air, hearing the night coming, and the blackbirds flying round in the briars crying to themselves, the time you'll hear one cart getting off a long way in the east, and another   30
cart getting off a long way in the west, and a dog barking maybe,

and a little wind turning the sticks. [*He listens and sighs heavily*] I'll
be destroyed sitting alone and losing my senses this time the way
I'm after losing my sight, for it'd make any person afeard to be
sitting up hearing the sound of his breath [*he moves his feet on the*   35
stones], and the noise of his feet, when it's a power of queer things
do be stirring, little sticks breaking, and the grass moving [*Mary*
Doul half sighs, and he turns on her in horror] till you'd take your
dying oath on sun and moon a thing was breathing on the stones.
[*He listens towards her for a moment, then starts up nervously, and*   40
gropes about for his stick] I'll be going now, I'm thinking, but I'm
not sure what place my stick's in, and I'm destroyed with terror
and dread. [*He touches her hand as he is groping about and cries out*]
There's a thing with a cold living hand on it sitting up at my side.
[*He turns to run away, but misses his path and stumbles in against the*   45
wall] My road is lost on me now! Oh, merciful God, set my foot
on the path this day, and I'll be saying prayers morning and night,
and not straining my ear after young girls, or doing any bad thing
till I die—

MARY DOUL [*indignantly*] Let you not be telling lies to the Almighty   50
   God.

MARTIN DOUL Mary Doul is it? [*Recovering himself with immense*
   relief] Is it Mary Doul, I'm saying?

MARY DOUL There's a sweet tone in your voice I've not heard for a
   space.° You're taking me for Molly Byrne, I'm thinking.   55

MARTIN DOUL [*coming towards her, wiping sweat from his face*] Well,
   sight's a queer thing for upsetting a man. It's a queer thing to think
   I'd live to this day to be fearing the like of you, but if it's shaken
   I am for a short while, I'll soon be coming to myself.

MARY DOUL You'll be grand then, and it's no lie.   60

MARTIN DOUL [*sitting down shyly, some way off*] You've no call to be
   talking, for I've heard tell you're as blind as myself.

MARY DOUL If I am I'm bearing in mind I'm married to a little dark
   stump of a fellow looks the fool of the world, and I'll be bearing
   in mind from this day the great hullabaloo he's after making from   65
   hearing a poor woman breathing quiet in her place.

MARTIN DOUL And you'll be bearing in mind, I'm thinking, what
   you seen a while back when you looked down into a well, or a clear
   pool, maybe, when there was no wind stirring and a good light in
   the sky.   70

MARY DOUL I'm minding° that surely, for if I'm not the way the
   liars were saying below I seen a thing in them pools put joy and
   blessing in my heart. [*She puts her hand to her hair again*]

84

MARTIN DOUL [*laughing ironically*] Well! They were saying below I
was losing my senses but I never went any day the length of that.°   75
. . . God help you, Mary Doul, if you're not a wonder for looks,
you're the maddest female woman is walking the counties of the
east.

MARY DOUL [*scornfully*] You were saying all times you'd a great ear
for hearing the lies in a word, a great ear, God help you, and you   80
think you're using it now!

MARTIN DOUL If it's not lies you're telling, would you have me
think you're not a wrinkled poor woman is looking like three
scores, maybe, or two scores and a half?

MARY DOUL I would not, Martin. [*She leans forward earnestly*] For   85
when I seen myself in them pools, I seen my hair would be grey,
or white maybe in a short while, and I seen with it that I'd a face
would be a great wonder when it'll have soft white hair falling
around it, the way when I'm an old woman there won't be the like
of me° surely in the seven counties of the east.   90

MARTIN DOUL [*with real admiration*] You're a cute thinking° woman,
Mary Doul, and it's no lie.

MARY DOUL [*triumphantly*] I am surely, and I'm telling you a
beautiful white-haired woman is a grand thing to see, for I'm told
when Kitty Bawn° was selling poteen below, the young men itself   95
would never tire to be looking in her face.

MARTIN DOUL [*taking off his hat and feeling his head, speaking with
hesitation*] Did you think to look, Mary Doul, would there be a
whiteness the like of that coming upon me?

MARY DOUL [*with extreme contempt*] On you, God help you? . . . In a   100
short while° you'll have a head on you as bald as an old turnip you'd
see rolling round in the muck. You need never talk again of your
fine looks, Martin Doul, for the day of that talk's gone for ever.

MARTIN DOUL That's a hard word to be saying, for I was thinking
if I'd a bit of comfort, the like of yourself, it's not far off we'd be   105
from the good days went before, and that'd be a wonder surely.
But I'll never rest easy, thinking you're a grey, beautiful woman,
and myself a pitiful show.

MARY DOUL I can't help your looks, Martin Doul. It wasn't myself
made you with your rat's eyes, and your big ears, and your griseldy   110
chin.

MARTIN DOUL [*rubs his chin ruefully, then beams with delight*] There's
one thing you've forgot, if you're a cute thinking woman itself!

MARY DOUL Your slouching feet, is it? Or your hooky neck, or your
two knees is black with knocking one on the other?   115

MARTIN DOUL [*with delighted scorn*] There's talking for a cute woman!° There's talking surely!

MARY DOUL [*puzzled at the joy of his voice*] If you'd anything but lies to say you'd be talking yourself.

MARTIN DOUL [*bursting with excitement*] I've this to say, Mary Doul.   120
I'll be letting my beard grow in a short while—a beautiful, long, white, silken, streamy beard, you wouldn't see the like of in the eastern world° . . . Ah, a white beard's a grand thing on an old man, a grand thing for making the quality° stop and be stretching out their hands with good silver or gold, and a beard's a thing   125
you'll never have, so you may be holding your tongue.

MARY DOUL [*laughing cheerfully*] Well, we're a great pair, surely, and it's great times we'll have yet, maybe, and great talking before we die.°

MARTIN DOUL Great times from this day, with the help of the   130
Almighty God, for a priest itself would believe the lies of an old man would have° a fine white beard growing on his chin.

MARY DOUL There's the sound of one of them twittering yellow birds do be coming in the spring-time from beyond the sea, and there'll be a fine warmth now in the sun, and a sweetness in the   135
air, the way° it'll be a grand thing to be sitting here quiet and easy, smelling the things growing up, and budding from the earth.

MARTIN DOUL I'm smelling the furze a while back sprouting on the hill, and if you'd hold your tongue you'd hear the lambs of Grianan, though it's near drowned their crying is with the full   140
river° making noises in the glen.

MARY DOUL [*listens*] The lambs is bleating, surely, and there's cocks and laying hens making a fine stir a mile off on the face of the hill.
[*She starts*]

MARTIN DOUL What's that is sounding in the west?   145
        [*A faint sound of a bell is heard*]

MARY DOUL It's not the churches,° for the wind's blowing from the sea.

MARTIN DOUL [*with dismay*] It's the old saint, I'm thinking, ringing his bell.

MARY DOUL The Lord protect us from the saints of God! [*They   150
listen*] He's coming this road, surely.

MARTIN DOUL [*tentatively*] Will we be running off,° Mary Doul?

MARY DOUL What place would we run?

MARTIN DOUL There's the little path going up through the sloughs.°
        . . . If we reached the bank above, where the elders do be growing,   155

no person would see a sight of us, if it was a hundred yeomen° were passing itself, but I'm afeard after the time we were with our sight we'll not find our way to it at all.

MARY DOUL [*standing up*] You'd find the way, surely. You're a grand man the world knows at finding your way if there was deep snow   160 itself lying on the earth.

MARTIN DOUL [*taking her hand*] Come a bit this way, it's here it begins. [*They grope about gap*] There's a tree pulled into the gap, or a strange thing happened since I was passing it before.

MARY DOUL Would we have a right to be crawling° in below under   165 the sticks?

MARTIN DOUL It's hard set I am to know what would be right. And isn't it a poor thing to be blind when you can't run off itself, and you fearing to see?°

MARY DOUL [*nearly in tears*] It's a poor thing, God help us, and what   170 good'll our grey hairs be itself, if we have our sight, the way we'll see them falling each day, and turning dirty in the rain?

[*The bell sounds near by*]

MARTIN DOUL [*in despair*] He's coming now, and we won't get off from him at all.

MARY DOUL Could we hide in the bit of a briar is growing at the   175 west butt of the church?

MARTIN DOUL We'll try that, surely. [*He listens a moment*] Let you make haste, I hear them trampling in the wood. [*They grope over to church*]

MARY DOUL It's the words of the young girls making a great stir in   180 the trees. [*They find the bush*] Here's the briar on my left, Martin; I'll go in first, I'm the big one, and I'm easy to see.

MARTIN DOUL [*turning his head anxiously*] It's easy heard you are, and will you be holding your tongue?

MARY DOUL [*partly behind bush*] Come in now beside of me. [*They   185 kneel down, still clearly visible*] Do you think can they see us now, Martin Doul?

MARTIN DOUL I'm thinking they can't, but I'm hard set to know, for the lot of them young girls, the devil save them, have sharp terrible eyes, would pick out a poor man I'm thinking, and he lying   190 below hid in his grave.

MARY DOUL Let you not be whispering sin, Martin Doul, or maybe it's the finger of God they'd see pointing to ourselves.

MARTIN DOUL It's yourself is speaking madness, Mary Doul, haven't you heard the saint say it's the wicked do be blind?   195

MARY DOUL If it is you'd have a right to speak a big terrible word
would make the water not cure us at all.

MARTIN DOUL What way would I find a big terrible word, and I
shook with the fear, and if I did itself, who'd know rightly if it's
good words or bad would save us this day from himself?   200

MARY DOUL They're coming. I hear their feet on the stones.
    [Saint comes in on right with Timmy and Molly Byrne in
    holiday clothes, the others [including Mat Simon and Patch
    Ruadh] as before]

TIMMY I've heard tell Martin Doul and Mary Doul were seen this
day about on the road, holy father, and we were thinking you'd
have pity on them and cure them again.

SAINT I would, maybe, but where are they at all? I'll have little time   205
left when I have the two of you wed in the church.

MAT SIMON [at their seat] There are the rushes they do have lying
round on the stones. It's not far off they'll be, surely.

MOLLY BYRNE [pointing with astonishment] Look beyond, Timmy.
    [They all look over and see Martin Doul]

TIMMY Well, Martin's a lazy fellow to be lying in there at the height 210
of the day. [He goes over shouting] Let you get up out of that. You
were near losing a great chance by your sleepiness this day, Martin
Doul. . . . The two of them's in it, God help us all!

MARTIN DOUL [scrambling up with Mary Doul] What is it you want,
Timmy, that you can't leave us in peace?   215

TIMMY The saint's come to marry the two of us, and I'm after
speaking a word for yourselves, the way he'll be curing you
now,° for if you're a foolish man itself, I do be pitying you, for
I've a kind heart, when I think of you sitting dark again, and you
after seeing a while, and working for your bread.°   220
    [Martin Doul takes Mary Doul's hand and tries to grope his
    way off right, he has lost his hat, and they are both covered with
    dust, and grass seeds]

PEOPLE You're going wrong. It's this way, Martin Doul.
    [They push him over in front of Saint near centre. Martin Doul
    and Mary Doul stand with piteous hang-dog dejection]

SAINT Let you not be afeard, for there's great pity with the Lord.

MARTIN DOUL We aren't afeard, holy father.

SAINT It's many a time° those that are cured with the well of the four
beauties of God lose their sight when a time is gone, but those I   225
cure a second time go on seeing till the hour of death. [He takes
the cover from his can] I've a few drops only left of the water, but,

with the help of God, it'll be enough for the two of you, and let
you kneel down now upon the road.

> [*Martin Doul wheels round with Mary Doul and tries to get
> away*]

SAINT You can kneel down here, I'm saying, we'll not trouble this 230
time going to the church.

TIMMY [*turning Martin Doul round angrily*] Are you going mad in
your head, Martin Doul? It's here you're to kneel. Did you not
hear his reverence, and he speaking to you now?

SAINT Kneel down, I'm saying, the ground's dry at your feet. 235

MARTIN DOUL [*with distress*] Let you go on your own way, holy
father. We're not calling you at all.

SAINT I'm not saying a word of penance, or fasting itself,° so you've
no call now to be fearing me, but let you kneel down till I give you
your sight. 240

MARTIN DOUL [*more troubled*] We're not asking our sight, holy
father, and let you be walking on and leaving us in our peace at
the crossing roads, for it's best we are this way, and we're not
asking to see.

SAINT [*to the People*] Is his mind gone that he's no wish to be cured 245
this day, and looking out on the wonders of the world?

MARTIN DOUL It's wonders enough I seen in a short space for the
life of one man only.

TIMMY Is it he see wonders?

PATCH RUADH He's making game. 250

MAT SIMON He's maybe drunk, holy father.

SAINT [*severely*] I never heard tell of any person wouldn't have great
joy to be looking on the earth, and the image of the Lord is thrown
upon men.

MARTIN DOUL [*raising his voice, by degrees*] That's great sights, holy 255
father. . . . What was it I seen my first day, but your own bleeding
feet and they cut with the stones, and my last day, but the villainy
of herself that you're wedding, God forgive you, with Timmy the
smith. That was great sights maybe. . . . And wasn't it great sights
seeing the roads when north winds would be driving and the skies 260
would be harsh, and you'd see the horses and the asses and the
dogs itself maybe with their heads hanging and they closing their
eyes—

TIMMY There's talking.

MAT SIMON He's right maybe, it's lonesome living when the days 265
are dark.

MOLLY BYRNE He's not right. Let you speak up, holy father, and confound him now.

SAINT [*coming close to Martin Doul and putting his hand on his shoulder*] Did you never set eyes on the summer and the fine spring in the 270 places where the holy men of Ireland have built up churches to the Lord, that you'd wish to be closed up and seeing no sight of the glittering seas, and the furze is opening above, will soon have the hills shining as if it was fine creels of gold they were, rising to the sky? 275

PATCH RUADH That's it, holy father.

MAT SIMON What have you now to say, Martin Doul?

MARTIN DOUL [*fiercely*] Isn't it finer sights ourselves had a while since and we sitting dark smelling the sweet beautiful smells do be rising in the warm nights and hearing the swift flying things racing 280 in the air [*Saint draws back from him*], till we'd be looking up in our own minds° into a grand sky, and seeing lakes, and broadening rivers, and hills are waiting for the spade and plough.

MAT SIMON [*roaring laughing*] It's songs he's making now, holy father. 285

PATCH It's mad he is.

MOLLY BYRNE It's not, but lazy he is, holy father, and not wishing to work, for a while since he was all times longing and screeching for the light of day.

MARTIN DOUL [*turning on her*] If I was, I seen my fill in a short while 290 with the look of my wife, and of your own wicked grin, Molly Byrne, the time you're making game with a man.

MOLLY BYRNE My grin, is it? Let you not mind him more, holy father, but leave him in darkness, if it's that is best fitting to the blackness of his heart. 295

TIMMY Cure Mary Doul, your reverence, who is a quiet poor woman never said a hard word but when she'd be vexed with himself, or with the young girls do be making game of her below.

PEOPLE That's it, cure Mary Doul your reverence.

SAINT There is little use, maybe, talking to the like of him, but if 300 you have any sense, Mary Doul, kneel down at my feet, and I'll bring the sight into your eyes.

MARTIN DOUL [*more defiantly*] You will not, holy father! Would you have her looking on me, and saying hard words to me, till the hour of death? 305

SAINT [*severely*] If she's wishing her sight it isn't the like of you'll stop her. [*To Mary*] Kneel down, I'm saying.

MARY DOUL [*doubtfully*] Let us be as we are, holy father, and then we'll be known again as the people is happy and blind, and we'll be having an easy time with no trouble to live, and we getting 310 halfpence on the road.

MOLLY BYRNE Let you not be raving. Kneel down and get your sight, and let himself be taking half-pence if he likes it best.

TIMMY If it's choosing a wilful blindness you are, there isn't any one will give you a hap'worth of meal or be doing the little things you 315 need to keep you at all living in the world.

MAT SIMON If you had your sight you could be keeping a watch that no other woman came near to him at all.

MARY DOUL [*half persuaded*] That's true, maybe. . . .

SAINT Kneel down for I must be hastening with the marriage and 320 going my own way before the fall of night.

PEOPLE [*all together*] Kneel down, Mary! Kneel down when you're bid by the saint!

MARY DOUL [*looking uneasily towards Martin Doul*] Maybe it's right they are, and I will if you wish it, holy father. . . . 325
[*She kneels down. Saint takes off his hat and gives it to someone near him. All the men take off their hats. He goes forward a step to take Martin Doul's hand away from Mary Doul*]

SAINT [*to Martin Doul*] Go aside now, we're not wanting you here.

MARTIN DOUL [*pushes him away roughly, and stands with his left hand on Mary Doul's shoulder*] Keep off yourself, holy father, and let you not be taking my rest from me in the darkness of my wife. . . . What call have the like of you to be coming in where you're not 330 wanted at all, and making a great mess with the holy water you have and the length of your prayers? [*Defiantly*] Go on, I'm saying, and leave us this place on the road.

SAINT If it was a seeing man I heard talking to me the like of that I'd put a black curse on him would weigh down his soul till it'd 335 be falling to hell; but you're a poor blind sinner, God forgive you, and I don't mind you at all. [*He raises his can*] Go aside now till I give the blessing to your wife, and if you won't go with your own will, there are those standing by will make you surely.

MARTIN DOUL [*pulling Mary Doul*] Make me, is it? Well, there's 340 cruel hardship in the pity of your like, and what is it you want coming for to break our happiness and hour of rest. Let you rise up, Mary, against them and not heed them more.

SAINT [*imperiously to People*] Let you take that man and drive him down upon the road. 345

MAT SIMON Come now, Martin, come on.

PATCH RUADH Come off now from talking badness to the holy saint.

MARTIN DOUL [*throwing himself down on the ground clinging to Mary Doul*] I'll not come, I'm saying, and let you take his holy water to cure the blackness of your souls today. 350

MARY DOUL [*putting her arm round him*] Leave him easy, holy father, when I'd liefer live dark all times beside him, than be seeing in new troubles now.

SAINT You've taken your choice. Drag him away.

PEOPLE That's it. Lift his head. [*They carry him to right*] 355

MARTIN DOUL [*screaming*] Make them leave me go, holy father. Make them leave me go, and let you have pity and forgive me for my heathen words, and you may cure her this day, holy father, and do anything that you will.

SAINT [*to People*] Let him be if his sense is come to him at all. 360
[*They put him down*]

MARTIN DOUL [*shakes himself loose, feels for Mary Doul, sinking his voice to a plausible whine*] You may cure herself, surely, holy father, I wouldn't stop you at all—and it's great joy she'll have looking on your face—but let you cure myself along with her, the way I'll see when it's lies she's telling, and be looking out day and 365 night upon the holy men of God.° [*He kneels down a little before Mary Doul*]

SAINT [*speaking half to the People*] Men who are dark a long while and thinking over queer thoughts in their heads, aren't the like of simple men, who do be working every day, and praying, and living 370 like ourselves, and with that it's my part to be showing a love to you would take pity on the worst that live. So if you've found a right mind at the last minute itself, I'll cure you, if the Lord will, and not be thinking of the hard, foolish words you're after saying this day to us all. 375

MARTIN DOUL [*listening eagerly*] I'm waiting now, holy father.

SAINT [*with can in his hand, close to Martin Doul*] With the power of the water from the grave of the four beauties of God, with the power of this water, I'm saying, that I put upon your eyes—
[*He raises can. Martin Doul with a sudden movement strikes the can from Saint's hand and sends it rocketing across stage*]

PEOPLE [*with a terrified murmur*] Will you look what he's done. Oh, 380 glory be to God. There's a villain surely.

MARTIN DOUL [*stands up triumphantly, and pulls Mary Doul up*] If I'm a poor dark sinner I've sharp ears, God help me, and it's well

I heard the little splash of the water you had there in the can. Go
on now, holy father, for if you're a fine saint itself, it's more sense   385
is in a blind man, and more power maybe than you're thinking at
all. Let you walk on now with your worn feet, and your welted
knees, and your fasting, holy ways have left you with a big head
on you and a thin pitiful arm.

PEOPLE Go on from this.°   390
　　　[*Saint looks at Martin Doul for a moment severely, then turns
　　　away and picks up his can*]

MARTIN DOUL We're going surely, for if it's right some of you have
to be working and sweating the like of Timmy the smith, and a
right some of you have to be fasting and praying and talking holy
talk the like of yourself, I'm thinking it's a good right ourselves
have to be sitting blind, hearing a soft wind turning round the little   395
leaves of the spring and feeling the sun, and we not tormenting
our souls with the sight of the grey days, and the holy men, and
the dirty feet is trampling the world. [*He gropes towards his stone
with Mary Doul*]

MAT SIMON It'd be an unlucky fearful thing, I'm thinking, to have   400
the like of that man living near us at all. Wouldn't he bring down
a curse upon us, holy father, from the heavens of God?

SAINT [*tying his girdle*] God has great mercy, but great wrath for
them that sin.

PEOPLE [*all together*] Go on now, Martin Doul. Go on from this   405
place. Let you not be bringing great storms or droughts on us
maybe from the power of the Lord.° [*Some of them throw things at
him*]

MARTIN DOUL [*turning round defiantly and picking up his stick*] Keep
off now the yelping lot of you, or it's more than one maybe will   410
get a bloody head on him from the welt of my stick. Keep off now,
and let you not be afeard; for we're going on the two of us to the
towns of the south, where the people will have kind voices maybe,
and we won't know their bad looks or their villainy at all.

MARY DOUL [*despondingly*] That's the truth, surely, and we'd have a   415
right to be gone, if it's a long way itself, where you do have to be
walking with a slough of wet° on the one side and a slough of wet
on the other, and you going a stony path with a north wind
blowing behind.

MEN Go on now. Go on from this place.   420

MARTIN DOUL Keep off I'm saying. [*He takes Mary Doul's hand
again*] Come along now and we'll be walking to the south, for

we've seen too much of everyone in this place, and it's small joy we'd have living near them, or hearing the lies they do be telling from the grey of dawn till the night. [*They go*]   425

TIMMY There's a power of deep rivers with floods in them where you do have to be lepping the stones and you going to the south, so I'm thinking the two of them will be drowned together in a short while, surely.

SAINT They have chosen their lot, and the Lord have mercy on their   430
souls. [*He rings his bell*] And let the two of you come up now into the church, Molly Byrne and Timmy the smith, till I make your marriage and put my blessing on you all.

[*He turns to the church, procession forms, and the curtain comes down, as they go slowly into the church*]

CURTAIN

THE PLAYBOY OF
THE WESTERN WORLD

A Comedy in Three Acts

(1905–1907)

PREFACE

In writing *The Playboy of the Western World*, as in my other plays, I
have used one or two words only, that I have not heard among the
country people of Ireland, or spoken in my own nursery before I
could read the newspapers. A certain number of the phrases I employ
I have heard also from herds and fishermen along the coast from   5
Kerry to Mayo, or from beggar-women and ballad-singers nearer
Dublin; and I am glad to acknowledge how much I owe to the
folk-imagination of these fine people. Anyone who has lived in real
intimacy with the Irish peasantry will know that the wildest sayings
and ideas in this play are tame indeed compared with the fancies one   10
may hear in any little hillside cabin in Geesala, or Carraroe, or Dingle
Bay.° All art is a collaboration; and there is little doubt that in the
happy ages of literature striking and beautiful phrases were as ready
to the story-teller's or the playwright's hand as the rich cloaks and
dresses of his time. It is probable that when the Elizabethan dramatist   15
took his ink-horn and sat down to his work he used many phrases that
he had just heard, as he sat at dinner, from his mother or his children.
In Ireland those of us who know the people have the same privilege.
When I was writing *The Shadow of the Glen*, some years ago, I got
more aid than any learning could have given me, from a chink in the   20
floor of the old Wicklow house where I was staying, that let me hear
what was being said by the servant girls in the kitchen. This matter,
I think, is of importance, for in countries where the imagination of
the people, and the language they use, is rich and living, it is possible
for a writer to be rich and copious in his words, and at the same time   25
to give the reality which is the root of all poetry, in a comprehensive
and natural form. In the modern literature of towns, however,
richness is found only in sonnets, or prose poems, or in one or two
elaborate books that are far away from the profound and common
interests of life. One has, on one side, Mallarmé and Huysmans   30
producing this literature; and on the other Ibsen and Zola° dealing
with the reality of life in joyless and pallid words. On the stage one
must have reality, and one must have joy, and that is why the
intellectual modern drama has failed, and people have grown sick of
the false joy of the musical comedy, that has been given them in place   35
of the rich joy found only in what is superb and wild in reality. In a
good play every speech should be as fully flavoured as a nut or apple,

and such speeches cannot be written by anyone who works among people who have shut their lips on poetry. In Ireland, for a few years more, we have a popular imagination that is fiery and magnificent, 40 and tender; so that those of us who wish to write start with a chance that is not given to writers in places where the springtime of the local life has been forgotten, and the harvest is a memory only, and the straw has been turned into bricks.

J. M. S.

January 21st, 1907

PERSONS

CHRISTOPHER MAHON

OLD MAHON, his father, a squatter°

MICHAEL JAMES FLAHERTY (called MICHAEL JAMES), a publican

MARGARET FLAHERTY (called PEGEEN MIKE), his daughter

SHAWN KEOGH, her second cousin, a young farmer

PHILLY O'CULLEN ⎫
JIMMY FARRELL ⎭   small farmers

WIDOW QUIN, a woman of about thirty

SARA TANSEY ⎫
SUSAN BRADY ⎪
HONOR BLAKE ⎬   village girls
NELLY MCLAUGHLIN ⎭

A BELLMAN

SOME PEASANTS

SCENE

The action takes place near a village, on a wild coast of Mayo.° The first Act passes on a dark evening of autumn, the other two Acts on the following day.

FIRST PRODUCTION
(Dublin, 26 January 1907)

Christopher Mahon	W. G. Fay
Old Mahon	A. Power
Michael James	Arthur Sinclair
Pegeen Mike	Maire O'Neill
Shawn Keogh	F. J. Fay
Philly O'Cullen	J. A. O'Rourke
Jimmy Farrell	J. M. Kerrigan
Widow Quin	Sara Allgood
Sara Tansey	Brigit O'Dempsey
Susan Brady	Alice O'Sullivan
Honor Blake	Mary Craig
Peasants	Harry Young and U. Wright

Act 1

*Country public house or shebeen,° very rough and untidy. There
is a sort of counter on the right with shelves, holding many bottles
and jugs, just seen above it. Empty barrels stand near the
counter. At back, a little to left of counter, there is a door into
the open air; then, more to the left, there is a settle with shelves
above it, with more jugs, and a table beneath a window. At the
left there is a large open fire-place, with turf fire, and a small
door into inner room. Pegeen, a wild-looking but fine girl of
about twenty, is writing at table. She is dressed in the usual
peasant dress°*

PEGEEN [*slowly, as she writes*] Six yards of stuff for to make a yellow
gown. A pair of lace boots with lengthy heels on them and brassy
eyes. A hat is suited for a wedding–day A fine tooth comb.° To be
sent with three barrels of porter in Jimmy Farrell's creel cart° on
the evening of the coming Fair to Mister Michael James Flaherty.   5
With the best compliments of this season: Margaret Flaherty.

SHAWN KEOGH [*a fat and fair young man comes in down right centre
as she signs and looks round awkwardly, when he sees she is alone*]
Where's himself?°

PEGEEN [*without looking at him*] He's coming. [*She directs letter*] To   10
Mister Sheamus Mulroy, Wine and Spirit Dealer, Castlebar.°

SHAWN [*uneasily*] I didn't see him on the road.

PEGEEN How would you see him [*licks stamp and puts it on letter*] and
it dark night this half an hour gone by?

SHAWN [*turning towards door again*] I stood a while outside wonder-   15
ing would I have a right to pass on or to walk in and see you,
Pegeen Mike [*comes to the fire*], and I could hear the cows
breathing, and sighing in the stillness of the air, and not a step
moving any place from this gate to the bridge.

PEGEEN [*putting letter in envelope*] It's above at the cross-roads he is,   20
meeting Philly O'Cullen and a couple more are going along with
him to Kate Cassidy's wake.

SHAWN [*looking at her blankly*] And he's going that length in the dark
night?

PEGEEN [*impatiently*] He is surely, and leaving me lonesome on the   25
scruff of the hill.° [*She gets up and puts envelope on dresser, then
winds clock*] Isn't it long the nights are now, Shawn Keogh, to be

leaving a poor girl with her own self counting the hours to the dawn of day?

SHAWN [*with awkward humour*] If it is, when we're wedded in a short   30
while you'll have no call to complain, for I've little will to be walking off to wakes or weddings in the darkness of the night.

PEGEEN [*with rather scornful good humour*] You're making mighty certain, Shaneen,° that I'll wed you now.

SHAWN Aren't we after making a good bargain, the way we're only   35
waiting these days on Father Reilly's dispensation° from the bishops or the Court of Rome.

PEGEEN [*looking at him teasingly, washing up at dresser*] It's a wonder, Shaneen, the Holy Father'd be taking notice of the likes of you, for if I was him, I wouldn't bother with this place where you'll   40
meet none but Red Linahan, has a squint in his eye, and Patcheen is lame in his heel, or the mad Mulrannies were driven from California and they lost in their wits. We're a queer° lot these times to go troubling the Holy Father on his sacred seat.

SHAWN [*scandalized*] If we are, we're as good this place as another,   45
maybe, and as good these times as we were for ever.

PEGEEN [*with scorn*] As good, is it? Where now will you meet the like of Daneen Sullivan knocked the eye from a peeler, or Marcus Quin, God rest him, got six months for maiming ewes, and he a great warrant to tell stories of holy Ireland till he'd have the old   50
women shedding down tears about their feet. Where will you find the like of them, I'm saying?

SHAWN [*timidly*] If you don't, it's a good job, maybe, for [*with peculiar emphasis on the words*] Father Reilly has small conceit to have that kind walking around and talking to the girls.   55

PEGEEN [*impatiently, throwing water from basin out of the door*] Stop tormenting me with Father Reilly [*imitating his voice*], when I'm asking only what way I'll pass these twelve hours of dark, and not take my death with the fear. [*Looking out of door*]

SHAWN [*timidly*] Would I fetch you the Widow Quin, maybe.   60

PEGEEN Is it the like of that murderer?° You'll not, surely.

SHAWN [*going to her, soothingly*] Then I'm thinking himself will stop along with you when he sees you taking on, for it'll be a long night and with great darkness, and I'm after feeling a kind of fellow° above in the furzy ditch,° groaning wicked like a madden-   65
ing dog, the way it's good cause you have, maybe, to be fearing now.

PEGEEN [*turning on him sharply*] What's that? Is it a man you seen?

SHAWN [*retreating*] I couldn't see him at all, but I heard him groaning out and breaking his heart. It should have been a young 70
man from his words speaking.

PEGEEN [*going after him*] And you never went near to see was he hurted or what ailed him at all?

SHAWN I did not, Pegeen Mike. It was a dark lonesome place to be hearing the like of him. 75

PEGEEN Well, you're a daring fellow!° And if they find his corpse stretched above in the dews of dawn, what'll you say then to the peelers or the Justice of the Peace?

SHAWN [*thunderstruck*] I wasn't thinking of that. For the love of God, Pegeen Mike, don't let on I was speaking of him. Don't tell your 80
father and the men is coming above, for if they heard that story they'd have great blabbing this night at the wake.

PEGEEN I'll maybe tell them, and I'll maybe not.

SHAWN They are coming at the door. Will you whisht, I'm saying. 85

PEGEEN Whisht yourself.

[*She goes behind counter. Michael James, fat jovial publican, comes in down right centre followed by Philly O'Cullen, who is thin and mistrusting, and Jimmy Farrell, who is fat and amorous, about forty-five*]

MEN [*together*] God bless you. The blessing of God on this place.

PEGEEN God bless you kindly.

MICHAEL [*to men, who go to the counter right*] Sit down now, and take your rest. [*Crosses to Shawn at the fire left*] And how is it you are, 90
Shawn Keogh? Are you coming over the sands to Kate Cassidy's wake?

SHAWN I am not, Michael James. I'm going home the short-cut to my bed.

PEGEEN [*speaking across from counter*] He's right too, and have you 95
no shame, Michael James, to be quitting off for the whole night and leaving myself lonesome in the shop?

MICHAEL [*good-humouredly*] Isn't it the same whether I go for the whole night or a part only? and I'm thinking it's a queer daughter you are if you'd have me crossing backward through the Stooks of 100
the Dead Women,° with a drop taken.

PEGEEN [*angrily*] If I am a queer daughter, it's a queer father'd be leaving me lonesome these twelve hours of dark, and I piling the turf with the dogs barking, and the calves mooing, and my own teeth rattling with the fear. 105

JIMMY [*flatteringly*] What is there to hurt you and you a fine, hardy girl would knock the head of any two men in the place.

PEGEEN [*working herself up*] Isn't there the harvest boys with their tongues red for drink, and the ten tinkers is camped in the east glen, and the thousand militia°—bad cess to them!°—walking idle   110 through the land? There's lots surely to hurt me, and I won't stop alone in it, let himself do what he will.

MICHAEL If you're that afeard, let Shawn Keogh stop along with you. It's the will of God, I'm thinking, himself should be seeing to you now. [*They all turn on Shawn*]   115

SHAWN [*in horrified confusion*] I would and welcome, Michael James; but I'm afeard of Father Reilly, and what at all would the Holy Father and the Cardinals of Rome be saying if they heard I did the like of that?

MICHAEL [*with contempt*] God help you! Can't you sit in by the   120 hearth with the light lit and herself beyond in the room? You'll do that surely, for I've heard tell there's a queer fellow above going mad or getting his death, maybe, in the gripe of the ditch, so she'd be safer this night with a person here.

SHAWN [*with plaintive despair*] I'm afeard of Father Reilly,   125 I'm saying. Let you not be tempting me and we near married itself.

PHILLY [*with cold contempt*] Lock him in the west room. He'll stay then and have no sin to be telling to the priest.

MICHAEL [*to Shawn, getting between him and the door*] Go up now.   130

SHAWN [*at the top of his voice*] Don't stop me, Michael James. Let me out of the door, I'm saying, for the love of the Almighty God. Let me out [*trying to dodge past him*]. Let me out of it and may God grant you His indulgence in the hour of need.

MICHAEL [*loudly*] Stop your noising and sit down by the hearth.   135 [*Gives him a push and goes to counter laughing*]

SHAWN [*turning back, wringing his hands*] Oh, Father Reilly and the saints of God, where will I hide myself today? Oh, St. Joseph and St. Patrick and St. Brigid and St. James, have mercy on me now! [*He turns round, sees door clear and makes a rush for it*]   140

MICHAEL [*catching him by the coat-tail*] You'd be going, is it?

SHAWN [*screaming*] Leave me go, Michael James, leave me go, you old Pagan, leave me go or I'll get the curse of the priests on you, and of the scarlet-coated bishops of the courts of Rome. [*With a sudden movement he pulls himself out of his coat and disappears out of   145 the door, leaving his coat in Michael's hands*]

MICHAEL [*turning round, and holding up coat*] Well, there's the coat of a Christian man. Oh, there's sainted glory this day in the lonesome west, and by the will of God I've got you a decent man, Pegeen, you'll have no call to be spying after if you've a score of   150 young girls, maybe, weeding in your fields.

PEGEEN [*taking up the defence of her property*] What right have you to be making game of a poor fellow for minding the priest when it's your own the fault is, not paying a penny pot-boy° to stand along with me and give me courage in the doing of my work? [*She snaps*   155 *the coat away from him, and goes behind counter with it*]

MICHAEL [*taken aback*] Where would I get a pot-boy? Would you have me send the bell-man screaming in the streets of Castlebar?

SHAWN [*opening the door a chink and putting in his head, in a small voice*] Michael James!   160

MICHAEL [*imitating him*] What ails you?

SHAWN The queer dying fellow's beyond looking over the ditch. He's come up, I'm thinking, stealing your hens. [*Looks over his shoulder*] God help me, he's following me now [*he runs into room*], and if he's heard what I said, he'll be having my life and I going   165 home lonesome in the darkness of the night.

[*For a perceptible moment they watch the door with curiosity. Someone coughs outside. Then Christy Mahon, a slight young man, comes in, very tired and frightened and dirty*]

CHRISTY [*in a small voice*] God save all here!

MEN God save you kindly.

CHRISTY [*going to counter*] I'd trouble you for a glass of porter, woman of the house. [*He puts down coin*]   170

PEGEEN [*serving him*] You're one of the tinkers, young fellow, is beyond camped in the glen?

CHRISTY I am not; but I'm destroyed walking.

MICHAEL [*patronizingly*] Let you come up then to the fire. You're looking famished with the cold.   175

CHRISTY God reward you. [*He takes up his glass, and goes a little way across to the left, then stops and looks about him*] Is it often the polis° do be coming into this place, master of the house?

MICHAEL If you'd come in better hours, you'd have seen 'Licensed for the Sale of Beer and Spirits, to be consumed on the Premises,'   180 written in white letters above the door, and what would the polis want spying on me, and not a decent house within four miles, the way every living Christian is a bona fide° saving one widow alone?

CHRISTY [*with relief*] It's a safe house, so. [*He goes over to the fire,*   185
sighing and moaning. Then he sits down putting his glass beside him
and begins gnawing a turnip, too miserable to feel the others staring at
him with curiosity]

MICHAEL [*going after him*] Is it yourself is fearing the polis? You're
wanting,° maybe?   190

CHRISTY There's many wanting.

MICHAEL Many surely, with the broken harvest° and the ended
wars.° [*He picks up some stockings etc. that are near the fire, and*
carries them away furtively] It should be larceny, I'm thinking?

CHRISTY [*dolefully*] I had it in my mind it was a different word and   195
a bigger.

PEGEEN There's a queer lad! Were you never slapped in school,
young fellow, that you don't know the name of your deed?

CHRISTY [*bashfully*] I'm slow at learning, a middling scholar only.

MICHAEL If you're a dunce itself, you'd have a right to know that   200
larceny's robbing and stealing. Is it for the like of that you're
wanting?

CHRISTY [*with a flash of family pride*] And I the son of a strong
farmer° [*with a sudden qualm*], God rest his soul, could have bought
up the whole of your old house a while since from the butt of his   205
tail-pocket° and not have missed the weight of it gone.

MICHAEL [*impressed*] If it's not stealing, it's maybe something big.

CHRISTY [*flattered*] Aye; it's maybe something big.

JIMMY He's a wicked-looking young fellow. Maybe he followed after
a young woman on a lonesome night.   210

CHRISTY [*shocked*] Oh, the saints forbid, mister. I was all times a
decent lad.

PHILLY [*turning on Jimmy*] You're a silly man, Jimmy Farrell. He
said his father was a farmer a while since, and there's himself now
in a poor state. Maybe the land was grabbed from him, and he did   215
what any decent man would do.°

MICHAEL [*to Christy, mysteriously*] Was it bailiffs?

CHRISTY The divil a one.°

MICHAEL Agents?°

CHRISTY The divil a one.   220

MICHAEL Landlords?

CHRISTY [*peevishly*] Ah, not at all, I'm saying. You'd see the like of
them stories on any little paper of a Munster town. But I'm not
calling to mind any person, gentle, simple,° judge or jury, did the
like of me.   225

[*They all draw nearer with delighted curiosity*]

PHILLY Well that lad's a puzzle-the-world.°

JIMMY He'd beat Dan Davies' Circus° or the holy missioners° making sermons on the villainy of man. Try him again, Philly.

PHILLY Did you strike golden guineas out of solder, young fellow, or shilling coins° itself?

CHRISTY I did not mister, not sixpence nor a farthing coin.

JIMMY Did you marry three wives maybe? I'm told there's a sprinkling have done that among the holy Luthers of the preaching North.°

CHRISTY [*shyly*] I never married with one, let alone with a couple or three.

PHILLY Maybe he went fighting for the Boers, the like of the man beyond, was judged to be hanged, quartered, and drawn.° Were you off east, young fellow, fighting bloody wars for Kruger° and the freedom of the Boers?

CHRISTY I never left my own parish till Tuesday was a week.

PEGEEN [*coming from counter*] He's done nothing, so. [*To Christy*] If you didn't commit murder or a bad nasty thing, or false coining, or robbery, or butchery or the like of them, there isn't anything would be worth your troubling for to run from now. You did nothing at all.

CHRISTY [*his feelings hurt*] That's an unkindly thing to be saying to a poor orphaned traveller, has a prison behind him, and hanging before, and hell's gap gaping below.

PEGEEN [*with a sign to the men to be quiet*] You're only saying it. You did nothing at all. A soft lad the like of you wouldn't slit the windpipe of a screeching sow.

CHRISTY [*offended*] You're not speaking the truth.

PEGEEN [*in mock rage*] Not speaking the truth, is it? Would you have me knock the head of you with the butt of the broom?

CHRISTY [*twisting round on her with a sharp cry of horror*] Don't strike me. . . . I killed my poor father, Tuesday was a week, for doing the like of that.

PEGEEN [*with blank amazement*] Is it killed your father?

CHRISTY [*subsiding*] With the help of God I did surely, and that the Holy Immaculate Mother may intercede for his soul.

PHILLY [*retreating with Jimmy*] There's a daring fellow.

JIMMY Oh, glory be to God!

MICHAEL [*with great respect*] That was a hanging crime, mister honey.° You should have had good reason for doing the like of that.

CHRISTY [*in a very reasonable tone*] He was a dirty man, God forgive him, and he getting old and crusty, the way I couldn't put up with him at all.

PEGEEN And you shot him dead?

CHRISTY [*shaking his head*] I never used weapons. I've no licence,   270
and I'm a law-fearing man.

MICHAEL It was with a hilted knife maybe? I'm told, in the big world, it's bloody knives they use.

CHRISTY [*loudly, scandalized*] Do you take me for a slaughter-boy?

PEGEEN You never hanged him, the way Jimmy Farrell hanged his   275
dog from the licence° and had it screeching and wriggling three hours at the butt of a string, and himself swearing it was a dead dog, and the peelers swearing it had life?

CHRISTY I did not then. I just riz the loy° and let fall the edge of it on the ridge of his skull, and he went down at my feet like an   280
empty sack, and never let a grunt or groan from him at all.

MICHAEL [*making a sign to Pegeen to fill Christy's glass*] And what way weren't you hanged, mister? Did you bury him then?

CHRISTY [*considering*] Aye. I buried him then. Wasn't I digging spuds in the field?   285

MICHAEL And the peelers never followed after you the eleven days that you're out?

CHRISTY [*shaking his head*] Never a one of them and I walking forward facing hog, dog, or divil on the highway of the road.

PHILLY [*nodding wisely*] It's only with a common week-day kind of   290
a murderer them lads would be trusting their carcase, and that man should be a great terror when his temper's roused.

MICHAEL He should then. [*To Christy*] And where was it, mister honey, that you did the deed?

CHRISTY [*looking at him with suspicion*] Oh, a distant place, master of   295
the house, a windy corner of high distant hills.

PHILLY [*nodding with approval*] He's a close man and he's right surely.

PEGEEN That'd be a lad with the sense of Solomon to have for a pot-boy, Michael James, if it's the truth you're seeking one at all.   300

PHILLY The peelers is fearing him, and if you'd that lad in the house there isn't one of them would come smelling around if the dogs itself were lapping poteen from the dung-pit of the yard.

JIMMY Bravery's a treasure in a lonesome place, and a lad would kill his father, I'm thinking, would face a foxy divil with a pitchpike°   305
on the flags of hell.

PEGEEN It's the truth they're saying, and if I'd that lad in the house, I wouldn't be fearing the loosèd khaki cut-throats,° or the walking dead.

CHRISTY [*swelling with surprise and triumph*] Well, glory be to God!   310

MICHAEL [*with deference*] Would you think well to stop here and be pot-boy, mister honey, if we gave you good wages, and didn't destroy you with the weight of work?

SHAWN [*coming forward uneasily*] That'd be a queer kind to bring into a decent quiet household with the like of Pegeen Mike.   315

PEGEEN [*very sharply*] Will you whisht. Who's speaking to you?

SHAWN [*retreating*] A bloody-handed murderer the like of. . . .

PEGEEN [*snapping at him*] Whisht, I'm saying, we'll take no fooling from your like at all. [*To Christy with a honeyed voice*] And you, young fellow, you'd have a right to stop I'm thinking, for we'd do   320 our all and utmost to content your needs.

CHRISTY [*overcome with wonder*] And I'd be safe this place from the searching law?

MICHAEL You would surely. If they're not fearing you itself, the peelers in this place is decent, droughty poor fellows, wouldn't   325 touch a cur dog and not give warning in the dead of night.

PEGEEN [*very kindly and persuasively*] Let you stop a short while anyhow. Aren't you destroyed walking with your feet in bleeding blisters, and your whole skin needing washing like a Wicklow sheep.

CHRISTY [*looking round with satisfaction*] It's a nice room, and if it's   330 not humbugging me you are, I'm thinking that I'll surely stay.

JIMMY [*jumps up*] Now, by the grace of God, herself will be safe this night, with a man killed his father holding danger from the door, and let you come on, Michael James, or they'll have the best stuff drunk at the wake.   335

MICHAEL [*going to the door with Men*] And begging your pardon, mister, what name will we call you for we'd like to know.

CHRISTY Christopher Mahon.

MICHAEL Well, God bless you Christy, and a good rest till we meet again when the sun'll be rising to the noon of day.   340

CHRISTY God bless you all.

MEN God bless you. [*They go out except Shawn who lingers at door*]

SHAWN [*to Pegeen*] Are you wanting me to stop along with you and keep you from harm?

PEGEEN [*gruffly*] Didn't you say you were fearing Father Reilly?   345

SHAWN There'd be no harm staying now, I'm thinking, and himself in it too.

PEGEEN You wouldn't stay when there was need for you, and let you step off nimble this time when there's none.

SHAWN Didn't I say it was Father Reilly. . . .   350

PEGEEN Go on then to Father Reilly [*in a jeering tone*], and let him put you in the holy brotherhoods and leave that lad to me.

SHAWN If I meet the Widow Quin. . . .

PEGEEN Go on, I'm saying, and don't be waking this place with your noise. [*She hustles him out and bolts door*] That lad would wear the 355 spirits from the saints of peace.° [*Bustles about, then takes off her apron and pins it up in the window as a blind, Christy watching her timidly. Then she comes to him and speaks with bland good humour*] Let you stretch out now by the fire, young fellow. You should be destroyed° travelling.   360

CHRISTY [*shyly again, drawing off his boots*] I'm tired surely, walking wild eleven days and waking fearful in the night. [*He holds up one of his feet, feeling his blisters and looking at it with compassion*]

PEGEEN [*standing beside him, watching him with delight*] You should 365 have had great people in your family, I'm thinking, with the little small feet you have, and you with a kind of a quality name,° the like of what you'd find on the great powers and potentates of France and Spain.

CHRISTY [*with pride*] We were great surely, with wide and windy 370 acres of rich Munster land.

PEGEEN Wasn't I telling you, and you a fine, handsome young fellow with a noble brow.

CHRISTY [*with a flash of delighted surprise*] Is it me?

PEGEEN Aye. Did you never hear that from the young girls where 375 you come from in the west or south?

CHRISTY [*with venom*] I did not then. . . . Oh, they're bloody liars in the naked parish where I grew a man.

PEGEEN If they are itself, you've heard it these days, I'm thinking, and you walking the world telling out your story to young girls or 380 old.

CHRISTY I've told my story no place till this night, Pegeen Mike, and it's foolish I was here, maybe, to be talking free, but you're decent people, I'm thinking, and yourself a kindly woman, the way I wasn't fearing you at all.   385

PEGEEN [*filling a sack with straw, right*] You've said the like of that, maybe, in every cot and cabin where you've met a young girl on your way.

CHRISTY [*going over to her, gradually raising his voice*] I've said it
nowhere till this night, I'm telling you, for I've seen none the like   390
of you the eleven days I am walking the world, looking over a low
ditch or a high ditch on my north or south, into stony scattered
fields, or scribes of bog, where you'd see young limber girls, and
fine prancing women making laughter with the men.

PEGEEN [*nodding with approval*] If you weren't destroyed travelling   395
you'd have as much talk and streeleen, I'm thinking, as Owen Roe
O'Sullivan° or the poets of the Dingle Bay,° and I've heard all
times it's the poets are your like, fine fiery fellows with great rages
when their temper's roused.

CHRISTY [*drawing a little nearer to her*] You've a power of rings, God   400
bless you, and would there be any offence if I was asking are you
single now?

PEGEEN What would I want wedding so young?

CHRISTY [*with relief*] We're alike, so.

PEGEEN [*putting sack on settle and beating it up*] I never killed my   405
father. I'd be afeard to do that, except I was the like of yourself
with blind rages tearing me within, for I'm thinking you should
have had great tussling when the end was come.

CHRISTY [*expanding with delight at the first confidential talk he has ever
had with a woman*] We had not then. It was a hard woman was   410
come over the hill, and if he was always a crusty° kind, when he'd
a hard woman setting him on, not the divil himself or his four
fathers could put up with him at all.

PEGEEN [*with curiosity*] And isn't it a great wonder that one wasn't
fearing you?   415

CHRISTY [*very confidentially*] Up to the day I killed my father, there
wasn't a person in Ireland knew the kind I was, and I there
drinking, waking, eating, sleeping, a quiet, simple poor fellow with
no man giving me heed.

PEGEEN [*getting a quilt out of cupboard and putting it on the sack*] It   420
was the girls were giving you heed maybe, and I'm thinking it's
most conceit you'd have to be gaming with their like.

CHRISTY [*shaking his head, with simplicity*] Not the girls itself, and I
won't tell you a lie. There wasn't anyone heeding me in that place
saving only the dumb beasts of the field. [*He sits down at fire*]   425

PEGEEN [*with disappointment*] And I thinking you should have been
living the like of a king of Norway or the Eastern world. [*She
comes and sits beside him after placing bread and mug of milk on the
table*]

CHRISTY [*laughing piteously*] The like of a king, is it! And I after   430
toiling, moiling, digging, dodging from the dawn till dusk with
never a sight of joy or sport saving only when I'd be abroad in the
dark night poaching rabbits on hills, for I was a divil to poach, God
forgive me [*very naïvely*], and I near got six months for going with
a dung-fork and stabbing a fish.°   435

PEGEEN And it's that you'd call sport is it, to be abroad in the
darkness with yourself alone?

CHRISTY I did, God help me, and there I'd be as happy as the
sunshine of St. Martin's Day,° watching the light passing the
north or the patches of fog, till I'd hear a rabbit starting to screech   440
and I'd go running in the furze. Then when I'd my full share I'd
come walking down where you'd see the ducks and geese stretched
sleeping on the highway of the road, and before I'd pass the
dunghill, I'd hear himself snoring out, a loud lonesome snore he'd
be making all times, the while he was sleeping, and he a man'd be   445
raging all times the while he was waking, like a gaudy officer°
you'd hear cursing and damning and swearing oaths.

PEGEEN Providence and Mercy, spare us all!

CHRISTY It's that you'd say surely if you seen him and he after
drinking for weeks, rising up in the red dawn, or before it maybe,   450
and going out into the yard as naked as an ash tree in the moon of
May, and shying clods again the visage of the stars till he'd put
the fear of death into the banbhs and the screeching sows.

PEGEEN I'd be well-nigh afeard of that lad myself, I'm thinking. And
there was no one in it but the two of you alone?   455

CHRISTY The divil a one, though he'd sons and daughters walking
all great states and territories of the world, and not a one of them°
to this day but would say their seven curses on him, and they
rousing up to let a cough or sneez , maybe, in the deadness of the
night.   460

PEGEEN [*nodding her head*] Well, you should have been a queer lot.
. . . I never cursed my father the like of that though I'm twenty
and more years of age.

CHRISTY Then you'd have cursed mine, I'm telling you, and he a
man never gave peace to any saving when he'd get two months or   465
three, or be locked in the asylum for battering peelers or assaulting
men [*with depression*], the way it was a bitter life he led me till I
did up a Tuesday° and halve his skull.

PEGEEN [*putting her hand on his shoulder*] Well, you'll have peace in
this place, Christy Mahon, and none to trouble you, and it's near   470

time a fine lad the like of you should have your good share of the earth.

CHRISTY It's time surely, and I a seemly fellow with great strength in me and bravery of. . . . [*Some one knocks*]

CHRISTY [*clinging to Pegeen*] Oh, glory! it's late for knocking, and this last while I'm in terror of the peelers, and the walking dead. . . . [*Knocking again*]

PEGEEN Who's there?

VOICE [*outside*] Me.

PEGEEN Who's me?

VOICE The Widow Quin.

PEGEEN [*jumping up and giving him the bread and milk*] Go on now with your supper, and let on to be sleepy, for if she found you were such a warrant to talk, she'd be stringing gabble till the dawn of day.

[*Christy takes bread and sits shyly with his back to the door*]

PEGEEN [*opening door, with temper*] What ails you, or what is it you're wanting at this hour of the night?

WIDOW QUIN [*coming in a step and peering at Christy*] I'm after meeting Shawn Keogh and Father Reilly below, who told me of your curiosity man, and they fearing by this time he was maybe roaring, romping on your hands with drink.

PEGEEN [*pointing to Christy*] Look now, is he roaring, and he stretched out drowsy with his supper, and his mug of milk. Walk down and tell that to Father Reilly and to Shaneen Keogh.

WIDOW QUIN [*coming forward*] I'll not see them again, for I've their word° to lead that lad forward for to lodge with me.

PEGEEN [*in blank amazement*] This night, is it?

WIDOW QUIN [*going over*] This night. 'It isn't fitting,' says the priesteen, 'to have his likeness lodging with an orphaned girl.' [*To Christy*] God save you, mister!

CHRISTY [*shyly*] God save you kindly.

WIDOW QUIN [*looking at him with half-amused curiosity*] Well, aren't you a little smiling fellow? It should have been great and bitter torments did rouse your spirits to a deed of blood.

CHRISTY [*doubtfully*] It should, maybe.

WIDOW QUIN It's more than 'maybe' I'm saying, and it'd soften my heart to see you sitting so simple with your cup and cake, and you fitter to be saying your catechism than slaying your da.

PEGEEN [*at counter, washing glasses*] There's talking when any'd see he's fit to be holding his head high with the wonders of the world.

Walk on from this, for I'll not have him tormented and he
destroyed travelling since Tuesday was a week.

WIDOW QUIN [*peaceably*] We'll be walking surely when his supper's
done, and you'll find we're great company, young fellow, when it's
of the like of you and me you'd hear the penny poets singing in   515
an August Fair.°

CHRISTY [*innocently*] Did you kill your father?

PEGEEN [*contemptuously*] She did not. She hit himself° with a worn
pick, and the rusted poison did corrode his blood the way he never
overed° it and died after. That was a sneaky kind of murder   520
did win small glory with the boys itself. [*She crosses to Christy's
left*]

WIDOW QUIN [*with good-humour*] If it didn't, maybe all knows a
widow woman has buried her children and destroyed her man is a
wiser comrade° for a young lad than a girl the like of you who'd   525
go helter-skeltering after any man would let you a wink° upon the
road.

PEGEEN [*breaking out into wild rage*] And you'll say that, Widow
Quin, and you gasping with the rage you had racing the hill
beyond to look on his face.   530

WIDOW QUIN [*laughing derisively*] Me, is it! Well, Father Reilly has
cuteness° to divide you now. [*She pulls Christy up*] There's great
temptation in a man did slay his da, and we'd best be going, young
fellow; so rise up and come with me.

PEGEEN [*seizing his arm*] He'll not stir. He's pot-boy in this place and   535
I'll not have him stolen off and kidnabbed while himself's abroad.

WIDOW QUIN It'd be a crazy pot-boy'd lodge him in the shebeen
where he works by day, so you'd have a right to come on, young
fellow, till you see my little houseen, a perch off on the rising hill.

PEGEEN Wait till morning, Christy Mahon, wait till you lay eyes on   540
her leaky thatch is growing more pasture for her buck goat than
her square of fields, and she without a tramp itself° to keep in
order her place at all.

WIDOW QUIN When you see me contriving° in my little gardens,
Christy Mahon, you'll swear the Lord God formed me to be living   545
lone and that there isn't my match in Mayo for thatching or
mowing or shearing a sheep.

PEGEEN [*with noisy scorn*] It's true the Lord God formed you to
contrive indeed! Doesn't the world know you reared a black ram
at your own breast, so that the Lord Bishop of Connaught felt the   550
elements of a Christian, and he eating it after in a kidney stew?°

Doesn't the world know you've been seen shaving the foxy skipper from France for a threepenny bit and a sop of grass tobacco° would wring the liver from a mountain goat you'd meet lepping the hills?

WIDOW QUIN [*with amusement*] Do you hear her now, young fellow? 555
Do you hear the way she'll be rating° at your own self when a week is by?

PEGEEN [*to Christy*] Don't heed her. Tell her to go on into her pigsty and not plague us here.

WIDOW QUIN I'm going; but he'll come with me. 560

PEGEEN [*shaking him*] Are you dumb, young fellow?

CHRISTY [*timidly to Widow Quin*] God increase you;° but I'm pot-boy in this place, and it's here I'd liefer stay.

PEGEEN [*triumphantly*] Now you've heard him, and go on from this.

WIDOW QUIN [*looking round the room*] It's lonesome this hour 565
crossing the hill, and if he won't come along with me, I'd have a right maybe to stop this night with yourselves. Let me stretch out on the settle, Pegeen Mike, and himself can lie by the hearth.

PEGEEN [*short and fiercely*] Faith I won't. Quit off or I will send you 570
now.

WIDOW QUIN [*gathering her shawl up*] Well, it's a terror to be aged a score! [*To Christy*] God bless you now, young fellow, and let you be wary, or there's right torment will await you here if you go romancing with her like, and she waiting only, as they bade me 575
say, on a sheep-skin parchment to be wed with Shawn Keogh of Killakeen. [*She goes out*]

CHRISTY [*going to Pegeen, as she bolts door*] What's that she's after saying?

PEGEEN Lies and blather, you've no call to mind. Well isn't Shawn 580
Keogh an impudent fellow to send up spying on me? Wait till I lay hands on him. Let him wait, I'm saying.

CHRISTY And you're not wedding him at all?

PEGEEN I wouldn't wed him if a bishop came walking for to join us here. 585

CHRISTY That God in glory may be thanked for that.

PEGEEN There's your bed now. I've put a quilt upon you I'm after quilting a while since with my own two hands, and you'd best stretch out now for your sleep, and may God give you a good rest till I call you in the morning when the cocks will crow. 590

CHRISTY [*as she goes to inner room*] May God and Mary and St. Patrick bless you and reward you for your kindly talk. [*She shuts

the door behind her. He settles his bed slowly, feeling the quilt with immense satisfaction] Well it's a clean bed and soft with it, and it's great luck and company I've won me in the end of time—two fine 595
women fighting for the likes of me—, till I'm thinking this night wasn't I a foolish fellow not to kill my father in the years gone by.

CURTAIN

Act 2

Scene as before. Brilliant morning light. Christy, looking bright and cheerful, is cleaning a girl's boot

CHRISTY [*to himself, counting jugs on dresser*] Half a hundred beyond. Ten there. A score that's above. Eighty jugs. Six cups and a broken one. Two plates. A power of glasses. Bottles, a school-master'd be hard set to count, and enough in them, I'm thinking, to drunken all the wealth and wisdom of the County Clare. [*He puts down the boot carefully*] There's her boots now, nice and decent for her evening use, and isn't it grand brushes she has? [*He puts them down and goes by degrees to the looking-glass*] Well, this'd be a fine place to be my whole life talking out with swearing Christians in place of my old dogs and cat, and I stalking around, smoking my pipe and drinking my fill, and never a day's work but drawing a cork an odd time, or wiping a glass, or rinsing out a shiny tumbler for a decent man. [*He takes the looking-glass from the wall and puts it on the back of a chair; then sits down in front of it and begins washing his face*] Didn't I know rightly I was handsome, though it was the divil's own mirror we had beyond, would twist a squint across an angel's brow, and I'll be growing fine from this day, the way I'll have a soft lovely skin on me and won't be the like of the clumsy young fellows do be ploughing all times in the earth and dung. [*He starts*] Is she coming again? [*He looks out*] Stranger girls. God help me, where'll I hide myself away and my long neck naked to the world. [*He looks out*] I'd best go to the room maybe till I'm dressed again.

> [*He gathers up his coat and the looking-glass, and runs into the inner room. The door is pushed open, and Susan Brady looks in, and knocks on door*]

SUSAN There's nobody in it. [*Knocks again*]

NELLY [*pushing her in and following her, with Honor Blake and Sara Tansey*] It'd be early for them both to be out walking the hill.

SUSAN I'm thinking Shawn Keogh was making game of us and there's no such man in it at all.

HONOR [*pointing to straw and quilt*] Look at that. He's been sleeping there in the night. Well, it'll be a hard case if he's gone off now, the way we'll never set our eyes on a man killed his father, and we after rising early and destroying ourselves running fast on the hill.

NELLY Are you thinking them's his boots?

SARA [*taking them up*] If they are, there should be his father's track
on them. Did you never read in the papers the way murdered men   35
do bleed and drip?

SUSAN Is that blood there, Sara Tansey?

SARA [*smelling it*] That's bog water, I'm thinking, but it's his own
they are surely, for I never seen the like of them for whity mud,
and red mud, and turf on them, and the fine sands of the sea. That   40
man's been walking, I'm telling you. [*She goes down right, putting
on one of his boots*]

SUSAN [*going to window*] Maybe he's stolen off to Belmullet° with the
boots of Michael James, and you'd have a right so to follow after
him, Sara Tansey, and you the one yoked the ass cart and drove   45
ten miles to set your eyes on the man bit the yellow lady's nostril
on the northern shore.° [*She looks out*]

SARA [*running to window, with one boot on*] Don't be talking, and we
fooled today. [*Putting on other boot*] There's a pair do fit me well,
and I'll be keeping them for walking to the priest, when you'd be   50
ashamed this place, going up winter and summer with nothing
worth while to confess at all.

HONOR [*who has been listening at inner door*] Whisht! there's some one
inside the room. [*She pushes door a chink open*] It's a man.
    [*Sara kicks off boots and puts them where they were. They all
    stand in a line looking through chink*]

SARA I'll call him. Mister! Mister! [*He puts in his head*] Is Pegeen   55
within?

CHRISTY [*coming in as meek as a mouse, with the looking-glass held
behind his back*] She's above on the cnuceen, seeking the nanny
goats, the way she'd have a sup of goat's milk for to colour my tea.

SARA And asking your pardon, is it you's the man killed his father?   60

CHRISTY [*sidling toward the nail where the glass was hanging*] I am,
God help me!

SARA [*taking eggs she has brought*] Then my thousand welcomes to
you, and I've run up with a brace of duck's eggs for your food
today. Pegeen's ducks is no use, but these are the real rich sort.   65
Hold out your hand and you'll see it's no lie I'm telling you.

CHRISTY [*coming forward shyly, and holding out his left hand*] They're
a great and weighty size.

SUSAN And I run up with a pat of butter, for it'd be a poor thing to
have you eating your spuds dry, and you after running a great way   70
since you did destroy your da.

CHRISTY Thank you kindly.

HONOR And I brought you a little cut of a cake, for you should have a thin stomach on you and you that length walking the world.

NELLY And I brought you a little laying pullet—boiled and all she is—was crushed at the fall of night by the curate's car. Feel the fat of that breast, Mister.   75

CHRISTY It's bursting, surely. [*He feels it with the back of his left hand, in which he holds the presents*]

SARA Will you pinch it? Is your right hand too sacred for to use at all? [*She slips round behind him*] It's a glass he has. Well I never seen to this day, a man with a looking-glass held to his back. Them that kills their fathers is a vain lot surely.   80

[*Girls giggle*]

CHRISTY [*smiling innocently and piling presents on glass*] I'm very thankful to you all today. . . .   85

WIDOW QUIN [*coming in quickly, at door*] Sara Tansey, Susan Brady, Honor Blake! What in glory has you here at this hour of day?

GIRLS [*giggling*] That's the man killed his father.

WIDOW QUIN [*coming to them*] I know well it's the man; and I'm after putting him down in the sports below for racing, lepping, pitching, and the Lord knows what.   90

SARA [*exuberantly*] That's right, Widow Quin. I'll bet my dowry that he'll lick the world.

WIDOW QUIN If you will, you'd have a right to have him fresh and nourished in place of nursing° a feast. [*Taking presents*] Are you fasting or fed, young fellow?   95

CHRISTY Fasting, if you please.

WIDOW QUIN [*loudly*] Well, you're the lot. Stir up now and give him his breakfast. [*To Christy*] Come here to me [*she puts him on bench beside her while the Girls make tea and get his breakfast*] and let you tell us your story before Pegeen will come, in place of grinning your ears off like the moon of May.   100

CHRISTY [*beginning to be pleased*] It's a long story you'd be destroyed listening.

WIDOW QUIN Don't be letting on to be shy, a fine, gamey, treacherous lad the like of you. Was it in your house beyond you cracked his skull?   105

CHRISTY [*shy, but flattered*] It was not. We were digging spuds in his cold, sloping, stony divil's patch of a field.

WIDOW QUIN And you went asking money of him, or making talk of getting a wife would drive him from his farm?   110

CHRISTY I did not, then; but there I was, digging and digging, and 'You squinting idiot,' says he, 'let you walk down now and tell the priest you'll wed the Widow Casey in a score of days.'

WIDOW QUIN And what kind was she?   115

CHRISTY [*with horror*] A walking terror from beyond the hills, and she two score and five years, and two hundredweights and five pounds in the weighing scales, with a limping leg on her, and a blinded eye, and she a woman of noted misbehaviour with the old and young. [*He begins gnawing a chicken leg*]   120

GIRLS [*clustering round him, serving him*] Glory be!

WIDOW QUIN And what did he want driving you to wed with her? [*She takes a bit of the chicken*]

CHRISTY [*eating with growing satisfaction*] He was letting on I was wanting a protector from the harshness of the world, and he   125 without a thought the whole while but how he'd have her hut to live in and her gold to drink.

WIDOW QUIN There's maybe worse than a dry hearth and a widow woman and your glass at night. So you hit him then?

CHRISTY [*getting almost excited*] I did not. 'I won't wed her,' says I,   130 'when all know she did suckle me for six weeks when I came into the world, and she a hag this day with a tongue on her has the crows and seabirds scattered, the way they wouldn't cast a shadow on her garden with the dread of her curse.'

WIDOW QUIN [*teasingly*] That one should be right company!   135

SARA [*eagerly*] Don't mind her. Did you kill him then?

CHRISTY 'She's too good for the like of you,' says he, 'and go on now or I'll flatten you out like a crawling beast has passed under a dray.' 'You will not if I can help it,' says I. 'Go on,' says he, 'or I'll have the divil making garters of your limbs tonight.'   140 'You will not if I can help it,' says I. [*He sits bolt up, brandishing his mug*]

SARA You were right surely.

CHRISTY [*impressively*] With that the sun came out between the cloud and the hill, and it shining green in my face. 'God have mercy on   145 your soul,' says he, lifting a scythe; 'or on your own,' says I, raising the loy.

SUSAN That's a grand story.

HONOR He tells it lovely.

CHRISTY [*flattered and confident, waving bone*] He gave a drive with   150 the scythe, and I gave a lep to the east. Then I turned around with my back to the north, and I hit a blow on the ridge of his skull, laid him stretched out, and he split to the knob of his gullet. [*He raises the chicken bone to his Adam's apple*]

GIRLS [*together*] Well, you're a marvel! Oh, God bless you! You're 155 the lad surely!

SUSAN I'm thinking the Lord God sent him this road to make a second husband to the Widow Quin, and she with a great yearning to be wedded though all dread her here. Lift him on her knee, Sara Tansey. 160

WIDOW QUIN Don't tease him.

SARA [*going over to dresser and counter very quickly, and getting two glasses and porter*] You're heroes surely, and let you drink a supeen with your arms linked like the outlandish° lovers in the sailor's song. [*She links their arms and gives them the glasses*] There now. 165 Drink a health to the wonders of the western world, the pirates, preachers, poteen-makers, with the jobbing jockies,° parching peelers, and the juries fill their stomachs selling judgments of the English law.° [*Brandishing the bottle*]

WIDOW QUIN That's a right toast, Sara Tansey. Now Christy. 170
[*They drink with their arms linked, he drinking with his left hand, she with her right. As they are drinking, Pegeen Mike comes in with a milk can and stands aghast. They all spring away from Christy. He goes down left. Widow Quin remains seated*]

PEGEEN [*angrily*] What is it you're wanting° [*to Sara*]?

SARA [*twisting her apron*] An ounce of tobacco.

PEGEEN Have you tuppence?

SARA I've forgotten my purse.

PEGEEN Then you'd best be getting it and not be fooling us here. 175 [*To the Widow Quin, with more elaborate scorn*] And what is it you're wanting, Widow Quin?

WIDOW QUIN [*insolently*] A penn'orth of starch.

PEGEEN [*breaking out*] And you without a white shift° or a shirt in your whole family since the drying of the flood.° I've no starch for 180 the like of you, and let you walk on now to Killamuck.°

WIDOW QUIN [*turning to Christy, as she goes out with the Girls*] Well, you're mighty huffy this day, Pegeen Mike, and you young fellow, let you not forget the sports and racing when the noon is by. [*They go out*] 185

PEGEEN [*imperiously*] Fling out that rubbish and put them cups away. [*Christy tidies away in great haste*] Shove in the bench by the wall. [*He does so*] And hang that glass on the nail. What disturbed it at all?

CHRISTY [*very meekly*] I was making myself decent only, and this a   190
fine country for young lovely girls.

PEGEEN [*sharply*] Whisht your talking of girls. [*Goes to counter right*]

CHRISTY Wouldn't any wish to be decent in a place. . . .

PEGEEN Whisht, I'm saying.

CHRISTY [*looks at her face for a moment with great misgivings, then as*   195
a last effort, takes up a loy, and goes towards her, with feigned
assurance] It was with a loy the like of that I killed my father.

PEGEEN [*still sharply*] You've told me that story six times since the
dawn of day.

CHRISTY [*reproachfully*] It's a queer thing you wouldn't care to be   200
hearing it and them girls after walking four miles to be listening
to me now.

PEGEEN [*turning round astonished*] Four miles!

CHRISTY [*apologetically*] Didn't himself say there were only bona
fides living in the place?   205

PEGEEN It's bona fides by the road they are, but that lot come over
the river lepping the stones.° It's not three perches when you go
like that and I was down this morning looking on the papers the
post-boy does have in his bag [*with meaning and emphasis*], for there
was great news this day, Christopher Mahon. [*She goes into room*   210
left]

CHRISTY [*suspiciously*] Is it news of my murder?

PEGEEN [*inside*] Murder indeed!

CHRISTY [*loudly*] A murdered da?

PEGEEN [*coming in again and crossing right*] There was not, but a story   215
filled half a page of the hanging of a man. Ah, that should be a
fearful end, young fellow, and it worst of all for a man destroyed
his da, for the like of him would get small mercies, and when
it's dead he is, they'd put him in a narrow grave, with cheap
sacking wrapping him round, and pour down quicklime on his   220
head, the way you'd see a woman pouring any frish-frash° from a
cup.

CHRISTY [*very miserably*] Oh, God help me. Are you thinking I'm
safe? You were saying at the fall of night, I was shut of jeo-
pardy° and I here with yourselves.   225

PEGEEN [*severely*] You'll be shut of jeopardy no place if you go
talking with a pack of wild girls the like of them, do be walking
abroad with the peelers, talking whispers at the fall of night.

CHRISTY [*with terror*] And you're thinking they'd tell?

PEGEEN [*with mock sympathy*] Who knows, God help you.   230

CHRISTY [*loudly*] What joy would they have to bring hanging to the
likes of me?

PEGEEN It's queer joys they have, and who knows the thing they'd
do, if it'd make the green stones cry itself to think of you swaying
and swiggling at the butt of a rope, and you with a fine, stout neck, 235
God bless you! the way you'd be a half an hour, in great anguish,
getting your death.

CHRISTY [*getting his boots and putting them on*] If there's that terror
of them, it'd be best, maybe, I went on wandering like Esau or
Cain and Abel on the sides of Neifin° or the Erris Plain.° 240

PEGEEN [*beginning to play with him*] It would, maybe, for I've heard
the Circuit Judges° this place is a heartless crew.

CHRISTY [*bitterly*] It's more than judges this place is a heartless crew.
[*Looking up at her*] And isn't it a poor thing to be starting again
and I a lonesome fellow will be looking out on women and girls 245
the way the needy fallen spirits do be looking on the Lord?

PEGEEN What call have you to be that lonesome when there's poor
girls walking Mayo in their thousands now?

CHRISTY [*grimly*] It's well you know what call I have. It's well you
know it's a lonesome thing to be passing small towns with the 250
lights shining sideways when the night is down, or going in strange
places with a dog nosing before you and a dog nosing behind, or
drawn to the cities where you'd hear a voice kissing and talking
deep love in every shadow of the ditch, and you passing on with
an empty hungry stomach failing from your heart. 255

PEGEEN I'm thinking you're an odd man, Christy Mahon. The
oddest walking fellow I ever set my eyes on to this hour today.

CHRISTY What would any be but odd men and they living lonesome
in the world?

PEGEEN I'm not odd, and I'm my whole life with my father only. 260

CHRISTY [*with infinite admiration*] How would a lovely handsome
woman the like of you be lonesome when all men should be
thronging around to hear the sweetness of your voice, and the little
infant children should be pestering your steps I'm thinking, and
you walking the roads. 265

PEGEEN I'm hard set to know what way a coaxing fellow the like of
yourself should be lonesome either.

CHRISTY Coaxing!

PEGEEN Would you have me think a man never talked with the girls
would have the words you've spoken today? It's only letting on you 270
are to be lonesome, the way you'd get around me now.

CHRISTY I wish to God I was letting on; but I was lonesome all times
and born lonesome, I'm thinking, as the moon of dawn. [*Going to
door*]

PEGEEN [*puzzled by his talk*] Well, it's a story I'm not understanding   275
at all why you'd be worse than another, Christy Mahon, and you
a fine lad with the great savagery to destroy your da.

CHRISTY It's little I'm understanding myself, saving only that my
heart's scalded this day, and I going off stretching out the earth
between us, the way I'll not be waking near you another dawn of   280
the year till the two of us do arise to hope or judgment with the
saints of God, and now I'd best be going with my wattle in my
hand, for hanging is a poor thing [*turning to go*], and it's little
welcome only is left me in this house today.

PEGEEN [*sharply*] Christy! [*He turns round*] Come here to me. [*He   285
goes towards her*] Lay down that switch and throw some sods on
the fire. You're pot-boy in this place, and I'll not have you mitch
off from us now.

CHRISTY You were saying I'd be hanged if I stay.

PEGEEN [*quite kindly at last*] I'm after going down and reading the   290
fearful crimes of Ireland for two weeks or three, and there
wasn't a word of your murder. [*Getting up and going over to the
counter*] They've likely not found the body. You're safe so with
ourselves.

CHRISTY [*astonished, slowly*] It's making game of me you were   295
[*following her with fearful joy*], and I can stay so, working at your
side, and I not lonesome from this mortal day.

PEGEEN What's to hinder you staying, except the widow woman or
the young girls would inveigle you off?

CHRISTY [*with rapture*] And I'll have your words from this day filling   300
my ears, and that look is come upon you meeting my two eyes,
and I watching you loafing around in the warm sun, or rinsing your
ankles when the night is come.

PEGEEN [*kindly, but a little embarrassed*] I'm thinking you'll be a loyal
young lad to have working around, and if you vexed me a while   305
since with your leaguing with the girls, I wouldn't give a thraneen
for a lad hadn't a mighty spirit in him and a gamey heart.

[*Shawn Keogh runs in carrying a cleeve on his back, followed
by the Widow Quin*]

SHAWN [*to Pegeen*] I was passing below and I seen your mountainy
sheep eating cabbages in Jimmy's field. Run up or they'll be
bursting surely.   310

PEGEEN Oh, God mend them! [*She puts a shawl over her head and runs out*]

CHRISTY [*looking from one to the other, still in high spirits*] I'd best go to her aid maybe. I'm handy with ewes.

WIDOW QUIN [*closing the door*] She can do that much, and there is   315
Shaneen has long speeches for to tell you now. [*She sits down with an amused smile*]

SHAWN [*taking something from his pocket and offering it to Christy*] Do you see that, Mister?

CHRISTY [*looking at it*] The half of a ticket to the Western States!°   320

SHAWN [*trembling with anxiety*] I'll give it to you and my new hat [*pulling it out of hamper*]; and my breeches with the double seat [*pulling it out*]; and my new coat is woven from the blackest shearings for three miles around [*giving him the coat*]; I'll give you the whole of them and my blessing and the blessing of Father   325
Reilly itself, maybe, if you'll quit from this and leave us in the peace we had till last night at the fall of dark.

CHRISTY [*with a new arrogance*] And for what is it you're wanting to get shut of me?

SHAWN [*looking to the Widow for help*] I'm a poor scholar with   330
middling faculties to coin a lie, so I'll tell you the truth, Christy Mahon. I'm wedding with Pegeen beyond, and I don't think well of having a clever fearless man the like of you dwelling in her house.

CHRISTY [*almost pugnaciously*] And you'd be using bribery for to   335
banish me?

SHAWN [*in an imploring voice*] Let you not take it badly, mister honey, isn't beyond the best place for you where you'll have golden chains and shiny coats and you riding upon hunters° with the ladies of the land. [*He makes an eager sign to the Widow Quin to   340
come to help him*]

WIDOW QUIN [*coming over*] It's true for him, and you'd best quit off and not have that poor girl setting her mind on you, for there's Shaneen thinks she wouldn't suit you though all is saying that she'll wed you now.   345
    [*Christy beams with delight*]

SHAWN [*in terrified earnest*] She wouldn't suit you, and she with the divil's own temper the way you'd be strangling one another in a score of days. [*He makes the movement of strangling with his hands*] It's the like of me only that she's fit for, a quiet simple fellow wouldn't raise a hand upon her if she scratched itself.   350

WIDOW QUIN [*putting Shawn's hat on Christy*] Fit them clothes on you anyhow, young fellow, and he'd maybe loan them to you for the sports. [*Pushing him towards inner door*] Fit them on and you can give your answer when you have them tried.

CHRISTY [*beaming, delighted with the clothes*] I will then, I'd like herself to see me in them tweeds and hat. [*He goes into room and shuts the door*]   355

SHAWN [*in great anxiety*] He'd like herself to see them! He'll not leave us, Widow Quin. He's a score of divils in him, the way it's well nigh certain he will wed Pegeen.   360

WIDOW QUIN [*jeeringly*] It's true all girls are fond of courage and do hate the like of you.

SHAWN [*walking about in desperation*] Oh, Widow Quin, what'll I be doing now? I'd inform again him, but he'd burst from Kilmainham° and he'd be sure and certain to destroy me. If I wasn't so God-fearing, I'd near have courage to come behind him and run a pike into his side. Oh, it's a hard case to be an orphan and not to have your father that you're used to, and you'd easy kill and make yourself a hero in the sight of all. [*Coming up to her*] Oh, Widow Quin, will you find me some contrivance when I've promised you a ewe?   365   370

WIDOW QUIN A ewe's a small thing, but what would you give me if I did wed him and did save you so?

SHAWN [*with astonishment*] You!

WIDOW QUIN Aye. Would you give me the red cow you have and the mountainy ram, and the right of way across your rye path, and a load of dung at Michaelmas,° and turbary° upon the western hill?   375

SHAWN [*radiant with hope*] I would surely, and I'd give you the wedding-ring I have, and the loan of the new suit, the way you'd have him decent on the wedding-day. I'd give you two kids for your dinner and a gallon of poteen, and I'd call the piper on the long car to your wedding from Crossmolina or from Ballina.° I'd give you . . .   380

WIDOW QUIN That'll do, so, and let you whisht, for he's coming now again.   385

[*Christy comes in very natty in the new clothes. Widow Quin goes to him admiringly*]

WIDOW QUIN If you seen yourself now, I'm thinking you'd be too proud to speak to us at all, and it'd be a pity surely to have your like sailing from Mayo to the Western World.

CHRISTY [*as proud as a peacock*] I'm not going. If this is a poor place   390
itself, I'll make myself contented to be lodging here.
    [*Widow Quin makes a sign to Shawn to leave them*]
SHAWN Well, I'm going measuring the race-course while the tide is
low,° so I'll leave you the garments and my blessing for the sports
today. God bless you! [*He wriggles out*]
WIDOW QUIN [*admiring Christy*] Well you're mighty spruce, young   395
fellow. Sit down now while you're quiet till you talk with me.
CHRISTY [*swaggering*] I'm going abroad on the hillside for to seek
Pegeen.
WIDOW QUIN You'll have time and plenty for to seek Pegeen, and
you heard me saying at the fall of night the two of us should be   400
great company.
CHRISTY From this out I'll have no want of company when all sorts
is bringing me their food and clothing [*he swaggers to the door,
tightening his belt*], the way they'd set their eyes upon a gallant
orphan cleft his father with one blow to the breeches belt. [*He*   405
opens door, then staggers back] Saints of glory! Holy angels from the
throne of light!
WIDOW QUIN [*going over*] What ails you?
CHRISTY It's the walking spirit of my murdered da!
WIDOW QUIN [*looking out*] Is it that tramper?   410
CHRISTY [*wildly*] Where'll I hide my poor body from that ghost of
hell?
    [*The door is pushed open, and Old Mahon appears on threshold.
    Christy darts in behind door*]
WIDOW QUIN [*in great amusement*] God save you, my poor man.
MAHON [*gruffly*] Did you see a young lad passing this way in the
early morning or the fall of night?   415
WIDOW QUIN You're a queer kind to walk in not saluting at all.°
MAHON Did you see the young lad?
WIDOW QUIN [*stiffly*] What kind was he?
MAHON An ugly young streeler with a murderous gob on him° and
a little switch in his hand. I met a tramper seen him coming this   420
way at the fall of night.
WIDOW QUIN There's harvest hundreds° do be passing these days
for the Sligo boat. For what is it you're wanting him, my poor
man?
MAHON I want to destroy him for breaking the head on me with the   425
clout of a loy. [*He takes off a big hat, and shows his head in a mass
of bandages and plaster, with some pride*] It was he did that, and

amn't I a great wonder to think I've traced him ten days with that
rent in my crown?

WIDOW QUIN [*taking his head in both hands and examining it with*   430
extreme delight] That was a great blow. And who hit you? A robber
maybe?

MAHON It was my own son hit me, and he the divil a robber or
anything else but a dirty, stuttering lout.

WIDOW QUIN [*letting go his skull and wiping her hands in her apron*]   435
You'd best be wary of a mortified scalp,° I think they call it,
lepping around with that wound in the splendour of the sun. It
was a bad blow surely, and you should have vexed him fearful to
make him strike that gash in his da.

MAHON Is it me?   440

WIDOW QUIN [*amusing herself*] Aye. And isn't it a great shame when
the old and hardened do torment the young?

MAHON [*raging*] Torment him is it? And I after holding out with the
patience of a martyred saint, till there's nothing but destruction on
me and I'm driven out in my old age with none to aid me?   445

WIDOW QUIN [*greatly amused*] It's a sacred wonder the way that
wickedness will spoil a man.

MAHON My wickedness, is it? Amn't I after saying it is himself has
me destroyed, and he a lier on walls, a talker of folly, a man you'd
see stretched the half of the day in the brown ferns with his belly   450
to the sun.

WIDOW QUIN Not working at all?

MAHON The divil a work, or if he did itself, you'd see him raising
up a haystack like the stalk of a rush or driving our last cow till he
broke her leg at the hip, and when he wasn't at that he'd be fooling   455
over little birds he had—finches and felts—or making mugs at his
own self in the bit of a glass we had hung on the wall.

WIDOW QUIN [*looking at Christy*] What way was he so foolish? It was
running wild after the girls maybe?

MAHON [*with a shout of derision*] Running wild, is it? If he seen a red   460
petticoat coming swinging over the hill, he'd be off to hide in the
sticks, and you'd see him shooting out his sheep's eyes between
the little twigs and leaves, and his two ears rising like a hare
looking out through a gap. Girls indeed!

WIDOW QUIN It was drink maybe?   465

MAHON And he a poor fellow would get drunk on the smell of a pint!
He'd a queer rotten stomach, I'm telling you, and when I gave
him three pulls from my pipe a while since, he was taken with

contortions till I had to send him in the ass cart to the females' nurse.   470

WIDOW QUIN [*clasping her hands*] Well, I never till this day heard tell of a man the like of that.

MAHON I'd take a mighty oath you didn't surely, and wasn't he the laughing joke of every female woman where four baronies meet, the way the girls would stop their weeding if they seen him coming   475
the road to let a roar at him, and call him the looney of Mahon's.

WIDOW QUIN I'd give the world and all to see the like of him. What kind was he?

MAHON A small low fellow.

WIDOW QUIN And dark?   480

MAHON Dark and dirty.

WIDOW QUIN [*considering*] I'm thinking I seen him.

MAHON [*eagerly*] An ugly young blackguard?

WIDOW QUIN A hideous, fearful villain, and the spit of you.

MAHON What way is he fled?   485

WIDOW QUIN Gone over the hills to catch a coasting steamer to the north or south.

MAHON Could I pull up on him now?

WIDOW QUIN If you'll cross the sands below where the tide is out, you'll be in it as soon as himself, for he had to go round ten miles   490
by the top of the bay. [*She points from the door*] Strike down by the head beyond and then follow on the roadway to the north and east.
    [*Mahon goes abruptly*]

WIDOW QUIN [*shouting after him*] Let you give him a good vengeance when you come up with him, but don't put yourself in the power of the law, for it'd be a poor thing to see a judge in his black cap   495
reading out his sentence on a civil warrior the like of you. [*She swings the door to and looks at Christy, who is cowering in terror, for a moment, then she bursts into a laugh*] Well, you're the walking playboy of the western world, and that's the poor man you had divided to his breeches belt.   500

CHRISTY [*looking out; then, to her*] What'll Pegeen say when she hears that story? What'll she be saying to me now?

WIDOW QUIN She'll knock the head of you, I'm thinking, and drive you from the door. God help her to be taking you for a wonder, and you a little schemer making up a story you destroyed your da.   505

CHRISTY [*turning to the door, nearly speechless with rage, half to himself*] To be letting on he was dead, and coming back to his life, and following me like an old weazel tracing a rat, and coming in here

laying desolation between my own self and the fine women of
Ireland, and he a kind of carcase that you'd fling upon the sea.° . . .   510
WIDOW QUIN [*more soberly*] There's talking for a man's one only
son.
CHRISTY [*breaking out*] His óne son, is it? May I meet him with one
tooth and it aching, and one eye to be seeing seven and seventy
divils in the twists of the road, and one old timber leg on him to   515
limp into the scalding grave. [*Looking out*] There he is now
crossing the strands, and that the Lord God would send a high
wave to wash him from the world.
WIDOW QUIN [*scandalized*] Have you no shame? [*Putting her hand
on his shoulder and turning him round*] What ails you? Near crying,   520
is it?
CHRISTY [*in despair and grief*] Amn't I after seeing the love-light of
the star of knowledge° shining from her brow, and hearing words
would put you thinking on the holy Brigid° speaking to the infant
saints, and now she'll be turning again, and speaking hard words   525
to me, like an old woman with a spavindy° ass she'd have, urging
on a hill.
WIDOW QUIN There's poetry talk for a girl you'd see itching and
scratching, and she with a stale stink of poteen on her from selling
in the shop.   530
CHRISTY [*impatiently*] It's her like is fitted to be handling merchand-
ise in the heavens above, and what'll I be doing now, I ask you,
and I a kind of wonder was jilted by the heavens when a day was by.
[*There is a distant noise of girls' voices. Widow Quin looks from
window and comes to him, hurriedly*]
WIDOW QUIN You'll be doing like myself, I'm thinking, when I did
destroy my man, for I'm above many's the day, odd times in great   535
spirits, abroad in the sunshine, darning a stocking or stitching a
shift, and odd times again looking out on the schooners, hookers,
trawlers is sailing the sea, and I thinking on the gallant hairy
fellows are drifting beyond, and myself long years living alone.
CHRISTY [*interested*] You're like me, so.   540
WIDOW QUIN I am your like, and it's for that I'm taking a fancy to
you, and I with my little houseen above where there'd be myself
to tend you, and none to ask were you a murderer or what at all.
CHRISTY And what would I be doing if I left Pegeen?
WIDOW QUIN I've nice jobs you could be doing, gathering shells to   545
make a whitewash for our hut within, building up a little goose-
house, or stretching a new skin on an old curagh I have, and if my

hut is far from all sides, it's there you'll meet the wisest old men,
I tell you, at the corner of my wheel,° and it's there yourself and
me will have great times whispering and hugging . . .   550

VOICES [*outside, calling far away*] Christy! Christy Mahon! Christy!

CHRISTY Is it Pegeen Mike?

WIDOW QUIN It's the young girls, I'm thinking, coming to bring you
to the sports below, and what is it you'll have me to tell them now?

CHRISTY Aid me for to win Pegeen. It's herself only that I'm seeking   555
now. [*Widow Quin gets up and goes to window*] Aid me for to win
her, and I'll be asking God to stretch a hand to you in the hour of
death, and lead you short cuts through the Meadows of Ease, and
up the floor of Heaven to the Footstool of the Virgin's Son.

WIDOW QUIN There's praying!   560

VOICES [*nearer*] Christy! Christy Mahon!

CHRISTY [*with agitation*] They're coming. Will you swear to aid and
save me for the love of Christ?

WIDOW QUIN [*looks at him for a moment*] If I aid you, will you swear
to give me a right of way I want, and a mountainy ram, and a load   565
of dung at Michaelmas, the time that you'll be master here?

CHRISTY I will, by the elements and stars of night.

WIDOW QUIN Then we'll not say a word of the old fellow, the way
Pegeen won't know your story till the end of time.

CHRISTY And if he chances to return again?   570

WIDOW QUIN We'll swear he's a maniac and not your da. I could
take an oath I seen him raving on the sands today.
        [*Girls run in*]

SUSAN Come on to the sports below. Pegeen says you're to come.

SARA TANSEY The lepping's beginning, and we've a jockey's suit to
fit upon you for the mule race on the sands below.   575

HONOR Come on, will you.

CHRISTY I will then if Pegeen's beyond.

SARA She's in the boreen making game of Shaneen Keogh.

CHRISTY Then I'll be going to her now. [*He runs out, followed by the
Girls*]   580

WIDOW QUIN Well, if the worst comes in the end of all, it'll be great
game to see there's none to pity him but a widow woman, the like
of me, has buried her children and destroyed her man. [*She goes
out*]

CURTAIN

Act 3

Scene, as before. Later in the day. Jimmy comes in, slightly drunk

JIMMY [*calls*] Pegeen! [*Crosses to inner door*] Pegeen Mike! [*Comes back again into the room*] Pegeen! [*Philly comes in in the same state*] [*To Philly*] Did you see herself?

PHILLY I did not; but I sent Shawn Keogh with the ass cart for to bear him home. [*Trying cupboards which are locked*] Well, isn't he 5 a nasty man to get into such staggers at a morning wake, and isn't herself the divil's daughter for locking, and she so fussy after that young gaffer, you might take your death with drought and none to heed you.

JIMMY It's little wonder she'd be fussy, and he after bringing 10 bankrupt ruin on the roulette man, and the trick-o'-the-loop° man, and breaking the nose of the cockshot-man,° and winning all in the sports below, racing, lepping, dancing, and the Lord knows what! He's right luck, I'm telling you.

PHILLY If he has he'll be rightly hobbled yet, and he not able to say 15 ten words without making a brag of the way he killed his father and the great blow he hit with the loy.

JIMMY A man can't hang by his own informing, and his father should be rotten by now.

[*Old Mahon passes window slowly*]

PHILLY Supposing a man's digging spuds in that field with a long 20 spade, and supposing he flings up the two halves of that skull, what'll be said then in the papers and the courts of law?

JIMMY They'd say it was an old Dane, maybe,° was drowned in the flood. [*Old Mahon comes in and sits down near door listening*] Did you never hear tell of the skulls they have in the city of Dublin, 25 ranged out like blue jugs in a cabin of Connaught?

PHILLY And you believe that?

JIMMY [*pugnaciously*] Didn't a lad see them and he after coming from harvesting in the Liverpool boat? 'They have them there,' says he, 'making a show of the great people there was one time 30 walking the world. White skulls and black skulls and yellow skulls, and some with full teeth and some haven't only but one.'

PHILLY It was no lie, maybe, for when I was a young lad, there was a graveyard beyond the house with the remnants of a man who had

thighs as long as your arm. He was a horrid man, I'm telling you, 35
and there was many a fine Sunday I'd put him together for fun,
and he with shiny bones you wouldn't meet the like of these days
in the cities of the world.

MAHON [*getting up*] You wouldn't is it? Lay your eyes on that skull,
and tell me where and when there was another the like of it, is 40
splintered only from the blow of a loy.

PHILLY Glory be to God! And who hit you at all?

MAHON [*triumphantly*] It was my own son hit me. Would you believe
that?

JIMMY Well there's wonders hidden in the heart of man! 45

PHILLY [*suspiciously*] And what way was it done?

MAHON [*wandering about the room*] I'm after walking hundreds and
long scores of miles, winning clean beds and the fill of my belly
four times in the day, and I doing nothing but telling stories of
that naked truth. [*He comes to them a little aggressively*] Give me a 50
supeen and I'll tell you now.

> [*Widow Quin comes in and stands aghast behind him. He is
> facing Jimmy and Philly, who are on the left*]

JIMMY Ask herself beyond. She's the stuff hidden in her shawl.

WIDOW QUIN [*coming to Mahon quickly*] You here, is it? You didn't
go far at all?

MAHON I seen the coasting steamer passing, and I got a drought 55
upon me and a cramping leg, so I said, 'The divil go along with
him,' and turned again. [*Looking under her shawl*] And let you give
me a supeen, for I'm destroyed travelling since Tuesday was a
week.

WIDOW QUIN [*getting a glass, in a cajoling tone*] Sit down then by 60
the fire and take your ease for a space. You've a right to be
destroyed indeed, with your walking, and fighting, and facing the
sun [*giving him poteen from a stone jar she has brought in*]. There
now is a drink for you, and may it be to your happiness and length
of life. 65

MAHON [*taking glass greedily, and sitting down by fire*] God increase
you!

WIDOW QUIN [*taking Men to the right stealthily*] Do you know what?
That man's raving from his wound today, for I met him a while
since telling a rambling tale of a tinker had him destroyed. Then 70
he heard of Christy's deed, and he up and says it was his son had
cracked his skull. Oh, isn't madness a fright, for he'll go killing
someone yet and he thinking it's the man has struck him so!

JIMMY [*entirely convinced*] It's a fright surely. I knew a party was
kicked in the head by a red mare, and he went killing horses a great   75
while, till he eat the insides of a clock and died after.

PHILLY [*with suspicion*] Did he see Christy?

WIDOW QUIN He didn't. [*With a warning gesture*] Let you not be
putting him in mind of him, or you'll be likely summoned if there's
murder done. [*Looking round at Mahon*] Whisht! He's listening.   80
Wait now till you hear me taking him easy and unravelling all. [*She
goes to Mahon*] And what way are you feeling, Mister? Are you in
contentment now?

MAHON [*slightly emotional from his drink*] I'm poorly only, for it's a
hard story the way I'm left today, when it was I did tend him from   85
his hour of birth, and he a dunce never reached his second book,
the way he'd come from school, many's the day, with his legs lamed
under him, and he blackened with his beatings like a tinker's ass.
It's a hard story, I'm saying, the way some do have their next and
nighest raising up a hand of murder on them, and some is   90
lonesome getting their death with lamentation in the dead of night.

WIDOW QUIN [*not knowing what to say*] To hear you talking so quiet,
who'd know you were the same fellow we seen pass today?

MAHON I'm the same surely. The wrack and ruin of three score
years; and it's a terror to live that length, I tell you, and to have   95
your sons going to the dogs against you, and you wore out scolding
them, and skelping them, and God knows what.

PHILLY [*to Jimmy*] He's not raving. [*To Widow Quin*] Will you ask
him what kind was his son?

WIDOW QUIN [*to Mahon, with a peculiar look*] Was your son that hit   100
you a lad of one year and a score maybe, a great hand at racing
and lepping and licking the world?

MAHON [*turning on her with a roar of rage*] Didn't you hear me say
he was the fool of men, the way from this out he'll know the
orphan's lot with old and young making game of him and they   105
swearing, raging, kicking at him like a mangy cur.

[*A great burst of cheering outside, some way off*]

MAHON [*putting his hands to his ears*] What in the name of God do
they want roaring below?

WIDOW QUIN [*with the shade of a smile*] They're cheering a young
lad, the champion playboy of the western world.   110

[*More cheering*]

MAHON [*going to window*] It'd split my heart to hear them, and I with
pulses in my brain-pan for a week gone by. Is it racing they are?

JIMMY [*looking from door*] It is then. They are mounting him for the mule race will be run upon the sands. That's the playboy on the winkered mule.   115

MAHON [*puzzled*] That lad, is it? If you said it was a fool he was, I'd have laid a mighty oath he was the likeness of my wandering son. [*Philly nods at Jimmy. Mahon, uneasily, putting his hand to his head*] Faith, I'm thinking I'll go walking for to view the race.

WIDOW QUIN [*stopping him, sharply*] You will not. You'd best take   120 the road to Belmullet,° and not be dilly-dallying in this place where there isn't a spot you could sleep.

PHILLY [*coming forward*] Don't mind her. Mount there on the bench and you'll have a view of the whole. They're hurrying before the tide will rise, and it'd be near over if you went down the pathway   125 through the crags below.

MAHON [*mounts on bench, Widow Quin beside him*] That's a right view again° the edge of the sea. They're coming now from the point. He's leading. Who is he at all?

WIDOW QUIN He's the champion of the world I tell you, and there   130 isn't a hap'orth isn't falling lucky to his hands today.

PHILLY [*looking out, interested in the race*] Look at that. They're pressing him now.

JIMMY He'll win it yet.

PHILLY Take your time, Jimmy Farrell. It's too soon to say.   135

WIDOW QUIN [*shouting*] Watch him taking the gate. There's riding.

JIMMY [*cheering*] More power to the young lad!

MAHON He's passing the third.

JIMMY He'll lick them yet.

WIDOW QUIN He'd lick them if he was running races with a score   140 itself.

MAHON Look at the mule he has kicking the stars.

WIDOW QUIN There was a lep! [*Catching hold of Mahon in her excitement*] He's fallen! He's mounted again! Faith, he's passing them all!   145

JIMMY Look at him skelping her!

PHILLY And the mountain girls hooshing him on!

JIMMY It's the last turn! The post's cleared for them now!°

MAHON Look at the narrow place. He'll be into the bogs! [*With a yell*] Good rider! He's through it again!   150

JIMMY He's neck and neck!

MAHON Good boy to him! Flames, but he's in!
   [*Great cheering, in which all join*]

MAHON [*with hesitation*] What's that? They're raising him up. They're coming this way. [*With a roar of rage and astonishment*] It's Christy! by the stars of God! I'd know his way of spitting and he astride the moon. [*He jumps down and makes a run for the door, but Widow Quin catches him and pulls him back*] 155

WIDOW QUIN Stay quiet, will you. That's not your son. [*To Jimmy*] Stop him, or you'll get a month for the abetting of manslaughter and be fined as well. 160

JIMMY I'll hold him.

MAHON [*struggling*] Let me out! Let me out the lot of you! till I have my vengeance on his head today.

WIDOW QUIN [*shaking him, vehemently*] That's not your son. That's a man is going to make a marriage with the daughter of this house, a place with fine trade, with a licence, and with poteen too. 165

MAHON [*amazed*] That man marrying a decent and a moneyed girl! Is it mad yous are? Is it in a crazy-house for females that I'm landed now?

WIDOW QUIN It's mad yourself is with the blow upon your head. That lad is the wonder of the western world. 170

MAHON I seen it's my son.

WIDOW QUIN You seen that you're mad. [*Cheering outside*] Do you hear them cheering him in the zig-zags of the road? Aren't you after saying that your son's a fool, and how would they be cheering a true idiot born? 175

MAHON [*getting distressed*] It's maybe out of reason that man's himself.° [*Cheering again*] There's none surely will go cheering him. Oh, I'm raving with a madness that would fright the world. [*He sits down with his hand to his head*] There was one time I seen ten scarlet divils letting on they'd cork my spirit in a gallon can; and one time I seen rats as big as badgers sucking the life blood from the butt of my lug;° but I never till this day confused that dribbling idiot with a likely man. I'm destroyed surely. 180 185

WIDOW QUIN And who'd wonder when it's your brain-pan that is gaping now?

MAHON Then the blight of the sacred drought upon myself and him, for I never went mad to this day, and I not three weeks with the Limerick girls drinking myself silly and parlatic from the dusk to dawn. [*To Widow Quin, suddenly*] Is my visage astray? 190

WIDOW QUIN It is then. You're a sniggering maniac, a child could see.

MAHON [*getting up more cheerfully*] Then I'd best be going to the Union beyond, and there'll be a welcome before me, I tell you [*with great pride*], and I a terrible and fearful case, the way that there I was one time screeching in a straitened waistcoat with seven doctors writing out my sayings in a printed book. Would you believe that?   195

WIDOW QUIN If you're a wonder itself, you'd best be hasty, for them lads caught a maniac one time and pelted the poor creature till he ran out raving and foaming and was drowned in the sea.   200

MAHON [*with philosophy*] It's true mankind is the divil when your head's astray. Let me out now and I'll slip down the boreen and not see them so.   205

WIDOW QUIN [*showing him out*] That's it. Run to the right, and not a one will see.

[*He runs off*]

PHILLY [*wisely*] You're at some gaming, Widow Quin; but I'll walk after him and give him his dinner and a time to rest, and I'll see then if he's raving or as sane as you.   210

WIDOW QUIN [*annoyed*] If you go near that lad, let you be wary of your head, I'm saying. Didn't you hear him telling he was crazed at times?

PHILLY I heard him telling a power; and I'm thinking we'll have right sport, before night will fall. [*He goes out*]   215

JIMMY Well, Philly's a conceited and foolish man. How could that madman have his senses and his brain-pan slit? I'll go after them and see him turn on Philly now.

[*He goes; Widow Quin hides poteen behind counter. Then hubbub outside*]

VOICES There you are! Good jumper! Grand lepper! Darlint boy! He's the racer! Bear him on, will you!   220

[*Christy comes in, in Jockey's dress, with Pegeen Mike, Sara, and other Girls, and Men*]

PEGEEN [*to Crowd*] Go on now and don't destroy him and he drenching with sweat. Go along, I'm saying, and have your tug-of-warring till he's dried his skin.

CROWD Here's his prizes! A bagpipes! A fiddle was played by a poet in the years gone by! A flat and three-thorned blackthorn would lick the scholars out of Dublin town!°   225

CHRISTY [*taking prizes from the Men*] Thank you kindly, the lot of you. But you'd say it was little only I did this day if you'd seen me a while since striking my one single blow.

TOWN CRIER [*outside, ringing a bell*] Take notice, last event of this   230
day! Tug-of-warring on the green below! Come on, the lot of you!
Great achievements for all Mayo men!

PEGEEN Go on, and leave him for to rest and dry. Go on, I tell you,
for he'll do no more. [*She hustles Crowd out; Widow Quin following
them*]   235

MEN [*going*] Come on then. Good luck for the while!

PEGEEN [*radiantly, wiping his face with her shawl*] Well you're the lad,
and you'll have great times from this out when you could win that
wealth of prizes, and you sweating in the heat of noon!

CHRISTY [*looking at her with delight*] I'll have great times if I win the   240
crowning prize I'm seeking now, and that's your promise that
you'll wed me in a fortnight, when our banns° is called.

PEGEEN [*backing away from him*] You've right daring to go ask me
that, when all knows you'll be starting to some girl in your own
townland, when your father's rotten in four months, or five.   245

CHRISTY [*indignantly*] Starting from you, is it! [*He follows her*] I will
not then, and when the airs is warming in four months or five, it's
then yourself and me should be pacing Neifin in the dews of
night,° the times sweet smells do be rising, and you'd see a little
shiny new moon maybe sinking on the hills.   250

PEGEEN [*looking at him playfully*] And it's that kind of a poacher's
love you'd make, Christy Mahon, on the sides of Neifin, when the
night is down?

CHRISTY It's little you'll think if my love's a poacher's or an earl's
itself when you'll feel my two hands stretched around you, and I   255
squeezing kisses on your puckered lips till I'd feel a kind of pity
for the Lord God is all ages sitting lonesome in his golden
chair.°

PEGEEN That'll be right fun, Christy Mahon, and any girl would
walk her heart out before she'd meet a young man was your like   260
for eloquence or talk at all.

CHRISTY [*encouraged*] Let you wait to hear me talking till we're
astray in Erris when Good Friday's by,° drinking a sup from a
well, and making mighty kisses with our wetted mouths, or gaming
in a gap of sunshine with yourself stretched back unto your   265
necklace in the flowers of the earth.

PEGEEN [*in a lower voice, moved by his tone*] I'd be nice so, is it?

CHRISTY [*with rapture*] If the mitred bishops seen you that time,
they'd be the like of the holy prophets, I'm thinking, do be
straining the bars of Paradise to lay eyes on the Lady Helen of   270

Troy,° and she abroad pacing back and forward with a nosegay in her golden shawl.

PEGEEN [*with real tenderness*] And what is it I have, Christy Mahon, to make me fitting entertainment for the like of you that has such poet's talking, and such bravery of heart?   275

CHRISTY [*in a low voice*] Isn't there the light of seven heavens in your heart alone, the way you'll be an angel's lamp to me from this out, and I abroad in the darkness spearing salmons in the Owen or the Carrowmore.°

PEGEEN If I was your wife, I'd be along with you those nights,   280
Christy Mahon, the way you'd see I was a great hand at coaxing bailiffs, or coining funny nicknames for the stars of night.

CHRISTY You, is it! Taking your death in the hailstones or the fogs of dawn.

PEGEEN Yourself and me would shelter easy in a narrow bush, [*with   285
a qualm of dread*] but we're only talking maybe, for this would be a poor thatched place to hold a fine lad is the like of you.

CHRISTY [*putting his arm round her*] If I wasn't a good Christian, it's on my naked knees I'd be saying my prayers and paters to every jackstraw you have roofing your head,° and every stony pebble is   290
paving the laneway to your door.

PEGEEN [*radiantly*] If that's the truth, I'll be burning candles from this out to the miracles of God have brought you from the south today, and I with my gowns bought ready the way that I can wed you, and not wait at all.   295

CHRISTY It's miracles and that's the truth. Me there toiling a long while, and walking a long while, not knowing at all I was drawing all times nearer to this holy day.

PEGEEN And myself a girl was tempted often to go sailing the seas till I'd marry a Jew-man with ten kegs of gold,° and I not knowing   300
at all there was the like of you drawing nearer like the stars of God.

CHRISTY And to think I'm long years hearing women talking that talk to all bloody fools, and this the first time I've heard the like of your voice talking sweetly for my own delight.

PEGEEN And to think it's me is talking sweetly, Christy Mahon, and   305
I the fright of seven townlands for my biting tongue. Well the heart's a wonder, and I'm thinking there won't be our like in Mayo for gallant lovers from this hour today. [*Drunken singing is heard outside*] There's my father coming from the wake, and when he's had his sleep we'll tell him, for he's peaceful then. [*They   310
separate*]

MICHAEL [*singing outside*]—
> The jailor and the turnkey
> They quickly ran us down,
> And brought us back as prisoners   315
> Once more to Cavan town.
> [*He comes in supported by Shawn*]
> There we lay bewailing
> All in a prison bound.° . . .
> [*He sees Christy. Goes and shakes him drunkenly by the hand,*
> *while Pegeen and Shawn talk on the left*]

MICHAEL [*to Christy*] The blessing of God and the holy angels on
your head, young fellow. I hear tell you're after winning all in the   320
sports below; and wasn't it a shame I didn't bear you along with
me to Kate Cassidy's wake, a fine, stout lad, the like of you, for
you'd never see the match of it for flows of drink, the way when
we sunk her bones at noonday in her narrow grave, there were five
men, aye, and six men, stretched out retching speechless on the   325
holy stones.

CHRISTY [*uneasily, watching Pegeen*] Is that the truth?

MICHAEL It is then, and aren't you a louty schemer to go burying
your poor father unbeknownst when you'd a right to throw him
on the crupper of a Kerry mule and drive him westwards, like holy   330
Joseph in the days gone by, the way we could have given him a
decent burial and not have him rotting beyond and not a Christian
drinking a smart drop to the glory of his soul.

CHRISTY [*gruffly*] It's well enough he's lying for the likes of him.

MICHAEL [*slapping him on the back*] Well, aren't you a hardened   335
slayer? It'll be a poor thing for the household man where you go
sniffing for a female wife; and [*pointing to Shawn*] look beyond at
that shy and decent Christian I have chosen for my daughter's
hand, and I after getting the gilded dispensation this day for to
wed them now.   340

CHRISTY And you'll be wedding them this day, is it?

MICHAEL [*drawing himself up*] Aye. Are you thinking, if I'm drunk
itself I'd leave my daughter living single with a little frisky rascal
is the like of you?

PEGEEN [*breaking away from Shawn*] Is it the truth the dispensation's   345
come?

MICHAEL [*triumphantly*] Father Reilly's after reading it in gallous
Latin, and 'It's come in the nick of time,' says he; 'so I'll wed them
in a hurry, dreading that young gaffer who'd capsize the stars.'

PEGEEN [*fiercely*] He's missed his nick of time, for it's that lad,   350
Christy Mahon, that I'm wedding now.

MICHAEL [*loudly, with horror*] You'd be making him a son to me and
he wet and crusted with his father's blood?

PEGEEN Aye. Wouldn't it be a bitter thing for a girl to go marrying
the like of Shaneen, and he a middling kind of a scarecrow with   355
no savagery or fine words in him at all?

MICHAEL [*gasping and sinking on a chair*] Oh, aren't you a heathen
daughter to go shaking the fat of my heart, and I swamped and
drownded with the weight of drink? Would you have them turning
on me the way that I'd be roaring to the dawn of day with the wind   360
upon my heart?° Have you not a word to aid me, Shaneen? Are
you not jealous at all?

SHAWN [*in great misery*] I'd be afeard to be jealous of a man did slay
his da.

PEGEEN Well, it'd be a poor thing to go marrying your like. I'm   365
seeing there's a world of peril for an orphan girl, and isn't it a great
blessing I didn't wed you, before himself came walking from the
west or south.

SHAWN It's a queer story you'd go picking a dirty tramp up from the
highways of the world.   370

PEGEEN [*playfully*] And you think you're a likely beau to go straying
along with, the shiny Sundays of the opening year, when it's
sooner on a bullock's liver you'd put a poor girl thinking than on
the lily or the rose.

SHAWN And have you no mind of my weight of passion, and the holy   375
dispensation, and the drift of heifers I am giving, and the golden
ring?

PEGEEN I'm thinking you're too fine for the like of me, Shawn Keogh
of Killakeen, and let you go off till you'd find a radiant lady with
droves of bullocks on the plains of Meath,° and herself bedizened   380
in the diamond jewelleries of Pharaoh's ma. That'd be your match,
Shaneen. So God save you now! [*She retreats behind Christy*]

SHAWN Won't you hear me telling you. . . .

CHRISTY [*with ferocity*] Take yourself from this, young fellow, or I'll
maybe add a murder to my deeds today.   385

MICHAEL [*springing up with a shriek*] Murder is it? Is it mad yous are?
Would you go making murder in this place, and it piled with
poteen for our drink tonight?° Go on to the foreshore if it's
fighting you want, where the rising tide will wash all traces from
the memory of man. [*Pushing Shawn towards Christy*]   390

SHAWN [*shaking himself free, and getting behind Michael*] I'll not fight
him, Michael James. I'd liefer live a bachelor simmering in
passions to the end of time, than face a lepping savage the like of
him has descended from the Lord knows where. Strike him
yourself, Michael James, or you'll lose my drift of heifers and my   395
blue bull from Sneem.°

MICHAEL Is it me fight him, when it's father-slaying he's bred to
now? [*Pushing Shawn*] Go on you fool and fight him now.

SHAWN [*coming forward a little*] Will I strike him with my hand?

MICHAEL Take the loy is on your western side.   400

SHAWN I'd be afeard of the gallows if I struck with that.

CHRISTY [*taking up the loy*] Then I'll make you face the gallows or
quit off from this. [*Shawn flies out of the door*]

CHRISTY Well, fine weather be after him, [*going to Michael, coaxingly*] and I'm thinking you wouldn't wish to have that quaking   405
blackguard in your house at all. Let you give us your blessing and
hear her swear her faith to me, for I'm mounted on the spring-tide
of the stars of luck the way it'll be good for any to have me in the
house.

PEGEEN [*at the other side of Michael*] Bless us now, for I swear to   410
God I'll wed him, and I'll not renege.

MICHAEL [*standing up in the centre, holding on to both of them*] It's the
will of God, I'm thinking, that all should win an easy or a cruel
end, and it's the will of God that all should rear up lengthy families
for the nurture of the earth. What's a single man, I ask you, eating   415
a bit in one house and drinking a sup in another, and he with no
place of his own, like an old braying jackass strayed upon the
rocks?° [*To Christy*] It's many would be in dread to bring your like
into their house for to end them maybe with a sudden end; but
I'm a decent man of Ireland, and I'd liefer face the grave untimely   420
and I seeing a score of grandsons growing up little gallant swearers
by the name of God, than go peopling my bedside with puny
weeds the like of what you'd breed, I'm thinking, out of Shaneen
Keogh. [*He joins their hands*] A daring fellow is the jewel of the
world, and a man did split his father's middle with a single clout   425
should have the bravery of ten, so may God and Mary and St.
Patrick bless you, and increase you from this mortal day.

CHRISTY and PEGEEN Amen, O Lord!

> [*Hubbub outside. Old Mahon rushes in, followed by all the
> Crowd and Widow Quin. He makes a rush at Christy, knocks
> him down, and begins to beat him*]

PEGEEN [*dragging back his arm*] Stop that, will you. Who are you at all?   430

MAHON His father, God forgive me!

PEGEEN [*drawing back*] Is it rose from the dead?

MAHON Do you think I look so easy quenched with the tap of a loy? [*Beats Christy again*]

PEGEEN [*glaring at Christy*] And it's lies you told, letting on you had   435
him slitted, and you nothing at all.

CHRISTY [*catching Mahon's stick*] He's not my father. He's a raving
maniac would scare the world. [*Pointing to Widow Quin*] Herself
knows it is true.

CROWD You're fooling Pegeen! The Widow Quin seen him this day   440
and you likely knew! You're a liar!

CHRISTY [*dumbfounded*] It's himself was a liar, lying stretched out
with an open head on him, letting on he was dead.

MAHON Weren't you off racing the hills before I got my breath with
the start I had seeing you turn on me at all?   445

PEGEEN And to think of the coaxing glory we had given him, and he
after doing nothing but hitting a soft blow and chasing northward
in a sweat of fear. Quit off from this.

CHRISTY [*piteously*] You've seen my doings this day, and let you save
me from the old man; for why would you be in such a scorch of   450
haste to spur me to destruction now?

PEGEEN It's there your treachery is spurring me, till I'm hard set to
think you're the one I'm after lacing in my heart-strings half-an-
hour gone by. [*To Mahon*] Take him on from this, for I think bad
the world should see me raging for a Munster liar and the fool   455
of men.

MAHON Rise up now to retribution, and come on with me.

CROWD [*jeeringly*] There's the playboy! There's the lad thought he'd
rule the roost in Mayo. Slate him now, Mister.

CHRISTY [*getting up in shy terror*] What is it drives you to torment   460
me here, when I'd ask the thunders of the might of God to blast
me if I ever did hurt to any saving only that one single blow.

MAHON [*loudly*] If you didn't, you're a poor good-for-nothing, and
isn't it by the like of you the sins of the whole world are
committed?   465

CHRISTY [*raising his hands*] In the name of the Almighty God. . . .

MAHON Leave troubling the Lord God. Would you have him
sending down droughts, and fevers, and the old hen° and the
cholera morbus?°

CHRISTY [*to Widow Quin*] Will you come between us and protect me   470
now?

WIDOW QUIN I've tried a lot, God help me! and my share is done.

CHRISTY [*looking round in desperation*] And I must go back into my
torment is it, or run off like a vagabond straying through the
Unions with the dusts of August making mudstains in the gullet   475
of my throat, or the winds of March blowing on me till I'd take
an oath I felt them making whistles of my ribs within.

SARA Ask Pegeen to aid you. Her like does often change.

CHRISTY I will not then, for there's torment in the splendour of her
like and she a girl any moon of midnight would take pride to   480
meet, facing southwards on the heaths of Keel.° But what did I
want crawling forward to scorch my understanding at her flaming
brow?

PEGEEN [*to Mahon, vehemently, fearing she will break into tears*] Take
him on from this or I'll set the young lads to destroy him here.   485

MAHON [*going to him, shaking his stick*] Come on now if you wouldn't
have the company to see you skelped.

PEGEEN [*half laughing, through her tears*] That's it, now the world will
see him pandied, and he an ugly liar was playing off the hero and
the fright of men!   490

CHRISTY [*to Mahon, very sharply*] Leave me go!

CROWD That's it. Now Christy. If them two set fighting, it will lick
the world.

MAHON [*making a grab at Christy*] Come here to me.

CHRISTY [*more threateningly*] Leave me go, I'm saying.   495

MAHON I will maybe when your legs is limping, and your back is
blue.

CROWD Keep it up, the two of you. I'll back the old one. Now the
playboy.

CHRISTY [*in low and intense voice*] Shut your yelling, for if you're   500
after making a mighty man of me this day by the power of a lie,
you're setting me now to think if it's a poor thing to be lonesome,
it's worse maybe go mixing with the fools of earth.

[*Mahon makes a movement towards him*]

CHRISTY [*almost shouting*] Keep off . . . lest I do show a blow unto
the lot of you would set the guardian angels winking in the clouds   505
above. [*He swings round with a sudden rapid movement and picks up
a loy*]

CROWD [*half frightened, half amused*] He's going mad! Mind yourselves! Run from the idiot!

CHRISTY If I am an idiot, I'm after hearing my voice this day saying   510
    words would raise the topknot on a poet in a merchant's town. I've
    won your racing and your lepping and. . . .

MAHON Shut your gullet and come on with me.

CHRISTY I'm going but I'll stretch you first.
    [*He runs at Old Mahon with the loy, chases him out of the door,
    followed by Crowd and Widow Quin. There is a great noise
    outside, then a yell, and dead silence for a moment. Christy
    comes in, half dazed, and goes to fire*]

WIDOW QUIN [*coming in, hurriedly, and going to him*] They're turning   515
    again you. Come on or you'll be hanged indeed.

CHRISTY I'm thinking from this out, Pegeen'll be giving me praises
    the same as in the hours gone by.

WIDOW QUIN [*impatiently*] Come by the back-door. I'd think bad to
    have you stifled on the gallows tree.   520

CHRISTY [*indignantly*] I will not then. What good'd be my life-time
    if I left Pegeen?

WIDOW QUIN Come on and you'll be no worse than you were last
    night; and you with a double murder this time to be telling to the
    girls.   525

CHRISTY I'll not leave Pegeen Mike.

WIDOW QUIN [*impatiently*] Isn't there the match of her in every
    parish public, from Binghamstown unto the plain of Meath?°
    Come on, I tell you, and I'll find you finer sweethearts at each
    waning moon.   530

CHRISTY It's Pegeen I'm seeking only, and what'd I care if you
    brought me a drift of chosen females, standing in their shifts itself
    maybe,° from this place to the Eastern World.

SARA [*runs in, pulling off one of her petticoats*] They're going to hang
    him. [*Holding out petticoat and shawl*] Fit these upon him and let   535
    him run off to the east.

WIDOW QUIN He's raving now; but we'll fit them on him and I'll
    take him in the ferry to the Achill boat.

CHRISTY [*struggling feebly*] Leave me go, will you, when I'm thinking
    of my luck today, for she will wed me surely and I a proven hero   540
    in the end of all. [*They try to fasten petticoat round him*]

WIDOW QUIN Take his left hand and we'll pull him now. Come on,
    young fellow.

CHRISTY [*suddenly starting up*] You'll be taking me from her? You're
    jealous, is it, of her wedding me? Go on from this. [*He snatches up   545
    a stool, and threatens them with it*]

WIDOW QUIN [*going*] It's in the mad-house they should put him not in jail at all. We'll go by the back-door to call the doctor and we'll save him so.

[*She goes out, with Sara, through inner room. Men crowd in the doorway. Christy sits down again by the fire*]

MICHAEL [*in a terrified whisper*] Is the old lad killed surely?   550

PHILLY I'm after feeling the last gasps quitting his heart. [*They peer in at Christy*]

MICHAEL [*with a rope*] Look at the way he is. Twist a hangman's knot on it and slip it over his head while he's not minding at all.

PHILLY Let you take it, Shaneen. You're the soberest of all that's   555 here.

SHAWN Is it me to go near him, and he the wickedest and worst with me? Let you take it, Pegeen Mike.

PEGEEN Come on, so. [*She goes forward with the others, and they drop the double hitch over his head*]   560

CHRISTY What ails you?

SHAWN [*triumphantly, as they pull the rope tight on his arms*] Come on to the peelers till they stretch you° now.

CHRISTY Me!

MICHAEL If we took pity on you, the Lord God would maybe bring   565 us ruin from the law today, so you'd best come easy, for hanging is an easy and a speedy end.

CHRISTY I'll not stir. [*To Pegeen*] And what is it you'll say to me and I after doing it this time in the face of all?

PEGEEN I'll say a strange man is a marvel with his mighty talk; but   570 what's a squabble in your back-yard and the blow of a loy, have taught me that there's a great gap between a gallous story and a dirty deed. [*To men*] Take him on from this, or the lot of us will be likely put on trial for his deed today.

CHRISTY [*with horror in his voice*] And it's yourself will send me off   575 to have a horny-fingered hangman hitching his bloody slip-knots at the butt of my ear?

MEN [*pulling rope*] Come on, will you?

[*He is pulled down on the floor*]

CHRISTY [*twisting his legs round the table*] Cut the rope, Pegeen, and I'll quit the lot of you and live from this out like the madmen of   580 Keel, eating muck and green weeds on the faces of the cliffs.

PEGEEN And leave us to hang, is it, for a saucy liar, the like of you? [*To Men*] Take him on out from this.

SHAWN Pull a twist on his neck, and squeeze him so.

PHILLY Twist yourself. Sure he cannot hurt you, if you keep your   585
distance from his teeth alone.

SHAWN I'm afeard of him. [*To Pegeen*] Lift a lighted sod° will you
and scorch his leg.

PEGEEN [*blowing the fire with a bellows*] Leave go now young fellow
or I'll scorch your shins.   590

CHRISTY You're blowing for to torture me? [*His voice rising and
growing stronger*] That's your kind, is it? Then let the lot of you be
wary, for if I've to face the gallows I'll have a gay march down, I
tell you, and shed the blood of some of you before I die.

SHAWN [*in terror*] Keep a good hold, Philly. Be wary for the love of   595
God, for I'm thinking he would liefest wreak his pains on me.

CHRISTY [*almost gaily*] If I do lay my hands on you, it's the way
you'll be at the fall of night hanging as a scarecrow for the fowls
of hell.° Ah, you'll have a gallous jaunt I'm saying, coaching out
through Limbo with my father's ghost.   600

SHAWN [*to Pegeen*] Make haste, will you. Oh, isn't he a holy terror,
and isn't it true for Father Reilly that all drink's a curse that has
the lot of you so shaky and uncertain now.

CHRISTY If I can wring a neck among you, I'll have a royal
judgment looking on the trembling jury in the courts of law.°   605
And won't there be crying out in Mayo the day I'm stretched
upon the rope with ladies in their silks and satins snivelling in
their lacy kerchiefs,° and they rhyming songs and ballads on the
terror of my fate? [*He squirms round on the floor and bites Shawn's
leg*]   610

SHAWN [*shrieking*] My leg's bit on me! He's the like of a mad dog,
I'm thinking, the way that I will surely die.

CHRISTY [*delighted with himself*] You will then, the way you can
shake out hell's flags of welcome for my coming in two weeks or
three, for I'm thinking Satan hasn't many have killed their da in   615
Kerry and in Mayo too.
[*Old Mahon comes in behind on all fours and looks on
unnoticed*]

MEN [*to Pegeen*] Bring the sod, will you.

PEGEEN [*coming over*] God help him so. [*Burns his leg*]

CHRISTY [*kicking and screaming*] Oh, glory be to God!
[*He kicks loose from the table, and they all drag him towards
the door*]

JIMMY [*seeing Old Mahon*] Will you look what's come in?   620
[*They all drop Christy and run left*]

CHRISTY [*scrambling on his knees face to face with Old Mahon*] Are you coming to be killed a third time or what ails you now?

MAHON For what is it they have you tied?

CHRISTY They're taking me to the peelers to have me hanged for slaying you.   625

MICHAEL [*apologetically*] It is the will of God that all should guard their little cabins from the treachery of law and what would my daughter be doing if I was ruined or was hanged itself?

MAHON [*grimly, loosening Christy*] It's little I care if you put a bag on her back and went picking cockles till the hour of death; but   630 my son and myself will be going our own way and we'll have great times from this out telling stories of the villainy of Mayo and the fools is here. [*To Christy, who is freed*] Come on now.

CHRISTY Go with you, is it! I will then, like a gallant captain with his heathen slave. Go on now and I'll see you from this day stewing   635 my oatmeal and washing my spuds, for I'm master of all fights from now. [*Pushing Mahon*] Go on, I'm saying.

MAHON Is it me?

CHRISTY Not a word out of you. Go on from this.

MAHON [*walking out and looking back at Christy over his shoulder*]   640 Glory be to God! [*With a broad smile*] I am crazy again! [*Goes*]

CHRISTY Ten thousand blessings upon all that's here, for you've turned me a likely gaffer in the end of all, the way I'll go romancing through a romping lifetime from this hour to the dawning of the judgment day. [*He goes out*]   645

MICHAEL By the will of God, we'll have peace now for our drinks. Will you draw the porter, Pegeen?

SHAWN [*going up to her*] It's a miracle Father Reilly can wed us in the end of all, and we'll have none to trouble us when his vicious bite is healed.   650

PEGEEN [*hitting him a box on the ear*] Quit my sight. [*Putting her shawl over her head and breaking out into wild lamentations.°*] Oh my grief, I've lost him surely. I've lost the only playboy of the western world.

                                                                                  655

CURTAIN

DEIRDRE OF THE SORROWS

A Play in Three Acts

(1907–1909)

PREFACE TO *DEIRDRE OF THE SORROWS*

by W. B. YEATS

It was Synge's practice to write many complete versions of a play, distinguishing them with letters, and running half through the alphabet before he finished. He read me a version of this play the year before his death, and would have made several more always altering and enriching. He felt that the story, as he had told it, required a 5 grotesque element mixed into its lyrical melancholy to give contrast and create an impression of solidity, and had begun this mixing with the character of Owen, who would have had some part in the first act also, where he was to have entered Lavarcham's cottage with Conchubor. Conchubor would have taken a knife from his belt to cut himself 10 free from threads of silk that caught in brooch or pin as he leant over Deirdre's embroidery frame, and forgotten this knife behind him. Owen was to have found it and stolen it. Synge asked that either I or Lady Gregory should write some few words to make this possible, but after writing in a passage we were little satisfied and thought it better 15 to have the play performed, as it is printed here, with no word of ours. When Owen killed himself in the second act, he was to have done it with Conchubor's knife. He did not speak to me of any other alteration, but it is probable that he would have altered till the structure had become as strong and varied as in his other plays; and 20 had he lived to do that, 'Deirdre of the Sorrows' would have been his masterwork, so much beauty is there in its course, and such wild nobleness in its end, and so poignant is an emotion and wisdom that were his own preparation for death.

W. B. YEATS.

April, 1910

DRAFT ESSAY

The following draft of an essay was written by Synge during the early stages of his work on *Deirdre of the Sorrows*, and might have served as the basis for a preface to the completed play:

Historical or Peasant Drama 18/3/07

The moment the sense of historical truth awoke in Europe, historical fiction became impossible. For a time it seemed otherwise. Antiquarian writers, fools now exploded. Old writers (Elizabethan Louis XIV) saw historical personages as living contemporaries. Now it is impossible to use our own language or feeling with perfect sincerity for personages we know to have been different from ourselves. Hence Hist. Fiction insincere. It is possible to use a national tradition a century or more old which is still alive in the soul of the people see Walter Scott.° But any one who is familiar with Elizabethan writings will not tolerate Kenilworth or Westward Ho.° Promessi Sposi (?)° To us now as *readers* the old literature itself is so priceless we look with disgust at imitations of it. As creators? It is impossible to use a legend [such] as Faust which from the outset defies historical reality—in the making up of an absolutely modern work. [That] is only to be done possibly in verse, as our modern spoken prose cannot be put into the mouths of antique persons. On stage this is so most of all. In thinking over the poems of the last century that one reads with most pleasure how many are historical? Browning, Rossetti.° For my own part I only care for personal lyrical modern poetry and little of that, but I am possibly exceptional. That is why lyrical poetry is now the only poetry. The real world is mostly unpoetical, fiction even in poetry is not totally sincere hence failure of modern poetry. This is to be taken with all reserve, there is always the poet's dream which makes itself a sort of world. When it is kept a dream is this possible on the stage? I think not. Maeterlinck, Pelleas and Melisande?° Is the drama—as a beautiful thing a lost art? The drama of swords is. Few of us except soldiers have seen swords in use, to drag them out on the stage is babyish. They are so rustic for us with the association of pseudo-antique fiction and drama. For the present the only possible beauty in drama is peasant drama, for the future we must await the making of life beautiful again before we can have beautiful drama. You cannot gather grapes of chimney pots.

PERSONS

LAVARCHAM,° a wise woman and servant of
  Conchubor, about fifty
OLD WOMAN, cook and Deirdre's foster-mother
CONCHUBOR,° High King of Ulster, about sixty
FERGUS, Conchubor's friend and warrior of the
  Red Branch of Ulster
DEIRDRE°
NAISI,° son of Usna, Deirdre's lover
AINNLE° ⎫ brothers to Naisi, with him heroes of the
ARDAN ⎭ Red Branch°
OWEN, Conchubor's spy
TWO SOLDIERS

SCENE

*The first Act takes place in Lavarcham's house on
Slieve Fuadh;° the second Act in a wood outside the
tent of Deirdre and Naisi in Alban; the third Act in
a tent below Emain Macha.°*

FIRST PRODUCTION
(Dublin, 13 January 1909)

Lavarcham	Sara Allgood
Old Woman	Eileen O'Doherty
Owen	J. A. O'Rourke
Conchubor	Arthur Sinclair
Fergus	Sydney J. Morgan
Deirdre	Maire O'Neill
Naisi	Fred O'Donovan
Ainnle	J. M. Kerrigan
Ardan	John Carrick
Two Soldiers	Ambrose Power and
	Harry Young

Act 1

Lavarcham's house on Slieve Fuadh. There is a door to the inner room on the left, and a door to the open air on the right. Window at back and a frame with a half-finished piece of tapestry; a high chair of state centre stage with a stool near it. There are also a large press° and heavy oak chest near the back wall. The place is neat and clean but bare. Lavarcham, a woman of fifty, is working at tapestry frame. Old Woman comes in from left

OLD WOMAN She hasn't come yet is it, and it falling to the night?

LAVARCHAM She has not. [*Concealing her anxiety*] It's dark with the clouds are coming from the west and south, but it isn't later than the common.°

OLD WOMAN It's later surely, and I hear tell the Sons of Usna,° Naisi and his brothers, are above chasing hares for two days or three, and the same a while since when the moon was full.   5

LAVARCHAM [*more anxiously*] The gods send° they don't set eyes on her [*with a sign of helplessness*] . . . yet if they do, itself, it wasn't *my* wish brought them or could send them away.   10

OLD WOMAN [*reprovingly*] If it was not, you'd do well to keep a check on her, and she turning a woman that was meant to be a queen.

LAVARCHAM Who'd check her like was made to have her pleasure only,° the way if there were no warnings told about her you'd see troubles coming when an old king is taking her, and she without   15 a thought but for her beauty and to be straying the hills.

OLD WOMAN The gods help the lot of us. . . . Shouldn't she be well pleased getting the like of Conchubor, and he middling settled in his years itself? I don't know what he wanted putting her this wild place to be breaking her in, or putting myself to be roasting   20 her suppers, and she with no patience for her food at all. [*She looks out*]

LAVARCHAM Is she coming from the glen?

OLD WOMAN She is not. But whisht . . . there's two men leaving the furze. . . . [*Crying out*] It's Conchubor and Fergus along with him!   25 Conchubor'll be in a blue stew° this night and herself abroad.

LAVARCHAM [*settling room hastily*] Are they close by?

OLD WOMAN Crossing the stream, and there's herself on the hillside with a load of twigs. Will I run out and put her in order before they'll set eyes on her at all?   30

LAVARCHAM You will nòt. Would you have him see you, and he a man would be jealous of a hawk would fly between her and the rising sun. [*She looks out*] Go up to the hearth and be as busy as if you hadn't seen them at all.

OLD WOMAN [*sitting down to polish vessels*] There'll be trouble this   35
night, for he should be in his tempers° from the way he's stepping out, and he swinging his hands.

LAVARCHAM [*wearied with the whole matter*] It'd be best of all maybe if he got in tempers with herself, and made an end quickly, for I'm in a poor way between the pair of them. [*Going back to tapestry*   40
frame] There they are now at the door.
    [*Conchubor and Fergus come in*]

CONCHUBOR and FERGUS The gods save you.

LAVARCHAM [*getting up and curtseying*] The gods save and keep you kindly, and stand between you and all harm forever.

CONCHUBOR [*looking around*] Where is Deirdre?   45

LAVARCHAM [*trying to speak with indifference*] Abroad upon Slieve Fuadh. She does be all times straying around picking flowers or nuts, or sticks itself, but so long as she's gathering new life I've a right not to heed her, I'm thinking, and she taking her will.
    [*Fergus talks to Old Woman*]

CONCHUBOR [*stiffly*] A night with thunder coming is no night to be   50
abroad.

LAVARCHAM [*more uneasily*] She's used to every track and pathway and the lightning itself wouldn't let down its flame to singe the beauty of her like.

FERGUS [*cheerfully*] She's right Conchubor, and let you sit down   55
and take your ease [*he takes a wallet from under his cloak*] . . . and I'll count out what we've brought, and put it in the presses within.
    [*He goes into the inner room with Old Woman*]

CONCHUBOR [*sitting down and looking about*] Where are the mats and hangings and the silver skillets I sent up for Deirdre?   60

LAVARCHAM The mats and hangings are in this press, Conchubor. She wouldn't wish to be soiling them, she said, running out and in with mud and grasses on her feet, and it raining since the night of Samhain. The silver skillets and the golden cups, we have beyond locked in the chest.   65

CONCHUBOR Bring them out and use them from this day.

LAVARCHAM We'll do it, Conchubor.

CONCHUBOR [*getting up and going to frame°*] Is this hers?

LAVARCHAM [*pleased to speak of it*] It is, Conchubor. All say there isn't her match at fancying figures and throwing purple upon crimson, and she edging them all times with her greens and gold. 70

CONCHUBOR [*a little uneasily*] Is she keeping wise and busy since I passed before, and growing ready for her life in Emain?

LAVARCHAM [*drily*] That's questions will give small pleasure to yourself or me. . . . [*She sits on a stool and faces him, making up her mind to speak out*] If it's the truth I'll tell you, she's growing too wise to marry a big king and she a score only. Let you not be taking it bad, Conchubor, but you'll get little good seeing her this night, for with all my talking it's wilfuller she's growing these two months or three. 75 80

CONCHUBOR [*severely, but relieved things are no worse*] Isn't it a poor thing that you're doing so little to school her to meet what is to come?

LAVARCHAM I'm after serving you two score of years, and I'll tell you this night, Conchubor, she's little call to mind an old woman when she has the birds to school her, and the pools in the rivers where she goes bathing in the sun. I'll tell you if you seen her that time, with her white skin, and her red lips, and the blue water and the ferns about her, you'd know maybe, and you greedy itself, it wasn't for your like she was born at all. 85 90

CONCHUBOR It's little I heed for what she was born; she'll be my comrade surely. [*He examines her workbox*]

LAVARCHAM [*sinking into sadness again*] I'm in dread, so, they were right saying she'd bring destruction on the world, for it's a poor thing when you see a settled man putting the love he has for a young child, and the love he has for a full woman, on a girl the like of her, and it's a poor thing, Conchubor, to see a High King the way you are this day, prying after her needles and numbering her lines of thread. 95 100

CONCHUBOR [*getting up*] Let you not be talking too far and you old itself.° [*Walks across the room and back*] . . . Does she know the troubles are foretold?

LAVARCHAM [*in the tone of the earlier talk*] I'm after telling her one time and another but I'd do as well speaking to a lamb of ten weeks and it racing the hills. . . . It's not the dread of death or troubles that would tame her like. 105

CONCHUBOR [*looking out*] She's coming now, and let you walk in and keep Fergus, till I speak with her a while.

LAVARCHAM [*going left*] If I'm after vexing you, itself, it'd be best   110
you weren't taking her hasty or scolding her at all.

CONCHUBOR [*very stiffly*] I've no call to. I'm well pleased she's light
and airy.°

LAVARCHAM [*offended at his tone*] Well pleased is it? [*With a snort of
irony*] It's a queer thing the way the likes of me do be telling the   115
truth and the wise are lying all times!

> [*She goes into room left. Conchubor arranges himself before a
> mirror for a moment, then goes a little to the left and waits.
> Deirdre comes in poorly dressed with a little bag and a bundle of
> twigs in her arms. She is astonished for a moment when she sees
> Conchubor; then she makes a curtsey to him, and goes to the
> hearth without any embarrassment*]

CONCHUBOR The gods save you, Deirdre. I have come up bringing
you rings and jewels from Emain Macha.

DEIRDRE The gods save you.

CONCHUBOR What have you brought from the hills?   120

DEIRDRE [*quite self-possessed*] A bag of nuts, and twigs for our fires at
the dawn of day.

CONCHUBOR [*showing annoyance in spite of himself*] And it's that way
you're picking up the manners will fit you to be Queen of Ulster?

DEIRDRE [*made a little defiant by his tone*] I have no wish to be a queen.   125

CONCHUBOR [*almost sneeringly*] You'd wish to be dressing in your
duns and grey,° and you herding your geese or driving your calves
to their shed . . . like the common lot scattered in the glens?

DEIRDRE [*very defiant*] I would not, Conchubor. [*She goes to tapestry
and begins to work*] A girl born, the way I'm born, is more likely   130
to wish for a mate who'd be her likeness . . . a man with his hair
like the raven maybe and his skin like the snow and his lips like
blood spilt on it.°

CONCHUBOR [*sees his mistake and after a moment takes a flattering tone,
looking at her work*] Whatever you wish there's no queen but   135
would be well pleased to have your skill at choosing colours and
making pictures on the cloth. [*Looking closely*] What is it you're
figuring?

DEIRDRE [*deliberately*] Three young men, and they chasing in the
green gap of a wood.°   140

CONCHUBOR [*now almost pleading*] It's soon you'll have dogs with
silver chains to be chasing in the woods of Emain, for I have white
hounds rearing up for you, and grey horses, that I've chosen from
the finest in Ulster and Britain and Gaul.

DEIRDRE [*unmoved, as before*] I've heard tell in Ulster and Britain and   145
Gaul, Naisi and his brothers have no match and they chasing in
the woods.

CONCHUBOR [*very gravely*] Isn't it a strange thing you'd be talking
of Naisi and his brothers or figuring them either, when you know
the things that are foretold about themselves and you! Yet you've   150
little knowledge and I'd do wrong taking it bad when it'll be my
share from this out to keep you the way you'll have little call to
trouble for knowledge or its want either.

DEIRDRE Yourself should be wise surely.

CONCHUBOR The like of me have a store of knowledge that's a   155
weight and terror; it's for that we do choose out the like of yourself
that are young and glad only. I'm thinking you're gay and lively
each day in the year?

DEIRDRE I don't know if that's true, Conchubor. There are lonesome
days and bad nights in this place like another.   160

CONCHUBOR You should have as few sad days I'm thinking as I have
glad and good ones.

DEIRDRE What is it has you that way, Conchubor? Ever this
place you hear the old women saying a good child's as happy as a
king.   165

CONCHUBOR How would I be happy seeing age come on me each
year when the dry leaves are blowing back and forward at the gate
of Emain, and yet this last while I'm saying out when I'd see the
furze breaking and the daws sitting two and two on ash-trees by
the Duns of Emain,° 'Deirdre's a year nearer her full age when   170
she'll be my mate and comrade,' and then I'm glad surely.

DEIRDRE [*almost to herself*] I will not be your mate in Emain.

CONCHUBOR [*not heeding her*] It's there you'll be proud and happy
and you'll learn that if young men are great hunters yet it's with
the like of myself you'll find a knowledge of what is priceless in   175
your own like. What we all need is a place is safe and splendid,
and it's that you'll get in Emain in two days or three.

DEIRDRE [*aghast*] Two days?

CONCHUBOR I've the rooms ready, and in a little while you'll be
brought down there, to be my queen, and queen of the five parts   180
of Ireland.°

DEIRDRE [*standing up frightened and pleading*] I'd liefer stay this place,
Conchubor. . . . Leave me this place where I'm well used to the
tracks and pathways and the people of the glens. . . . It's for this
life I'm born surely.   185

CONCHUBOR You'll be happier and greater with myself in Emain. It is I will be your comrade, and I will stand between you and the great troubles are foretold.

DEIRDRE I will not be your queen in Emain when it's my pleasure to be having my freedom on the edges of the hills.   190

CONCHUBOR It's my wish to have you quickly, and I'm sick and weary thinking of the day you'll be brought down to me and seeing you walking into my big empty halls. I've made all sure to have you—and yet all said there's a fear in the back of my mind I'd miss you and have great troubles in the end. It's for that, Deirdre,   195
I'm praying that you'll come quickly. And you may take the word of a man has no lies° you'll not find with any other the like of what I'm bringing you in wildness and confusion in my own mind.

DEIRDRE I cannot go, Conchubor.

CONCHUBOR [taking a triumphant tone] It is my pleasure to have you   200
and I a man is waiting a long while on the throne of Ulster. Wouldn't you liefer be my comrade growing up the like of Emer and Maeve,° than to be in this place and you a child always?

DEIRDRE You don't know me, and you'd have little joy taking me, Conchubor.... I'm too long watching the days getting a great   205
speed passing me by, I'm too long taking my will and it's that way I'll be living always.

CONCHUBOR [drily] Call Fergus to come with me. This is your last night upon Slieve Fuadh.

DEIRDRE [now pleadingly] Leave me a short space longer, Conchubor.   210
Isn't it a poor thing I should be hastened away when all these troubles are foretold? Leave me a year Conchubor, it isn't much I'm asking.

CONCHUBOR It's much to have me two score and two weeks waiting for your voice in Emain, and you in this place growing lonesome   215
and shy. I'm a ripe man and I've great love and yet, Deirdre, I'm the King of Ulster. [He gets up] I'll call Fergus and we'll make Emain ready in the morning. [He goes towards door on left]

DEIRDRE [clinging to him] Do not call him, Conchubor.... Promise me a year of quiet.... It's one year I'm asking only.   220

CONCHUBOR You'd be asking a year next year, and the years that follow. [Calling] Fergus ... Fergus.... [To Deirdre] Young girls are slow always; it is their lovers that must say the word. [Calling] Fergus!

[Deirdre springs away from him as Fergus comes in with Lavarcham and Old Woman]

CONCHUBOR [*to Fergus*] There is a storm coming and we'd best be   225
going to our people when the night is young.

FERGUS [*cheerfully*] The gods shield you, Deirdre. [*To Conchubor*]
We're late already, and it's no work the High King to be slipping
on stepping stones,° and hilly pathways when the floods are rising
with the rain. [*He helps Conchubor into his cloak*]   230

CONCHUBOR [*glad that he has made his decision, to Lavarcham*] Keep
your rules a few days longer and you'll be brought down to Emain,
you and Deirdre with you.

LAVARCHAM [*obediently*] Your rules are kept always.

CONCHUBOR The gods shield you.   235

> [*He goes out with Fergus. Old Woman bolts the door. Deirdre
> covers her face*]

LAVARCHAM [*looking at Deirdre*] Wasn't I saying you'd do it? . . .
You've brought your marriage a sight nearer° not heeding those
are wiser than yourself.

DEIRDRE [*with agitation*] It wasn't I did it. Will you take me from
this place, Lavarcham, and keep me safe in the hills?   240

LAVARCHAM He'd have us tracked in the half of a day, and then
you'd be his queen in spite of you, and I and mine would be
destroyed forever.

DEIRDRE [*terrified with the reality that is before her*] Are there none
can go against Conchubor?   245

LAVARCHAM Maeve of Connaught only, and those that are her like.

DEIRDRE Would Fergus go against him?

LAVARCHAM He would maybe and his temper roused.

DEIRDRE [*in a lower voice, with sudden excitement*] Would Naisi and
his brothers?   250

LAVARCHAM [*impatiently*] Let you not be dwelling on Naisi and his
brothers. . . . In the end of all there is none can go against Conchubor,
and it's folly that we're talking, for if any went against Conchubor it's
sorrows he'd earn and the shortening of his day of life.

> [*She turns away, and Deirdre stands up stiff with excitement,
> then goes to the window and looks out*]

DEIRDRE Are the stepping stones flooding, Lavarcham? Will the   255
night be stormy in the hills?

LAVARCHAM [*looking at her curiously*] The stepping stones are flooding surely, and the night will be the worst I'm thinking we've seen
these years gone by.

DEIRDRE [*tearing open the press and pulling out clothes and tapestries*]   260
Lay these mats and hangings by the windows, and at the tables for

our feet, and take out the skillets of silver, and the golden cups we
have, and our two flasks of wine.

LAVARCHAM What ails you?

DEIRDRE [*gathering up a dress*] Lay them out quickly Lavarcham,   265
we've no call dawdling this night. Lay them out quickly; I'm going
into the room to put on the rich dresses and jewels have been sent
from Emain.

LAVARCHAM Putting on dresses at this hour and it dark and
drenching with the weight of rain! Are you away in your head?°   270

DEIRDRE [*gathering her things together with an outburst of excitement*] I
will dress like Emer in Dundealgan° or Maeve in her house in
Connaught. If Conchubor'll make me a queen I'll have the right
of a queen who is a master, taking her own choice and making a
stir to the edges of the seas. . . . Lay out your mats and hangings   275
where I can stand this night and look about me. Lay out the skins
of the rams of Connaught and of the goats of the west. I'll put on
my robes that are the richest for I will not be brought down to
Emain as Cuchulain° brings his horse to its yoke, or Conall
Cearneach° puts his shield upon his arm. And maybe from this day   280
I will turn the men of Ireland like a wind blowing on the heath.

[*She goes into inner room. Lavarcham and Old Woman look at
each other; then Old Woman goes over, looks in at Deirdre
through chink of the door, and then closes it carefully*]

OLD WOMAN [*in a frightened whisper*] She's thrown off the rags she
had about her, and there she is in her skin° putting her hair in
shiny twists. Is she raving Lavarcham, or has she a good right
turning to a queen like Maeve?   285

LAVARCHAM [*putting up hangings, very anxiously*] It's more than
raving's in her mind, or I'm the more astray,° and yet she's as good
a right as another, maybe, having her pleasure though she'd spoil
the world.

OLD WOMAN [*helping her*] Be quick before she'll come back. . . .   290
Who'd have thought we'd run before her and she so quiet till
tonight. Will the High King get the better of her, Lavarcham? If
I was Conchubor I wouldn't marry with her like at all.

LAVARCHAM Hang that by the window. That should please her
surely. . . . When all's said it's her like will be the master till the   295
ends of time.

OLD WOMAN [*at the window*] There's a mountain of blackness in the
sky, and the greatest rain falling has been these long years on the
earth. The gods help Conchubor, he'll be a sorry man this night

reaching his Dun, and he with all his spirits, thinking to himself   300
he'll be putting his arms around her in two days or three.

LAVARCHAM It's more than Conchubor'll be sick and sorry, I'm
thinking, before this story is told to the end.

[*Loud knocking on door at right*]

LAVARCHAM [*startled*] Who is that?

NAISI [*outside*] Naisi and his brothers.   305

LAVARCHAM We are lonely women. What is it you're wanting in the
blackness of the night?

NAISI We met a young girl in the woods who told us we might
shelter this place if the rivers rose on the pathways and the floods
gathered from the butt of the hills.   310

[*Old Woman claps her hands in horror*]

LAVARCHAM [*with great alarm*] You cannot come in. . . . There is no
one let in here, and no young girl with us.

NAISI Let us in from the great storm. Let us in and we will go
further when the cloud will rise.

LAVARCHAM Go round east to the shed and you'll have shelter. You   315
cannot come in.

NAISI [*knocking loudly*] Open the door, or we will burst it.

[*The door is shaken*]

OLD WOMAN [*in a timid whisper*] Let them in, and keep Deirdre in
her room tonight.

AINNLE AND ARDAN [*outside*] Open. . . . Open. . . .   320

LAVARCHAM [*to old woman*] Go in and keep her.

OLD WOMAN I couldn't keep her. I've no hold on her. . . . Go in
yourself and I will free the door.

LAVARCHAM I must stay and turn them out. [*She pulls her hair and
cloak over her face*°] Go in and keep her.   325

OLD WOMAN The gods help us. [*She runs into inner room*]

VOICES Open!

LAVARCHAM [*opening the door*] Come in then, and ill luck if you'll
have it so.

[*Naisi and Ainnle and Ardan come in, and look around with
astonishment*]

NAISI It's a rich man has this place and no herd at all.   330

LAVARCHAM [*sitting down with her head half-covered*] It is not, and
you'd do best going quickly.

NAISI [*hilariously, shaking rain from his clothes*] When we've the pick
of luck finding princely comfort in the darkness of the night? Some
rich man of Ulster should come here and he chasing in the woods.   335

May we drink? [*He takes up flask*] Whose wine is this that we may drink his health?

LAVARCHAM It's no one's that you've call to know.

NAISI [*pouring out wine for the three*] Your own health then and length of life. [*They drink*]   340

LAVARCHAM [*very crossly*] You're great boys taking a welcome where it isn't given, and asking questions where you've no call to. . . . If you'd a quiet place settled up to be playing yourself maybe with a gentle queen, what'd you think of young men prying around and carrying tales? When I was a bit of a girl, the big men of Ulster   345 had better manners and they the like of your three selves in the top folly of youth. That'll be a great story to tell out in Tara° that Naisi is a tippler and stealer, and Ainnle the drawer of a stranger's cork.

NAISI [*quite cheerfully, sitting down beside her*] At your age you should   350 know there are nights when a king like Conchubor would spit upon his arm ring and queens will stick their tongues out at the rising moon. We're that way this night, and it's not wine we're asking only. . . . Where is the young girl told us we might shelter here?

LAVARCHAM Asking me you'd be? . . . We're decent people, and I   355 wouldn't put you tracking a young girl, not if you gave me the gold clasp you have, hanging on your coat.

NAISI [*giving it to her*] Where is she?

LAVARCHAM [*in a confidential whisper, putting her hand on his arm*] Let you walk back into the hills, and turn up by the second   360 cnuceen where there are three together. You'll see a path running on the rocks and you'll hear the dogs barking in the houses and their noise will guide you till you come to a bit of cabin at the foot of an ash-tree. It's there there is a young and flighty girl that I'm thinking is the one you've seen.   365

NAISI [*hilariously*] Here's health then to herself and you!

ARDAN Here's to the years when you were young as she!

AINNLE [*in a frightened whisper*] Naisi. . . .

    [*Naisi looks up and Ainnle beckons to him. He goes over and Ainnle points to something on the golden mug he holds in his hand*]

NAISI [*looking at it in astonishment*] This is the High King's. . . . I see his mark on the rim. Does Conchubor come lodging here?   370

LAVARCHAM [*jumping up with extreme annoyance*] Who says it's Conchubor's? How dare young fools the like of you [*speaking with vehement insolence*] come prying around, running the world into troubles for some slip of a girl? What brings you this place straying from Emain? [*Very bitterly*] Though you think maybe young men can do their fill of foolery and there is none to blame them. 375

NAISI [*very soberly*] Is the rain easing?

ARDAN The clouds are breaking. . . . I can see Orion° in the gap of the glen.

NAISI [*still cheerfully*] Open the door and we'll go forward to the little cabin between the ash-tree and the rocks. Lift the bolt and pull it. 380

> [*Deirdre comes in on left royally dressed and very beautiful. She stands for a moment, and then as the door opens she calls softly*]

DEIRDRE Naisi. . . . Do not leave me, Naisi, I am Deirdre of the Sorrows.

NAISI [*transfixed with amazement*] And it is you who go around in the woods, making the thrushes bear a grudge against the heavens for the sweetness of your voice?' 385

DEIRDRE It is with me you've spoken surely. [*To Lavarcham and Old Woman*] Take Ainnle and Ardan, these two princes, into the little hut where we eat, and serve them with what is best and sweetest. I have many things for Naisi only. 390

LAVARCHAM [*overawed by her tone*] I will do it, and I ask their pardon I have fooled them here.

DEIRDRE [*to Ainnle and Ardan*] Do not take it badly, that I am asking you to walk into our hut for a little. You will have a supper that is cooked by the cook of Conchubor, and Lavarcham will tell you stories of Maeve and Nessa and Rogh.° 395

AINNLE We'll ask Lavarcham to tell us stories of yourself, and with that we'll be well pleased to be doing your wish.

> [*They all go out except Deirdre and Naisi*]

DEIRDRE [*sitting in the high chair in the centre for the first time*] Come to this stool, Naisi. [*Pointing to the stool*] If it's low itself the High King would sooner be on it this night, than on the throne of Emain Macha. 400

NAISI [*sitting down*] You are Fedlimid's° daughter that Conchubor has walled up from all the men of Ulster?

DEIRDRE Do many know what is foretold, that Deirdre will be the ruin of the Sons of Usna, and have a little grave by herself, and a story will be told forever? 405

NAISI It's a long while men have been talking of Deirdre the child who had all gifts, and the beauty that has no equal. Many know it, and there are kings would give a great price to be in my place this night, and you grown to a queen. 410

DEIRDRE It isn't many I'd call, Naisi. . . . I was in the woods at the full moon and I heard a voice singing. Then I gathered up my skirts, and I ran on a little path I have to the verge of a rock, and I saw you pass by underneath, in your crimson cloak, singing a song, and you standing out beyond your brothers are called the flower of Ireland. 415

NAISI [*in a low voice*] It's for that you called us in the dusk?

DEIRDRE [*in a low voice also*] Since that, Naisi, I have been one time the like of a ewe looking for a lamb that had been taken away from her, and one time seeing new gold on the stars and a new face on the moon, and all times dreading Emain. 420

NAISI [*pulling himself together and beginning to draw back a little*] Yet it should be a lonesome thing to be in this place and you born for great company. 425

DEIRDRE [*softly*] This night I have the best company in the whole world.

NAISI [*still a little formally*] It's yourself is your best company, for when you're queen in Emain you will have none to be your match or fellow. 430

DEIRDRE I will not be queen in Emain.

NAISI Conchubor has made an oath you will surely.

DEIRDRE It's for that maybe I'm called Deirdre, the girl of many sorrows [*she looks up at him*] . . . for it's a sweet life you and I could have Naisi. . . . It should be a sweet thing to have what is best and richest if it's for a short space only. 435

NAISI [*very distressed*] And we've a short space only to be triumphant and brave.

DEIRDRE You must not go Naisi, and leave me to the High King, a man is ageing in his Dun, with his crowds round him and his silver and gold. [*More quickly*] I will not live to be shut up in Emain, and wouldn't we do well paying, Naisi, with silence, and a near death? [*She stands up and walks away from him*] I'm a long while in the woods with my own self, and I'm in little dread of death, and it earned with richness would make the sun red with envy and he going up the heavens, and the moon pale and lonesome and she wasting away. [*She comes to him and puts her hands on his shoulders*] Isn't it a small thing is foretold about the ruin of ourselves, Naisi, when all men have age coming and great ruin in the end? 440 445 450

NAISI Yet it's a poor thing it's I should bring you to a tale of blood, and broken bodies and the filth of the grave. . . . Wouldn't we do well to wait, Deirdre, and I each twilight meeting you on the side of the hills?

DEIRDRE Messengers are coming tomorrow morning or the next 455 morning to bring me down to Conchubor to be his mate in Emain.

NAISI Messengers are coming?

DEIRDRE Tomorrow morning or the next surely.

NAISI Then it isn't I will give your like to Conchubor, not if the grave was dug to be my lodging when a week was by. [*He looks* 460 *out*] The stars are out Deirdre, and let you come with me quickly, for it is the stars will be our lamps many nights and we abroad in Alban,° and taking our journeys among the little islands in the sea. There has never been the like of the joy we'll have Deirdre, you and I having our fill of love at the evening and the morning till the 465 sun is high.

DEIRDRE [*sinking on his shoulder, a little shaken by what has passed*] And yet I'm in dread leaving this place where I have lived always. Won't I be lonesome and I thinking on the little hill beyond and the apple trees do be budding in the springtime by the post of the 470 door? ... Won't I be in great dread to bring you to destruction, Naisi, and you so happy and young?

NAISI Are you thinking I'd go on living after this night, Deirdre, and you with Conchubor in Emain? Are you thinking I'd go out after hares on the hillside when I've had your lips in my sight? 475

[*Lavarcham comes in as they cling to each other*]

LAVARCHAM Are you raving, Deirdre? ... Are you choosing this night to destroy the world?

DEIRDRE [*very deliberately, letting go of Naisi slowly*] It's Conchubor has chosen this night, calling me to Emain. [*To Naisi*] Bring in Ainnle and Ardan, and take me from this place where I'm in dread 480 from this out° of the footstep of a hare passing.

[*Naisi goes*]

DEIRDRE [*clinging to Lavarcham*] Do not take it bad I'm going, Lavarcham. It's you have been a good friend and given me great freedom and joy, and I living on Slieve Fuadh, and maybe you'll be well pleased one day, saying you have nursed Deirdre. 485

LAVARCHAM [*moved*] It isn't I'll be well pleased and I far away from you. Isn't it a hard thing you're doing, but who can help it? Birds go mating in the spring of the year, and ewes at the leaves falling, but a young girl must have her lover in all the courses of the sun and moon. 490

DEIRDRE Will you go to Emain in the morning?

LAVARCHAM I will not, I'll go to Brandon° in the south, and in the course of a piece° maybe I'll be sailing back and forward on the seas to be looking on your face, and the little ways you have that none can equal.   495

[*Naisi comes back with Ainnle and Ardan and Old Woman*]

DEIRDRE [*taking Naisi's hand*] My two brothers, I am going with Naisi to Alban and the north, to face the troubles are foretold. Will you take word to Conchubor in Emain?

AINNLE We will go with you.

ARDAN We will be your servants and your huntsmen, Deirdre.   500

DEIRDRE It isn't one brother only of you three, is brave and courteous. . . . Will you wed us Lavarcham, you have the words and customs?

LAVARCHAM I will not then. . . . What would I want meddling in the ruin you will earn?   505

NAISI Let Ainnle wed us. . . . He has been with wise men and he knows their ways.

AINNLE [*joining their hands*] By the sun and moon and the whole earth, I wed Deirdre to Naisi. [*He steps back and holds up his hands*] May the air bless you, and water and the wind, the sea, and all the   510 hours of the sun and moon.°

CURTAIN

Act 2

Alban, early morning in the beginning of winter. A wood, outside the tent of Deirdre and Naisi. Lavarcham comes in, muffled in a cloak

LAVARCHAM [*calling*] Deirdre . . . Deirdre. . . .

DEIRDRE [*coming from tent, radiant and mature*] My welcome, Lavarcham. . . . Whose curagh is rowing from Ulster? I saw the oars through the tops of the trees, and I thought it was you were coming towards us.   5

LAVARCHAM I came in the shower was before the dawn.

DEIRDRE And who is coming?

LAVARCHAM [*mournfully*] Let you not be startled or taking it bad, Deirdre. It's Fergus bringing messages of peace from Conchubor to take Naisi and his brothers back to Emain. [*Sitting down*]   10

DEIRDRE [*lightly*] Naisi and his brothers are well pleased this place and what would take them back to Conchubor in Ulster?

LAVARCHAM Their like would go any place where they'd see death standing. [*With more agitation*] I'm in dread Conchubor wants to have yourself, and to kill Naisi, and that that'll be the ruin of the   15
Sons of Usna. I'm silly maybe to be dreading the like, but those have a great love for yourself have a right to be in dread always.

DEIRDRE [*more anxiously*] Emain should be no safe place for myself and Naisi, and isn't it a hard thing, they'll leave us no peace Lavarcham, and we so quiet in the woods?   20

LAVARCHAM [*impressively*] It's a hard thing surely, but let you take my word and swear Naisi by the earth, and the sun over it, and the four quarters of the moon he'll not go back to Emain for good faith, or bad faith, the time Conchubor's keeping the high throne of Ireland. . . . It's that would save you surely.   25

DEIRDRE [*without hope*] There's little power in oaths to stop what's coming, and little power in what I'd do Lavarcham, to change the story of Conchubor and Naisi and the things old men foretold.

LAVARCHAM [*aggressively*] Was there little power in what you did the night you dressed in your finery and ran Naisi off along with you,   30
in spite of Conchubor, and the big nobles did dread the blackness of your luck? It was power enough you had that night to bring distress and anguish, and now I'm pointing you a way to save Naisi, you'll not stir stick or straw to aid me.

DEIRDRE [*a little haughtily*] Let you not raise your voice against me 35
Lavarcham, if you have great will itself to guard Naisi.

LAVARCHAM [*breaking out in anger*] Naisi is it? I didn't care° if the
crows were stripping his thigh-bones at the dawn of day. It's to
stop your own despair and wailing, and you waking up in a cold
bed, without the man you have your heart on, I am raging now. 40
[*Starting up with temper*] Yet there's more men than Naisi in it,
and maybe I was a big fool thinking his dangers, and this day,
would fill you up with dread.

DEIRDRE [*sharply*] Let you end such talking is a fool's only, when it's
well you know if a thing harmed Naisi it isn't I would live after 45
him. [*With distress*] It's well you know it's this day I'm dreading
seven years, and I, fine nights, watching the heifers walking to the
haggard with long shadows on the grass [*with a thickening in her
voice*], or the time I've been stretched in the sunshine when I've
heard Ainnle and Ardan stepping lightly, and they saying, 'Was 50
there ever the like of Deirdre for a happy and a sleepy queen?'

LAVARCHAM [*not fully pacified*] And yet you'll go and welcome is it,
if Naisi chooses?

DEIRDRE I've dread going or staying, Lavarcham. It's lonesome this
place having happiness like ours till I'm asking each day, will this 55
day match yesterday, and will tomorrow take a good place beside
the same day in the year that's gone, and wondering all times is it
a game worth playing, living on until you're dried and old, and our
joy is gone forever.

LAVARCHAM If it's that ails you, I tell you there's little hurt getting 60
old, though young girls and poets do be storming at the shapes of
age. [*Passionately*] There's little hurt getting old, saving when
you're looking back, the way I'm looking this day, and seeing the
young you have a love for breaking up their hearts with folly.
[*Going to Deirdre, making a last attempt*] Take my word and stop 65
Naisi, and the day'll come you'll have more joy having the senses
of an old woman and you with your little grandsons shrieking
round you, than I'd have this night putting on the red mouth, and
the white arms you have, to go walking lonesome byeways with a
gamey° king. 70

DEIRDRE It's little joy of a young woman or an old woman I'll have
from this day surely. But what use is in our talking when there's
Naisi on the foreshore, and Fergus with him.

LAVARCHAM [*getting up despairingly*] I'm late so with my warnings,
for Fergus'd talk the moon over to take a new path in the sky. 75

166

[*With reproach*] You'll not stop him this day, and isn't it a strange story you were a plague and torment since you were that height to those did hang their life-times on your voice. . . . [*Overcome with trouble, gathering her cloak about her*] Don't think bad of my crying. I'm not the like of many and I'd see a score of naked corpses and 80 not heed them at all, but I'm destroyed seeing yourself in your hour of joy, when the end is coming surely.

[*Owen comes in quickly, rather ragged, bows to Deirdre*]

OWEN [*to Lavarcham*] Fergus's men are calling you. You were seen on the path and he and Naisi want you for their talk below.

LAVARCHAM [*looking at him with dislike*] Yourself's an ill-lucky thing 85 to meet a morning is the like of this. Yet if you are a spy itself I'll go and give my word that's wanting surely. [*She goes out slowly*]

OWEN [*to Deirdre*] So I've found you alone, and I after waiting three weeks getting ague and asthma in the chill of the bogs, till I saw Naisi caught with Fergus. 90

DEIRDRE I've heard news of Fergus, what brought you from Ulster?

OWEN [*who has been searching, finds a loaf and sits down eating greedily*] The full moon I'm thinking and it squeezing the crack in my skull.° Was there ever a man crossed nine waves after a fool's wife and he not away in his head? 95

DEIRDRE [*absently*] It should be a long time since you left Emain, where there's civility in speech with queens.

OWEN It's a long while surely. It's three weeks I am losing my manners beside the Saxon° bull-frogs at the head of the bog. Three weeks is a long space, and yet you're seven years spancelled° with 100 Naisi and the pair!

DEIRDRE [*beginning to fold up her jewels*] Three weeks of your days might be long surely; yet seven years are a short space for the like of Naisi and myself.

OWEN [*derisively*] If they're a short space there aren't many the like 105 of you. Wasn't there a queen in Tara° had to walk out every morning till she'd meet a stranger and see the flame of courtship leaping up within his eye? Tell me now [*leaning towards her*], . . . are you well pleased that length with the same man snorting next you at the dawn of day? 110

DEIRDRE [*very quietly*] Am I well pleased seven years seeing the same sun throwing light across the branches at the dawn of day? [*With abstracted feeling*] It's a heart-break to the wise that it's for a short space we have the same things only. [*With contempt*] Yet the earth itself is a silly place maybe, when a man's a fool and talker. 115

167

OWEN [*sharply*] Well go take your choice. Stay here and rot with
Naisi, or go to Conchubor in Emain. Conchubor's a swelling belly,
and eyes falling down from his shining crown, Naisi should be
stale and weary; yet there are many roads, Deirdre [*he goes towards
her*], and I tell you I'd liefer be bleaching in a bog-hole than living on   120
without a touch of kindness from your eyes and voice. It's a poor
thing to be so lonesome you'd squeeze kisses on a cur dog's nose.

DEIRDRE Are there no women like yourself could be your friends in
Emain?

OWEN [*vehemently*] There are none like you, Deirdre. It's for that   125
I'm asking are you going back this night with Fergus?

DEIRDRE I will go where Naisi chooses.

OWEN [*with a burst of rage*] It's Naisi, Naisi is it? Then I tell you
you'll have great sport one day seeing Naisi getting a harshness in
his two sheep's eyes and he looking on yourself. Would you credit   130
it, my father used to be in the broom and heather kissing
Lavarcham, with a little bird chirping out above their heads, and
now she'd scare a raven from a carcass on a hill. [*With a sad cry
that brings dignity into his voice*] Queens get old Deirdre, with their
white and long arms going from them, and their backs hooping. I   135
tell you it's a poor thing to see a queen's nose reaching down to
scrape her chin.

DEIRDRE [*looking out, a little uneasy at his tone*] Naisi and Fergus are
coming on the path.

OWEN I'll go so . . . for if I had you seven years I'd be jealous of the   140
midges and the dust is in the air. [*With a sort of warning in his voice,
muffling himself in his cloak*] I'll give you a riddle, Deirdre. Why
isn't my father as ugly and as old as Conchubor? You've no
answer? . . . It's because Naisi killed him. [*With a curious expression*] Think of that and you awake at night hearing Naisi snoring,   145
or the night you'll hear strange stories of the things I've done in
Alban or in Ulster either.

[*He goes out, and in a moment Naisi and Fergus come in on the
other side*]

NAISI [*gaily*] Fergus has brought messages of peace from Conchubor!

DEIRDRE [*greeting Fergus*] He is welcome. Let you rest Fergus, you
should be hot and thirsty after mounting the rocks.   150

FERGUS It's a sunny nook you've found in Alban, yet any man would
be well pleased mounting higher rocks, to fetch yourself and Naisi
back to Emain.

DEIRDRE [*with keenness*] They've answered? They would go?

FERGUS [*benignly*] They have not [*Deirdre begins to net°*], but when I   155
   was a young man we'd have given a lifetime to be in Ireland a score
   of weeks, and to this day the old men have nothing so heavy as
   knowing it's in a short while they'll lose the high skies are over
   Ireland, and the lonesome mornings with birds crying on the bogs.
   Let you come this day for there's no place but Ireland where the   160
   Gael can have peace always.°

NAISI [*gruffly*] It's true surely. Yet we're better this place while
   Conchubor's in Emain Macha.

FERGUS [*giving him parchments*] These are your sureties with Conchubor's seal. [*To Deirdre, who stops netting during his speech*]   165
   You'll not be young always, and it's time you were making
   yourselves ready for the years will come, building up a homely
   Dun beside the seas of Ireland, and getting in your children from
   the princes' wives.° It's little joy wandering till age is on you and
   your youth is gone away, so you'd best come this night, for you'd   170
   have great pleasure putting out your foot and saying 'I am in
   Ireland surely'.

DEIRDRE It isn't pleasure I'd have while Conchubor is king in Emain.

FERGUS [*almost annoyed*] Would you doubt the seals of Conall
   Cearneach and the kings of Meath? [*More gently*] It's easy being   175
   fearful and you alone in the woods yet it would be a poor thing if
   a timid woman [*taunting her a little*] could turn away the Sons of
   Usna° from the life of kings. Let you be thinking on the years to
   come, Deirdre, and the way you'd have a right to see Naisi a high
   and white-haired Justice beside some king of Emain. Wouldn't it   180
   be a poor story if a queen the like of you should have no thought
   but to be scraping up her hours dallying in the sunshine with the
   sons of kings?

DEIRDRE [*turning away a little haughtily*] I leave the choice to Naisi.
   [*Turning back towards Fergus*] Yet you'd do well Fergus to go on your   185
   own way, for the sake of your own years, so you'll not be saying till
   your hour of death, maybe it was yourself brought Naisi and his
   brothers to a grave was scooped by treachery. [*She goes into tent*]

FERGUS It's a poor thing to see a queen so lonesome and afraid. [*He
   watches till he is sure Deirdre cannot hear him*] Listen now to what   190
   I'm saying. You'd do well to come back to men and women are
   your match and comrades, and not be lingering until the day that
   you'll grow weary, and hurt Deirdre showing her the hardness in
   your eyes. . . . You've been here years and plenty to know it's truth
   I'm saying.   195

[*Deirdre comes out of tent with a horn of wine. She catches the beginning of Naisi's speech and stops with stony wonder*]

NAISI [*very thoughtfully*] I'll not tell you a lie. There have been days a while past when I've been throwing a line for salmon, or watching for the run of hares, that I've had a dread upon me a day'd come I'd weary of her voice [*very slowly*] . . . and Deirdre'd see I'd wearied.°   200

FERGUS [*sympathetic but triumphant*] I knew it, Naisi. . . . And take my word Deirdre's seen your dread and she'll have no peace from this out in the woods.

NAISI [*with confidence*] She's not seen it. . . . Deirdre's no thought of getting old or wearied, it's that puts wonder in her ways, and she   205 with spirits would keep bravery and laughter in a town with plague.

[*Deirdre drops the horn of wine and crouches down where she is*]

FERGUS That humour'll leave her. But we've no call going too far, with one word borrowing another. Will you come this night to Emain Macha?   210

NAISI I'll not go, Fergus. I've had dreams of getting old and weary, and losing my delight in Deirdre, but my dreams were dreams only. What are Conchubor's seal and all your talk of Emain and the fools of Meath beside one evening in Glen Masain?° We'll stay this place till our lives and time are worn out. It's that word you   215 may take in your curagh to Conchubor in Emain.

FERGUS [*gathering up his parchments*] And you won't go surely?

NAISI [*gaily*] I will not. . . . I've had dread, I tell you, dread winter and summer, and the autumn and the spring-time, even when there's a bird in every bush making his own stir till the fall of   220 night. But this talk's brought me ease, and I see we're as happy as the leaves on the young trees and we'll be so ever and always though we'd live the age of the eagle and the salmon and the crow of Britain.°

FERGUS [*very much annoyed*] Where are your brothers? My message   225 is for them also.

NAISI You'll see them above chasing otters by the stream.

FERGUS [*bitterly*] It isn't much I was mistaken, thinking you were hunters only.

[*He goes. Naisi turns towards tent, and sees Deirdre crouching down with her cloak round her face. Deirdre comes out*]

NAISI You've heard my words to Fergus? [*She does not answer. A*   230 *pause. He puts his arm round her*] Leave troubling, and we'll go this night to Glen da Ruadh° where the salmon will be running with the tide.

[*Deirdre crosses and sits down*]

DEIRDRE [*in a very low voice*] With the tide in a little while we will be journeying again, or it is our own blood maybe will be running away. [*She turns and clings to him*] The dawn and evening are a little while, the winter and the summer pass quickly, and what way would you and I Naisi, have joy forever? 235

NAISI We'll have the joy is highest till our age is come, for it isn't Fergus's talk of great deeds could take us back to Emain. 240

DEIRDRE It isn't to great deeds you're going but to near troubles, and the shortening of your days the time that they are bright and sunny and isn't it a poor thing that I, Deirdre, could not hold you away?

NAISI I've said we'd stay in Alban always?

DEIRDRE There's no place to stay always. . . . It's a long time we've had, pressing the lips together, going up and down, resting in our arms, Naisi, waking with the smell of June in the tops of the grasses, and listening to the birds in the branches that are highest. . . . It's a long time we've had, but the end has come surely. 245

NAISI Would you have us go to Emain, though if any ask the reason we do not know it, and we journeying as the thrushes come from the north, or young birds fly out on a dark sea? 250

DEIRDRE There's reason all times for an end that's come. . . . And I'm well pleased, Naisi, we're going forward in the winter the time the sun has a low place, and the moon has her mastery in a dark sky, for it's you and I are well lodged our last day, where there is a light behind the clear trees, and the berries on the thorns are a red wall. 255

NAISI [*with a new rush of love, eagerly*] If our time this place is ended, come away without Ainnle and Ardan to the woods of the East, for it's right to be away from all people when two lovers have their love only. Come away and we'll be safe always. 260

DEIRDRE [*broken-hearted*] There's no safe place, Naisi, on the ridge of the world. . . . And it's in the quiet woods I've seen them digging our grave, throwing out the clay on leaves are bright and withered. 265

NAISI [*still more eagerly*] Come away, Deirdre, and it's little we'll think of safety or the grave beyond it, and we resting in a little corner between the daytime and the long night.

DEIRDRE [*clearly and gravely*] It's this hour we're between the daytime and a night where there is sleep forever, and isn't it a 270

better thing to be following on to a near death, than to be bending
the head down, and dragging with the feet, and seeing one day, a
blight showing upon love where it is sweet and tender?

NAISI [*his voice broken with distraction*] If a near death is coming what   275
will be my trouble losing the earth and the stars over it, and you
Deirdre are their flame and bright crown? Come away into the
safety of the woods.

DEIRDRE [*shaking her head slowly*] There are as many ways to wither
love as there are stars in a night of Samhain, but there is no way   280
to keep life or love with it a short space only. . . . It's for that
there's nothing lonesome like a love is watching out the time most
lovers do be sleeping. . . . It's for that we're setting out for Emain
Macha when the tide turns on the sand.

NAISI [*giving in*] You're right maybe. . . . It should be a poor thing   285
to see great lovers and they sleepy and old.

DEIRDRE [*with a more tender intensity*] We're seven years without
roughness or growing weary, seven years so sweet and shining,
the gods would be hard set to give us seven days the like of
them. . . . It's for that we're going to Emain where there'll be a rest   290
forever, or a place for forgetting, in great crowds and they making
a stir.

NAISI [*very softly*] We'll go surely, in place of keeping a watch on a
love had no match and it wasting away.

> [*They cling to each other for a moment, then Deirdre stands up
> slowly, and goes into the tent with her head bowed down without
> looking at Naisi. Naisi sits with his head bowed. Owen runs in
> stealthily, comes behind Naisi and seizes him round the arms;
> Naisi shakes him off and whips out his sword*]

OWEN [*screaming with derisive laughter and showing his empty hands*]   295
Ah Naisi, wasn't it well I didn't kill you that time! There was
a fright you got. I've been watching Fergus above—don't be
frightened—and I've come down to see him getting the cold
shoulder and going off alone. . . . There he is.

> [*Voices are heard on the right, and Ainnle, Ardan, Fergus and
> Lavarcham come in. They are all subdued like men at a queen's
> wake*]

NAISI [*goes to Fergus, putting up his sword*] We are going back when   300
the tide turns, I and Deirdre with yourself.

ALL Going back?

FERGUS You've a choice wise men will be glad of in the five ends of
Ireland.

OWEN Wise men is it and they going back to Conchubor? I could   305
stop them only Naisi put in his sword among my father's ribs and
when a man's done that he'll not credit your oath.° Going to
Conchubor! I could tell of plots and tricks and spies were well paid
for their play. [*He throws up a bag of gold*] Are you paid, Fergus?
[*He scatters gold pieces over Fergus*]   310

FERGUS He is raving. . . . Seize him. . . .

OWEN [*flying between them*] You won't. Let the lot of you be off to
Emain but I'll be off before you. . . . Dead men, dead men, men
who'll die for Deirdre's beauty, I'll be before you in the grave!
[*Owen runs out with his knife in his hand. They all run after
him except Lavarcham, who looks out and then clasps her hands.
Deirdre comes out to her in a dark cloak*]

DEIRDRE What has happened?   315

LAVARCHAM It's Owen gone raging mad and he's after splitting his
gullet beyond at the butt of the stone. There was ill luck this day
in his eye. And he knew a power if he'd said it all.
[*Naisi comes back followed by the others*]

AINNLE [*coming in very excited*] That man knew plots of Conchubor's. . . . We'll not go to Emain where Conchubor may love her   320
and has hatred for yourself.

FERGUS Would you mind a fool and raver?

AINNLE It's many times there's more sense in madmen than the wise.
We will not obey Conchubor.

NAISI I and Deirdre have chosen, we will go back with Fergus.   325

ARDAN We will not go back. . . . We will burn your curaghs by the sea.

FERGUS My sons and I will guard them.

AINNLE We will blow the horn of Usna and our friends will come to
aid us.

NAISI It is my friends will come.   330

AINNLE Your friends will bind your hands and you out of your wits.
[*Deirdre comes forward quickly and comes between Ainnle and
Naisi*]

DEIRDRE [*in a low voice*] For seven years the Sons of Usna have not
raised their voices in a quarrel.

AINNLE We will not take you to Emain.

ARDAN It is Conchubor has broken our peace.   335

AINNLE Stop Naisi going. What way would we live if Conchubor
should take you from us?

DEIRDRE [*winningly putting her hands on his shoulders*] There is no one
could take me from you. . . . I have chosen to go back with Fergus.

Will you quarrel with me Ainnle, though I have been your queen   340
these seven years in Alban?

AINNLE [*subsiding suddenly*] Naisi has no call to take you.

ARDAN Why are you going?

DEIRDRE [*to both of them and the others*] It is my wish. . . . It may be
I will not have Naisi growing an old man in Alban with an old   345
woman at his side, and young girls pointing out and saying 'that
is Deirdre and Naisi, had great beauty in their youth'. . . . It may
be we do well putting a sharp end to the day is brave and glorious,
as our fathers put a sharp end to the days of the kings of Ireland,
. . . or that I'm wishing to set my foot on Slieve Fuadh where I   350
was running one time and leaping the streams [*to Lavarcham*], and
that I'd be well pleased to see our little apple-trees Lavarcham,
behind our cabin on the hill, or that I've learned Fergus, it's a
lonesome thing to be away from Ireland always.

AINNLE [*giving in*] There is no place but will be lonesome to us from   355
this out and we thinking on our seven years in Alban.

DEIRDRE It's in this place we'd be lonesome in the end. . . . [*To
Naisi*] Take down Fergus to the sea. . . . He has been a guest had
a hard welcome and he bringing messages of peace.

FERGUS We will make your curagh ready and it fitted for the voyage   360
of a king. [*He goes with Naisi*]

DEIRDRE Take your spears Ainnle and Ardan, and go down before
me, and take your horse-boys to be carrying my cloaks are on the
threshold.

AINNLE [*obeying*] It's with a poor heart we'll carry your things this   365
day, we have carried merrily so often and we hungry and cold.

[*They gather up things and go out*]

DEIRDRE [*to Lavarcham*] Go you too, Lavarcham. You are old and I
will follow quickly.

LAVARCHAM I'm old surely, and the hopes I had my pride in, are
broken and torn. [*She goes out, with a look of awe at Deirdre*]   370

DEIRDRE [*clasping her hands*] Woods of Cuan,° woods of Cuan. . . .
It's seven years we've had a life was joy only and this day we're
going west, this day we're facing death maybe, and [*goes and looks
towards Owen*] death should be a poor untidy thing, though it's a
queen that dies. [*She goes out slowly*]   375

CURTAIN

Act 3

Tent below Emain, with shabby skins and benches. There is an opening at each side and at back, the latter closed. Old Woman comes in with food and fruits and arranges them on table. Conchubor comes in on right

CONCHUBOR [*sharply*] Has no one come with news for me?

OLD WOMAN I've seen no one at all, Conchubor.

CONCHUBOR [*watches her working for a moment, then makes sure opening at back is closed*] Go up then to Emain, you're not wanting here. [*A noise is heard left*] Who is that? 5

OLD WOMAN [*going left*] It's Lavarcham coming again. . . . She's a great wonder for jogging back and forward through the world and I made certain she'd be off to meet them, but she's coming alone, Conchubor, my dear child Deirdre isn't with her at all.

CONCHUBOR Go up so and leave us. 10

OLD WOMAN [*pleadingly*] I'd be well pleased to set my eyes on Deirdre if she's coming this night, as we're told.

CONCHUBOR [*impatiently*] It's not long till you'll see her. But I've matters with Lavarcham and let you go on now I'm saying.

[*He shows her out right, as Lavarcham comes in on the left*]

LAVARCHAM [*looking round her, with suspicion*] This is a queer place 15
to find you, and it's a queer place to be lodging Naisi and his brothers, and Deirdre with them, and the lot of us tired out with the long way we have been walking.

CONCHUBOR You've come along with them the whole journey?

LAVARCHAM I have then, though I've no call now to be wandering 20
that length to a wedding or a burial or the two together. [*She sits down wearily*] . . . It's a poor thing the way me and you is getting old, Conchubor, and I'm thinking you yourself have no call to be loitering this place getting your death, maybe, in the cold of night.

CONCHUBOR I'm waiting only to know is Fergus stopped in the 25
north.

LAVARCHAM [*more sharply*] He's stopped surely, and that's a trick°
has me thinking you have it in mind to bring trouble this night on Emain and Ireland and the big world's east beyond them. [*She goes to him*] . . . And yet you'd do well to be going to your Dun, and 30
not putting shame on her meeting the High King, and she seamed and sweaty, and in great disorder from the dust of many roads.

[*Laughing derisively*] Ah, Conchubor, my lad, beauty goes quickly in the woods, and you'd let a great gasp, I tell you, if you set your eyes this night on Deirdre.

CONCHUBOR [*fiercely*] It's little I care if she's white and worn, for it's I did rear her from a child should have a good right to meet and see her always.

LAVARCHAM [*put back*] A good right is it? Haven't the blind a good right to be seeing and the lame to be dancing, and the dummies° singing tunes? It's that right you have to be looking for gaiety on Deirdre's lips. [*Coaxingly*] Come on to your Dun, I'm saying, and leave her quiet for one night itself.

CONCHUBOR [*with sudden anger*] I'll not go, when it's long enough I am above in my Dun stretching east and west without a comrade, and I more needy maybe than the thieves of Meath. . . . You think I'm old and wise, but I tell you the wise know the old must die, and they'll leave no chance for a thing slipping from them, they've set their blood to win.

LAVARCHAM [*nodding her head*] If you're old and wise, it's I'm the same, Conchubor, and I'm telling you, you'll *not* have her though you're ready to destroy mankind, and skin the gods to win her. . . . There's things a king can't have, Conchubor, and if you go rampaging this night you'll be apt to win nothing but death for many, and a sloppy face of trouble on your own self before the day will come.

CONCHUBOR It's too much talk you have. [*Goes right, anxiously*] Where is Owen, did you see him no place and you coming the road?

LAVARCHAM [*stiffly*] I seen him surely. . . . He went spying on Naisi, and now the worms is spying on his own inside.

CONCHUBOR [*exultingly°*] Naisi killed him?

LAVARCHAM He did not then. . . . It was Owen destroyed himself, running mad because of Deirdre. . . . Fools and kings and scholars are all one in a story with her like, and Owen thought he'd be a great man, being the first corpse in the game you'll play this night in Emain.

CONCHUBOR [*turning to her with excitement*] It's yourself should be the first corpse, but my other messengers are coming, men from the clans that hated Usna.

LAVARCHAM [*drawing back hopelessly*] Then the gods have pity on us all.

[*Men come in with weapons*]

CONCHUBOR Are Ainnle and Ardan separate from Naisi?

MEN They are, Conchubor. We've got them off, saying they were needed to make ready Deirdre's house.

CONCHUBOR And Naisi and Deirdre are coming?

SOLDIER Naisi's coming surely, and a woman with him is putting out the glory of the moon is rising, and the sun is going down.

CONCHUBOR [*triumphant, to Lavarcham*] That's your story that she's seamed and ugly?

SOLDIER I have more news. When that woman heard you were bringing Naisi this place, she sent a horse-boy to call Fergus from the north.

CONCHUBOR [*to Lavarcham*] It's for that you've been playing your tricks, but what you've won is a nearer death for Naisi. [*To Soldiers*] Go up and call my fighters, and take that woman up to Emain.

LAVARCHAM I'd liefer stay this place. I've done my best but if a bad end is coming surely, it would be a good thing maybe I was here to tend her.

CONCHUBOR [*fiercely*] Take her to Emain; it's too many tricks she's tried this day already.

[*A Soldier goes to her*]

LAVARCHAM Don't touch me. [*She puts her cloak round her and catches Conchubor's arm*] . . . I thought to stay your hand with my stories till Fergus would come to be beside them, the way I'd save yourself, Conchubor, and Naisi and Emain Macha, but I'll walk up now into your halls and I'll say [*with a gesture*] . . . it's here nettles will be growing, and beyond thistles and docks. I'll go into your High Chambers, where you've been figuring° yourself stretching out your neck for the kisses of a queen of women, and I'll say it's here there'll be deer stirring, and goats scratching, and sheep, waking and coughing when there is a great wind from the north.

CONCHUBOR [*shaking himself loose*] Take her away.

LAVARCHAM I'm going surely, and in a short space I'll be sitting up with many listening to the flames crackling, and the beams breaking, and I looking on the great blaze will be the end of Emain. [*She goes out*]

CONCHUBOR [*looking out left*] I see two people in the trees. It should be Naisi and Deirdre. [*To Soldier*] Let you tell them they'll lodge here tonight.

[*He goes off right. Naisi and Deirdre come in on left, very weary*]

NAISI Is it this place he's made ready for myself and Deirdre?

SOLDIER The Red Branch House° is being aired and swept and
you'll be called there when a space is by. Till then you'll find fruits
and drink on this table, and so the gods be with you. [*Goes right*]

NAISI [*looking round*] It's a strange place he's put us camping and we
come back as his friends.   115

DEIRDRE He's likely making up a welcome for us, having curtains
shaken out and rich rooms put in order; and it's right he'd have
great state to meet us, and you his sister's sons.

NAISI [*gloomy*] It's little we want with state or rich rooms or curtains,
when we're used to the ferns only, and cold streams and they   120
making a stir.

DEIRDRE [*roaming round room*] We want what is our right in Emain
[*looking at hangings*] . . . and though he's riches in store for us it's
a shabby ragged place he's put us waiting, with frayed rugs and
skins are eaten by the moths.   125

NAISI [*a little impatiently*] There are few would worry over skins and
moths on this first night that we've come back to Emain.

DEIRDRE [*brightly*] You should be well-pleased it's for that I'd worry
all times, when it's I have kept your tent these seven years, as tidy
as a bee-hive or a linnet's nest. If Conchubor'd a queen like me in   130
Emain he'd not have stretched these rags to meet us. [*She pulls
hanging, and it opens*] . . . There's new earth on the ground and a
trench dug. . . . It's a grave Naisi, that is wide and deep.

NAISI [*goes over and pulls back curtain showing grave*] And that'll be
our home in Emain. . . . He's dug it wisely at the butt of a hill with 135
fallen trees to hide it. . . . He'll want to have us killed and buried
before Fergus comes.

DEIRDRE [*in a faint voice*] Take me away. . . . Take me to hide in the
rocks, for the night is coming quickly.

NAISI [*pulling himself together*] I will not leave my brothers.   140

DEIRDRE [*vehemently*] It's of us two he's jealous. Come away to the
places where we're used to have our company. . . . Wouldn't it be
a good thing to lie hid in the high ferns together? [*She pulls him
left*] I hear strange words in the trees.

NAISI It should be the strange fighters of Conchubor, . . . I saw them 145
passing as we came.

DEIRDRE [*pulling him towards the right*] Come to this side; listen,
Naisi!

NAISI There are more of them. . . . We are shut in and I have not
Ainnle and Ardan to stand near me. Isn't it a hard thing that we   150
three who have conquered many may not die together?

DEIRDRE [*sinking down*] And isn't it a hard thing that you and I are this place by our opened grave, though none have lived had happiness like ours those days in Alban that went by so quick.

NAISI It's a hard thing surely we've lost those days forever, and yet 155 it's a good thing maybe that all goes quick, for when I'm in that grave it's soon a day'll come you'll be too wearied to be crying out, and that day'll bring you ease.

DEIRDRE I'll not be here to know if that is true.

NAISI It's our three selves he'll kill tonight, and then in two months, 160 or three, you'll see him walking down for courtship with yourself.

DEIRDRE I'll not be here.

NAISI [*hard*] You'd best keep him off maybe, and then, when the time comes, make your way to some place west in Donegal, and it's there you'll get used to stretching out lonesome at the fall of 165 night, and waking lonesome for the day.

DEIRDRE Let you not be saying things are worse than death.

NAISI [*a little recklessly*] I've one word left. . . . If a day comes in the west that the larks are cocking their crests on the edge of the clouds, and the cuckoos making a stir, and there's a man you'd fancy, let 170 you not be thinking that day, I'd be well pleased you'd go on keening always.

DEIRDRE [*half-surprised, turning to look at him*] And if it was I that died, Naisi, would you take another woman to fill up my place?

NAISI [*very mournfully*] It's little I know. . . . Saving only that it's a 175 hard and bitter thing leaving the earth, and a worse and harder thing leaving yourself alone and desolate to be making lamentation on its face always.

DEIRDRE I'll die when you do, Naisi. I'd not have come from Alban but I knew I'd be along with you in Emain, and you living or dead. 180 . . . Yet this night it's strange and distant talk you're making only.

NAISI There's nothing surely the like of a new grave of open earth for putting a great space between two friends that love.

DEIRDRE If there isn't maybe it's that grave when it's closed will make us one forever, and we two lovers have had a great space 185 without weariness or growing old or any sadness of the mind.

[*Conchubor comes in on right*]

CONCHUBOR I'd bid you welcome, Naisi.

NAISI [*standing up, watching himself*] You're welcome, Conchubor. . . . I'm well pleased you've come.

CONCHUBOR [*blandly*] Let you not think bad of this place where I've 190 put you, till other rooms are readied.

NAISI [*breaking out*] We know the room you've readied. We know
what stirred you to send your seals, and Fergus into Alban, and to
stop him in the north [*opening curtain, and pointing to the grave*] . . .
and dig that grave before us. Now I ask what brought you here?   195

CONCHUBOR I've come to look on Deirdre.

NAISI Look on her. You're a knacky fancier° and it's well you chose
the one you'd lure from Alban. Look on her, I tell you, and when
you've looked I've got ten fingers will squeeze your mottled goose
neck though you're king itself.   200

DEIRDRE [*coming between them*] Hush Naisi, maybe Conchubor'll
make peace. . . . Do not mind him Conchubor, he has cause to
rage.

CONCHUBOR It's little I heed his raging, when a call would bring my
fighters from the trees. . . . But what do you say, Deirdre?   205

DEIRDRE I'll say so near that grave we seem three lonesome people,
and by a new made grave there's no man will keep brooding on a
woman's lips, or on the man he hates. It's not long till your own
grave will be dug in Emain and you'd go down to it more easy if
you'd let call Ainnle and Ardan, the way we'd have a supper all   210
together, and fill that grave, and you'll be well pleased from this
out having four new friends the like of us in Emain.

CONCHUBOR [*looking at her for a moment*] That's the first friendly
word I've heard you speaking, Deirdre. A game the like of
yours° should be the proper thing for softening the heart and   215
putting sweetness in the tongue, and yet this night when I hear
you, I've small blame left for Naisi that he stole you off from
Ulster.

DEIRDRE [*to Naisi*] Now, Naisi, answer gently and we'll be friends
tonight.   220

NAISI [*doggedly*] I have no call but to be friendly, I'll answer what
you will.

DEIRDRE [*taking Naisi's hand*] Then you'll call Conchubor your
friend and king, the man who reared me up upon Slieve Fuadh.

[*As Conchubor is going to clasp Naisi's hand, cries are heard
behind*]

CONCHUBOR What noise is that?   225

AINNLE [*behind*] Naisi . . . Naisi. . . . Come to us, we are betrayed
and broken.

NAISI It's Ainnle crying out in a battle!

CONCHUBOR I was near won this night, but death's between us now.

[*He goes out*]   230

DEIRDRE [*clinging to Naisi*] There is no battle. . . . Do not leave me, Naisi.

NAISI I must go to them.

DEIRDRE [*beseechingly*] Do not leave me, Naisi. Let us creep up in the darkness behind the grave. . . . If there's a battle, maybe the   235
strange fighters will be destroyed, when Ainnle and Ardan are against them.

[*Cries are heard*]

NAISI [*wildly*] I hear Ardan crying out. Do not hold me from my brothers.

DEIRDRE [*broken after the strain*] Do not leave me, Naisi. Do not   240
leave me broken and alone.

NAISI I cannot leave my brothers when it is I who have defied the king.

DEIRDRE I will go with you.

NAISI You cannot come. . . . Do not hold me from the fight. [*He*   245
throws her aside almost roughly]

DEIRDRE [*with restraint*] Go to your brothers. . . . For seven years you have been kindly, but the hardness of death has come between us.

NAISI [*looking at her aghast*] And you'll have me meet death with a   250
hard word from your lips in my ear?

DEIRDRE We've had a dream, but this night has waked us surely. In a little while we've lived too long, Naisi, and isn't it a poor thing we should miss the safety of the grave, and we trampling its edge?

AINNLE [*behind*] Naisi, Naisi, we are attacked and ruined.   255

DEIRDRE Let you go where they are calling! [*She looks at him for an*
instant coldly] Have you no shame loitering and talking and a cruel death facing Ainnle and Ardan in the woods?

NAISI [*frantic*] They'll not get a death that's cruel and they with men alone. It's women that have loved are cruel only, and if I went on   260
living from this day I'd be putting a curse on the lot of them I'd meet walking in the east or west, putting a curse on the sun that gave them beauty, and on the madder and the stone-crop° put red upon their cloaks.

DEIRDRE [*bitterly*] I'm well pleased there's no one this place to make   265
a story that Naisi was a laughing-stock the night he died.

NAISI There'd not be many'd make a story, for that mockery is in your eyes this night will spot the face of Emain with a plague of pitted graves. [*He draws out his sword, throws down belt and cloak,*
and goes out]   270

CONCHUBOR [*outside*] That is Naisi. Strike him.

[*Tumult. Deirdre crouches down on Naisi's cloak. Conchubor comes in hurriedly, and closes tent so that the grave is not seen any more*]

CONCHUBOR They've met their death, the three that stole you Deirdre, and from this out you'll be my queen in Emain.

[*A keen of men's voices is heard behind*]

DEIRDRE [*bewildered and terrified*] It is not I will be a queen.

CONCHUBOR Make your lamentation a short while if you will, but it   275
isn't long till a day'll come when you'll begin pitying a man is old and desolate and High King also. . . . Let you not fear me for it's I'm well pleased you have a store of pity for the three that were your friends in Alban.

DEIRDRE I have pity surely . . . It's the way pity has me this night,   280
when I think of Naisi, that I could set my teeth into the heart of a king.

CONCHUBOR I know well pity's cruel, when it was my pity for my own self destroyed Naisi.

DEIRDRE [*more wildly*] It was my words without pity gave Naisi a   285
death will have no match until the ends of life and time. [*Breaking out into a keen*] But who'll pity Deirdre has lost the lips of Naisi from her neck, and from her cheek forever: who'll pity Deirdre has lost the twilight in the woods with Naisi, when beech-trees were silver and copper, and ash-trees were fine gold?   290

CONCHUBOR [*bewildered*] It's I'll know the way to pity and care you, and I with a share of troubles has me thinking this night, it would be a good bargain if it was I was in the grave, and Deirdre crying over me, and it was Naisi who was old and desolate.

[*A keen rises loudly over the grave*]

DEIRDRE [*wild with sorrow*] It is I who am desolate, I, Deirdre, that   295
will not live till I am old.

CONCHUBOR It's not long you'll be desolate, and I seven years saying, 'It's a bright day for Deirdre in the woods of Alban,' or saying again, 'what way will Deirdre be sleeping this night, and wet leaves and branches driving from the north?' Let you not break   300
the thing I've set my life on, and you giving yourself up to your sorrow when it's joy and sorrow do burn out like straw blazing in an east wind.

DEIRDRE [*turning on him*] Was it that way with *your* sorrow, when I and Naisi went northward from Slieve Fuadh and let raise our sails   305
for Alban?

CONCHUBOR [*after a moment*] There's one sorrow has no end surely, that's being old and lonesome. [*With extraordinary pleading*] But you and I will have a little peace in Emain, with harps playing, and old men telling stories at the fall of night. . . . I've let build rooms° for our two selves Deirdre, with red gold upon the walls, and ceilings that are set with bronze. There was never a queen in the east had a house the like of your house, that's waiting for yourself in Emain.

SOLDIER [*running in*] Emain is in flames. Fergus has come back and is setting fire to the world. Come up Conchubor, or your state will be destroyed.

CONCHUBOR [*angry and regal again*] Are the Sons of Usna buried?

SOLDIER They are in their grave, but no earth is thrown.

CONCHUBOR Let me see them. Open the tent. [*Soldier opens back of tent and shows grave*] . . . Where are my fighters?

SOLDIER They are gone to Emain.

CONCHUBOR [*to Deirdre*] There are none to harm you. Stay here until I come again. [*Goes out with Soldier*]

> [*Deirdre looks round for a moment, then goes up slowly and looks into grave. She crouches down and begins swaying herself backwards and forwards keening softly. At first her words are not heard, then they become clear*]

DEIRDRE It's you three will not see age or death coming, you that were my company when the fires on the hill-tops were put out and the stars were our friends only. I'll turn my thoughts back from this night—that's pitiful for want of pity—to the time it was your rods and cloaks made a little tent for me where there'd be a birch tree making shelter, and a dry stone: though from this day my own fingers will be making a tent for me, spreading out my hairs and they knotted with the rain.

> [*Lavarcham and Old Woman come in stealthily on right*]

DEIRDRE [*not seeing them*] It is I Deirdre will be crouching in a dark place, I Deirdre that was young with Naisi, and brought sorrow to his grave in Emain.

OLD WOMAN Is that Deirdre broken down that was so light and airy?

LAVARCHAM It is, surely, crying out over their grave. [*She goes to Deirdre*]

DEIRDRE It will be my share from this out to be making lamentation on his stone always, and I crying for a love will be the like of a star shining on a little harbour by the sea.

LAVARCHAM [*coming forward*] Let you rise up Deirdre, and come off while there are none to heed us the way I'll find you shelter, and some friend to guard you. 345

DEIRDRE To what place would I go away from Naisi? What are the woods without Naisi, or the seashore?

LAVARCHAM [*very coaxingly*] If it's keening you'd be come till I find you a sunny place where you'll be a great wonder they'll call the queen of sorrows, and you'll begin taking a pride to be sitting up 350 pausing and dreaming when the summer comes.

DEIRDRE It was the voice of Naisi that was strong in summer, the voice of Naisi that was sweeter than pipes playing, but from this day will be dumb always.

LAVARCHAM [*to Old Woman, also sobbing*] She doesn't heed us at all. 355 We'll be hard set to rouse her.

OLD WOMAN If we don't the High King will rouse her coming down beside her with the rage of battle in his blood, for how could Fergus stand against him.

LAVARCHAM [*touching Deirdre with her hand*] There's a score of 360 woman's years in store for you, and you'd best choose will you start living them beside the man you hate, or being your own mistress in the west or south.

DEIRDRE It is not I will go on living after Ainnle and after Ardan. After Naisi I will not have a lifetime in the world. 365

OLD WOMAN [*with excitement*] Look, Lavarcham! There's a light leaving the Red Branch. Conchubor and his lot will be coming quickly with a torch of bog-deal° for her marriage throwing a light on her three comrades.

DEIRDRE [*startled*] Let us throw down clay on my three comrades. 370 Let us cover up Naisi along with Ainnle and Ardan, they that were the pride of Emain. [*Throwing in clay*] There is Naisi was the best of three, the choicest of the choice of many. It was a clean death was your share° Naisi, and it is not I will quit your head when it's many a dark night among the snipe and plover that you 375 and I were whispering together. It is not I will quit your head Naisi, when it's many a night we saw the stars among the clear trees of Glen da Ruadh, or the moon pausing on the edges of the hills.

OLD WOMAN Conchubor is coming surely. I see the glare of flames 380 throwing a light upon his cloak.

LAVARCHAM [*eagerly*] Rise up Deirdre and come to Fergus, or be the High King's slave forever.

DEIRDRE [*imperiously*] I will not leave Naisi who has left the whole world scorched and desolate, I will not go away when there is no 385 light in the heavens, and no flower in the earth under them, but is saying to me, that it is Naisi who is gone forever.

CONCHUBOR [*behind*] She is here . . . Stay a little back.

[*Lavarcham and Old Woman go into the shadow on left as Conchubor comes in*]

CONCHUBOR [*with excitement, to Deirdre*] Come forward and leave Naisi the way I've left charred timber and a smell of burning in 390 Emain Macha, and a heap of rubbish in the storehouse of many crowns.

DEIRDRE [*more awake to what is round her*] What are crowns and Emain Macha when the head that gave them glory is this place Conchubor, and it stretched upon the gravel will be my bed 395 tonight?

CONCHUBOR Make an end with talk of Naisi, for I've come to bring you to Dundealgan since Emain is destroyed. [*Makes a movement towards her*]

DEIRDRE [*with a tone that stops him*] Draw a little back from 400 Naisi who is young forever. Draw a little back from the white bodies I am putting under a mound of clay and grasses that are withered—a mound will have a nook for my own self when the end is come.

CONCHUBOR [*roughly*] Let you rise up and come along with me in 405 place of growing crazy with your wailings here.

DEIRDRE It's yourself has made a crazy story, and let you go back to your arms, Conchubor, and to councils where your name is great, for in this place you are an old man and a fool only.

CONCHUBOR If I've folly I've sense left not to lose the thing 410 I've bought with sorrow and the deaths of many. [*He moves towards her*]

DEIRDRE Do not raise a hand to touch me.

CONCHUBOR There are other hands to touch you. My fighters are set round in among the trees. 415

DEIRDRE [*almost mockingly*] Who'll fight the grave, Conchubor, and it opened on a dark night?

LAVARCHAM [*eagerly*] There are steps in the wood. . . . I hear the call of Fergus and his men.

CONCHUBOR [*furiously*] Fergus cannot stop me. . . . I am more 420 powerful than he is though I am defeated and old.

[*A red glow is seen behind the grave*]

FERGUS [*comes in to Deirdre*] I have destroyed Emain, and now I'll guard you all times, Deirdre, though it was I, without knowledge, brought Naisi to his grave.

CONCHUBOR It's not you will guard her, for my whole armies are 425 gathering. Rise up, Deirdre, for you are mine surely.

FERGUS [*coming between them*] I am come between you.

CONCHUBOR [*wildly*] When I've killed Naisi and his brothers is there any man that I will spare? . . . And is it you will stand against me, Fergus, when it's seven years you've seen me getting my death 430 with rage in Emain?

FERGUS It's I surely will stand against a thief and traitor.°

DEIRDRE [*stands up and sees the light from Emain*] Draw a little back with the squabbling of fools when I am broken up with misery. [*She turns round*] . . . I see the flames of Emain starting upward in 435 the dark night, and because of me there will be weasels and wild cats crying on a lonely wall where there were queens and armies, and red gold, the way there will be a story told of a ruined city and a raving king and a woman will be young forever. [*A pause. She looks round*] . . . I see the trees naked and bare, and the moon 440 shining. Little moon, little moon of Alban, it's lonesome you'll be this night, and tomorrow night, and long nights after, and you pacing the woods beyond Glen Laid, looking every place for Deirdre and Naisi, the two lovers who slept so sweetly with each other. 445

FERGUS [*going to Conchubor's right and whispering*] Keep back or you will have the shame of pushing a bolt on a queen who is out of her wits.

CONCHUBOR It is I am out of my wits, with Emain in flames, and Deirdre raving, and my own heart gone within me. 450

DEIRDRE [*in a high and quiet tone*] I have put away sorrow like a shoe that is worn out and muddy, for it is I have had a life that will be envied by great companies. It was not by a low birth I made kings uneasy, and they sitting in the halls of Emain. It was not a low thing to be chosen by Conchubor, who was wise, and Naisi had no 455 match for bravery. . . . It is not a small thing to be rid of grey hairs and the loosening of the teeth. [*With a sort of triumph*] . . . It was the choice of lives we had in the clear woods, and in the grave we're safe surely. . . .

CONCHUBOR She will do herself harm.° 460

DEIRDRE [*showing Naisi's knife*] I have a little key to unlock the prison of Naisi, you'd shut upon his youth forever. Keep back

Conchubor, for the High King who is your master° has put his
hands between us. [*She half turns to the grave*] . . . It was sorrows
were foretold, but great joys were my share always, yet it is a cold   465
place I must go to be with you, Naisi, and it's cold your arms will
be this night that were warm about my neck so often. . . . It's a
pitiful thing to be talking out when your ears are shut to me. It's
a pitiful thing, Conchubor, you have done this night in Emain, yet
a thing will be a joy and triumph to the ends of life and time.   470

> [*She presses knife to her heart and sinks into the grave.
> Conchubor and Fergus go forward; the red glow fades leaving
> the stage very dark*]

FERGUS Four white bodies are laid down together, four clear lights
are quenched in Ireland. [*He throws his sword into the grave*] . . .
There is my sword that could not shield you, my four friends that
were the dearest always. The flames of Emain have gone out:
Deirdre is dead and there is none to keen her. That is the fate of   475
Deirdre and Naisi next the Children of Usna and for this night
Conchubor, our war is ended. [*He goes out*]

LAVARCHAM I have a little hut where you can rest Conchubor, there
is a great dew falling.

CONCHUBOR [*with the voice of an old man*] Take me with you, I'm   480
hard set to see the way before me.

OLD WOMAN This way, Conchubor.

LAVARCHAM Deirdre is dead, and Naisi is dead, and if the oaks and
stars could die for sorrow it's a dark sky and a hard and naked
earth we'd have this night in Emain.   485

CURTAIN

EXPLANATORY NOTES

See the Glossary for words frequently used by Synge. References to Synge's works are to the four volumes of *Works*; see Select Bibliography for these and other relevant texts cited.

Riders to the Sea

Scene *An Island off the West of Ireland*: almost certainly Inishmaan, the middle-sized of the three Aran Islands in Galway Bay, where Synge spent most of his time when visiting Aran. Most of the incidents and details of the play are taken from Synge's observations in *The Aran Islands*.

Opening S.D.: *cake . . . in the pot-oven*: the staple soda bread was baked in an iron pot with embers from the turf fire piled on top of the lid.

6 *Donegal*: a seaport town in Donegal Bay, in the furthest north-west county of Ireland.

S.D. *leans out*: that is, across the wheel. Synge was insistent that the actress playing Cathleen know how to spin.

17 *the Galway fair*: the closest market town on the mainland.

23 *when the tide's turned to the wind*: when the tide is against the wind, and the waves will be higher.

30 *turf-loft*: an opening for the storage of sods of peat used as fuel.

31 *the way*: 'so that'; also used by Synge to mean 'so that s/he can or should', 'as' or 'as if', and (in 'what way') 'how could'.

46 *the green head*: a grassy headland overlooking the sea; most of the island has steep cliffs of rock.

47 *the hooker's tacking from the east*: because of the steep cliffs and strong winds on the two smaller islands, even the small sailing cutters (hookers) carrying passengers and produce could not come in to shore, which meant that islanders had to go out to meet them in frail rowing-boats called curaghs, encouraging their tethered (and terrified) animals to swim alongside.

54 *the pig with the black feet was eating it*: pigs were a valued source of food and commerce on the islands, but the repetition of the familiar description takes on further significance here in that pigs are associated with death in Irish folklore and black with ill luck or even evil.

68 *and I after giving . . . in Connemara*: trees were almost non-existent on Aran and boards would also be expensive in rocky Connemara, 10 miles

north of Aran on the mainland; Synge recalls the borrowing of some boards 'that a man below has had this two years to bury his mother' (*Works* ii. 158).

79 *jobber*: commercial traveller or small tradesman.

84 *cock for the kelp*: because of the lack of soil on Aran, islanders gathered and burned seaweed (kelp), then stacked it to dry in conical heaps (cocks) for use as fertilizer.

111 *Isn't it sorrow enough . . . word in his ear?*: the practical Cathleen is impatient with her mother's lengthy grieving, but also it was considered unlucky not to return a blessing, even more dangerous here because Maurya withholds the traditional blessing of the eldest to someone going on a journey.

115 *destroyed*: from the Irish meaning injured or harmed, in this case from hunger, but prophetic in the context of the play; see Glossary for the frequency and range of meanings.

132 *the big world*: outside the immediate region, beyond their experience, frequently referring to reports of large cities brought back by travellers.

137 *she's that sorry . . . you wouldn't know the thing she'd do*: Maurya is now so distracted with grief that she has lost her strength of will, and may not be able to turn the tide of ill luck threatening to engulf them all.

142 *The young priest said he'd be passing tomorrow*: the priest does not live on the smaller island; note the emphasis on his youth and inexperience.

147 *poteen*: illicitly distilled whiskey.

152 *the string's perished . . . in a week*: black is traditionally associated with death; in this case the stiff string and unyielding knot convey additional poignancy as a reminder of the manner of Michael's death. The omens have by now accumulated to such an extent that it is impossible to ignore them.

160 *a queer hard thing*: very difficult.

179 *to keen*: the traditional lament for the dead, usually, as later in the play, sung by a chorus of women.

black hags: a direct translation from the Irish for cormorants, but elsewhere Synge records a flock of black birds encountered by fishermen which were supernatural (*Works* ii. 181).

216 *Bride Dara seen the dead man with the child in his arms*: in folklore the dead return when ill at ease or jealous of the living; Synge records a story of a young mother returning to feed her child and promising to be 'on a grey horse, riding behind a young man' (*Works* ii. 159). Bride, pronounced 'Bride-ee', is short for Bridget.

235 *the grey pony, and there was Michael upon it*: the grey horse, its colour ghost-like, is reminiscent of the Pale Horse in Revelations, but in Irish folklore it is also the *puca*, a spirit in the form of a horse which lures

people to their death; in this case the vision is compounded because it was believed that the dead can return to claim a companion (see note to l. 216 above).

236 *and new shoes on his feet*: further proof that Michael's body was discovered on the mainland, for as an Irelander he would normally be wearing pampooties, shoes made of uncured skin; again Synge records hearing of a man taken by the fairies who was seen wearing leather boots and a new suit (*Works* ii. 165).

238 *It's destroyed, surely*: such is the belief in the supernatural that Cathleen readily accepts the implications of her mother's vision and faces the ruin of the family.

250 *the Bay of Gregory of the Golden Mouth*: perhaps Gregory Sound, which separates the two larger Aran islands.

259 *curagh*: a small rowing boat covered in canvas, keel-less with an upturned bow especially designed for the waves of the bay.

266 S.D. *with red petticoats over their heads*: the traditional skirt of the island women was red, a strikingly rare use of colour reflecting the red sail of Maurya's narrative; in this case their haste in running to the shore is indicated by their reaching for the closest piece of clothing to use as a shawl.

290 *no call . . . to*: no need for.

295 *getting Holy Water in the dark nights after Samhain*: either water from a holy well or water blessed by the clergy in preparation for the sacrament she is now performing, more likely during the storms of winter (after Samhain or 1 November). The double ambiguity reflects Maurya's attitude towards the young priest: the sea is an older power than his God, and Samhain (pronounced 'sow'in', as in allow), the feast of the Dead, was originally the Celtic festival when, it was believed, the spirits of the dead moved freely among the living.

297 *a small sup*: a small quantity, a few drops.

310 *a new cake*: the soda bread baked for Bartley's journey has now come full circle, even as he and Michael will share a coffin.

325 S.D. *puts the empty cup . . . on Bartley's feet*: the finality of Maurya's gestures not only reflects her acceptance of the death of her two sons, but becomes symbolic of her tragic acknowledgement of the power of fate.

335 *No man at all can be living for ever, and we must be satisfied*: Déclan Kiberd (*Synge and the Irish Language* (1979), 206–7) has pointed out that this magnificent concluding line to Maurya's internal battle with her grief is Synge's direct translation from a letter by Martin McDonough, a friend on Inishmaan, reporting of the death of his brother's wife: 'we must be satisfied because nobody can be living forever', and later in the same letter, 'he must be satisfied'. With these final words of blessing on both the dead and the living, Maurya comes to terms with her own

earlier weakness, when 'something choked' the words of the blessing in her throat, and with the grief she bears for all her sons in their hard and losing battle for life.

The Shadow of the Glen

Persons *his wife*: early drafts add 'a much younger woman'.

a young herd: a shepherd only, rather than a farmer who might keep some sheep or cattle as part of his farm.

Opening S.D.: *She takes up . . . the table*: Synge records the common habit of hoarding money in a stocking (*Works* ii. 219).

1 *lady of the house*: like 'woman' or 'master of the house', a direct translation of the Irish greeting upon entry.

5 *to Brittas from the Aughrim fair*: villages in County Wicklow 20 miles apart.

16 *no turf drawn for the winter*: no turf brought in before winter comes.

17 *a queer look*: a strange or odd appearance. The word 'queer' takes on greater significance as the play progresses, implying the strangeness of life's circumstances.

22 *and he not tidied, or laid out itself*: traditionally the dead body would have been prepared for the wake and burial by women of the neighbourhood before nightfall; 'not . . . itself' means 'not even'.

34 *Lough Nahanagan*: a deep lake in the hills about 18 miles from the town of Wicklow.

37 *the like of him*: his kind.

50 *The Almighty God reward you*: the beggar's traditional thanks.

60 *and no one to taste them but a woman only*: the tradition of the wake, when the community gathered round the corpse in the kitchen celebrating the dead with prayers, entertainment, whiskey, and new clay pipes, was strong in rural Ireland well into the twentieth century.

88 *the Richmond Asylum*: now St Lawrence's Hospital in Dublin. Synge reflects on the effect of the 'peculiar climate' of Ireland on a 'tendency to nervous depression' (*Works* ii. 209).

104 *Rathvanna*: probably a combination of Rathdrum and Aughavanna, two villages in County Wicklow.

119 *A piece only*: a short distance only.

121 *himself*: her husband, a variation on 'man of the house'; see also 'herself', the wife or woman of the house.

140 *there's great safety in a needle*: Synge was advised by his old mentor on Aran to ward off evil fairies by sticking a sharp needle under the collar of his coat (*Works* ii. 80).

152 s.d. *saying the 'De Profundis' under his breath*: it was a common belief that repeating Psalm 130 would protect one from evil spirits (*Works* ii. 180).

153 *your honour*: thinking Dan is dead, the frightened Tramp politely uses the formal address to placate the spirit. Later Nora and Michael Dara express the same uncertainty about Dan's condition.

156 *the devil mend her*: a mild oath or curse, 'the devil improve her'.

165 *letting on*: pretending.

174 *a black stick*: probably a blackthorn.

180 *and she a grand woman to talk?*: a characteristic reminiscent of the late Patch Darcy which the Tramp himself displays by the end of the play.

234 *Glen Malure . . . Glen Imaal*: Glenmalure is a wild valley west of Rathdrum, separated from the Glen of Imaal, some 10 miles away, by a high divide.

236 *and miss one of them . . . at all*: and notice one missing although he is not deliberately counting.

266 *What way . . . back hills?*: 'back hills' refers to the most distant hills of the farm used for grazing sheep, beyond the land cleared for cultivation. John Butler Yeats defended the play as a realistic presentation of the loveless marriages arranged in Ireland; Nora's question not only emphasizes the emotional and spiritual poverty of her situation, but points to the answer supplied by the Tramp in the play's denouement.

297 *turning a cake*: baking soda bread in the pot-oven.

310 *the Seven Churches*: Glendalough, a religious centre founded under St Kevin in the sixth century, where the ruins of churches can still be seen.

356 *the like of her would never go there*: Nicholas Grene (*Synge: A Critical Study of the Plays* (1975), 90) points out that a farmer's wife would never tolerate the Union or workhouse.

368 *and you half in your skin*: and you half-naked.

399 *the black lakes*: even the dark, gloomy aspects are lightened by the Tramp's emphasis on the sounds of nature.

421 *since the turn of the day*: since noon.

The Tinker's Wedding

Preface 1 *serious—in the French sense*: important, to be taken seriously.

14 *the pharmacopoeia of Galen*: the Greek Claudius Galenus (AD 129–99), was physician to the Roman emperor Marcus Aurelius and author of many treatises advising old-fashioned remedies made of vegetable components.

15 *look at Ibsen and the Germans*: Synge disliked the realism of the so-called 'problem play' which dealt primarily with contemporary life, although

he seems to have read the work of the Norwegian dramatist Henrik Ibsen (1828–1906) only in German translation (see the dismissal of Ibsen's 'joyless and pallid words' in his preface to *The Playboy*), and his knowledge of contemporary German theatre was limited to the few works by Gerhart Hauptmann (1862–1946) and Hermann Sudermann (1857–1928) that were performed in translation by English touring companies.

19 *Baudelaire calls laughter . . . in man*: Synge is paraphrasing the words of French poet and critic Charles Baudelaire (1821–67), who wrote on the essence of laughter and the comic in relation to the plastic arts in an essay published posthumously in *Curiosités ésthetiques* (1868).

31 *re-written it since*: see Introduction, p. xix.

Scene *A road-side near a village*: given the various place-names mentioned in the play, the village is probably Rathdrum in County Wicklow.

Opening S.D.: *near the ditch*: a high bank with a hollow at the bottom.

1.1 *his reverence*: the local priest.

2 *and he passing backward*: when he returns.

8 *the divil's job* 'a difficult piece of work', one of the rare times when Synge indicates pronunciation by spelling.

15 *And it's you'll go talking of fools*: you're no one to talk.

17 *even of your like*: even like the ones you tell.

18 *going beside me a great while, and rearing a lot of them*: the plot rests on Michael's comment, for the tinkers' traditional marriage ceremony is without benefit of clergy, and he and Sarah have obviously been together for some time. Early drafts of the play include two tinker children.

25 *at whiles*: at times.

26 *It's hard set you'd be to think queerer than welcome*: no matter how strange your thoughts I am prepared to welcome them.

32 *from Tibradden to the Tara Hill*: from Tibradden mountain in County Dublin to the ancient seat of kings in County Meath.

34 *the back of you*: anyone's back.

49 *wary*: 'careful', a word recorded by Synge in his Kerry notebook.

53 *the divil mend you*: a mild curse, as in *The Shadow of the Glen*, l. 156.

57 *porter*: malt beer.

61 *Rathvanna*: see note to *The Shadow of the Glen*, l. 104.

64 *a great clout in the lug*: a box on the ear.

68 *Ballinaclash*: a small village just 2 miles from Rathdrum, the setting for Act 2 of *The Well of the Saints*.

76 *Ballinacree*: a village in County Meath.

79 *Arklow*: a Wicklow market town some 50 miles south of Dublin.

85 *Glen Malure*: the setting of the cottage in *The Shadow of the Glen*.

93 *a high cart*: the tinker's wagon, indicative of Jaunting Jim's place in the tinkers' hierarchy, especially his economic superiority over Michael Byrne who must sleep in a makeshift tent in the ditch.

103 *a big boast of a man*: one of the phrases recorded by Synge in his Kerry notebook, a combination of 'a fine figure of a man' with references to the priest's size and vanity.

139 *a sight cheaper*: a good deal cheaper.

148 *half a sovereign*: ten shillings.

173 *Larry was a fine lad*: a line from the ballad 'The Night before Larry was Stretched', i.e. hanged.

176 *destroyed*: half-killed.

181 *Begob*: by God.

192 *a smart drop*: a strong and sufficient amount.

194 *for it's a middling drouthy man you are at all times*: you're usually or fairly eager for a drink any time.

cruel dry: terribly thirst-making.

254 *it should be . . . to the saints above*: what Mary asks for here in apparently simple innocence is, like most of the actions of the play, turned on its head when the tinkers flee in terror from the priest's curse at the end. Nor does she see any irony in offering the priest her own blessing in the next speech.

285 *flighty*: changeable, with the added implication of flirtatious.

308 *Dundalk*: a large coastal town between Dublin and Belfast.

310 *shifts*: chemises, the word which acted as a lightning-rod for objections to *The Playboy of the Western World*. See Introduction, p. xvii.

334 *coppers*: pennies.

336 *stretch yourself out*: in his Kerry notebook Synge records the phrase 'does be stretched back sleeping'.

346 *the time her hour was come*: the onset of labour pains.

2.4 *after spending*: have been spending.

7 *tackle*: 'tie up', again a word heard by Synge in Kerry.

43 *turn of day*: noon.

74 *put down a head . . . with your clothes*: hid the cabbage you stole from the parson in the pot in which you were washing your clothes.

117 *tight*: capable, well-made, and healthy.

118 *a black born fool*: an utter fool.

120 *go licking the wind*: faster than the wind.

129 *speckled*: freckled.

130 *sleeping . . . would choke a mule*: sleeping in old shacks so dusty and musty even a mule would choke.

181 *Greenane*: Grianan, a village just 2 miles from Ballinaclash, mentioned again in *The Well of the Saints*, I.224.

219 *differ*: difference.

240 *cute*: clever.

252 *bet*: beaten.

274 *you'll be getting . . . blinking at the girls*: 'all the tinkers from miles around will be needed to replace the broken glass in your windows with sheets of tin so you'll no longer be able to spy on young women passing by'. The mood turns ugly as Sarah's threats become more violent and her blandishments turn to insults, so that it is no wonder the priest finally loses his temper.

278 *the Lords of Justice*: the magistrates and judges.

280 *if you'd run . . . the rope itself*: the priest in his turn threatens to report the tinkers' villainies to the law, which could lead not only to Kilmainham jail in Dublin but perhaps even hanging.

289 *Take it then, your reverence, and God help you so*: Michael sees no irony in his invocation of God while threatening to beat the priest.

296 *Tie the bag around his head*: since this conclusion comes in a late draft in 1906, it is highly likely that Synge was recalling the poem 'The Lout and his Mother', published that year by Douglas Hyde in his *Religious Songs of Connacht*. The Lout of the poem also questions the sincerity of the clergy, and although there is some ambiguity in the lines 'Sure if you were dead tomorrow morning | And I were to bring you to a priest tied up in a bag, | He would not read a Mass for you without hand-money'—is it the Lout's mother or the priest who is tied up in a bag?—the image is clear.

309 *airy*: lively.

317 *I'm told there's swearing with it*: Mary deliberately puns on the word, enjoying the irony of the slanging-match between the free-ranging tinkers, who have their own traditions, and the priest whose province is rightly with the villagers who say their prayers at night and attend church on Sundays, as she described them in Act I.

337 *in the bias of the sacks*: in the folds of the sack.

354 *fooling*: spending foolishly.

355 *Clash*: a diminutive of Ballinaclash.

The Well of the Saints

Note: those explanations identified as Synge's come from his letters to the German translator Max Meyerfeld, printed in *Works* II. and *The Collected Letters*.

Title *The Well of the Saints*: Other titles Synge considered were *The Crossroads of Grianan* and *When the Blind See*.

Preface 1 *Six years ago*: Yeats first published this Preface in the 1905 edition of the play, and although they actually met in 1896, Synge never bothered correcting his friend. Yeats finally gave the correct date for their meeting in *The Bounty of Sweden* (1925).

16 *playing his fiddle to Italian sailors*: Synge studied the violin in Germany and perhaps played it in Paris, but again, he did not correct Yeats's fanciful picture.

23 *some undiscoverable country*: in the corrected version of his Preface, printed in *Essays and Introductions* (1961), Yeats added the note: 'Since writing this I have, with Lady Gregory's help, put *Red Hanrahan* into the common speech.'

24 *Racine*: while a student in Paris, Synge closely analysed several plays by the French tragic poet and dramatist Jean Racine (1639–99).

Arthur Symons: (1865–1945), English critic and poet, whose book *The Symbolist Movement in Literature* (1899) had a profound influence on his close friend Yeats.

33 *Malory*: Sir Thomas Malory (d. 1471), author of the cycle of Arthurian legends printed as *Le Morte d'Arthur* in 1485.

36 *Dr Hyde's lyrics*: Douglas Hyde (1860–1949), founding president of the Gaelic League and future president of Ireland, collaborated with Lady Gregory on several plays produced during the early years of the Irish Literary Theatre, but was best known for his translations published in *The Love Songs of Connacht* (1893), for which he created a language similar to Synge's and, to a lesser extent, Lady Gregory's.

50 *the players were puzzled by the rhythm*: see Introduction, p. xi.

71 *Rabelais . . . Blake*: Synge frequently referred to the works of the French physician and satirist François Rabelais (*c.* 1495–1553), whose exuberance and extravagance in his works *Gargantua* and *Pantagruel* gave an adjective to the language; Synge wrote several prose poems based on the work of the French poet François Villon (1431–*c.* 1463) (see *Poems*, 79–80); Yeats himself was an editor and admirer of the English visionary poet and engraver William Blake (1757–1827).

101 *their Scandinavian master*: Henrik Ibsen; see note to l. 15 of the Preface to *The Tinker's Wedding*.

139 *says Oisin in the story*: Yeats is referring here to the legendary Irish hero who celebrated the warrior Finn and his followers and of whom Yeats himself wrote in his long narrative poem 'The Wanderings of Oisin' (1889).

Persons *Doul*: Irish for blind, not a surname; Synge notes that the 'ou' is pronounced as in 'out'.

The Saint: clearly intended to be an archetypal figure, as the phrase 'wandering Friar' suggests, rather than a specific saint.

Scene *Some lonely mountainous district in the east of Ireland*: County Wicklow near the village of Grianan.

1.6 *that length*: that long a time.

7 *plaiting your yellow hair*: the contrast between what the audience sees and what it hears not only intensifies the underlying irony of the play but encourages close attention to every word.

8 *Clash*: Ballinaclash, see note to *The Tinker's Wedding* l. 68.

13 S.D. *beginning to shred rushes she gives him*: the pith of the rushes would be offered for sale to be dipped in grease and used as the wicks for rush-lights.

25 *I do be thinking odd times*: once in a while I think.

30 *Patch Ruadh*: Red Pat, pronounced 'roo'a', so-named for the colour of his hair.

32 *dark*: blind.

33 *Ballinatone*: the township or parish next to Grianan.

34 *If it was itself*: even if that was so.

48 *the way we'd know . . . the finest woman*: this is an early indication that Martin and Mary have, in part consciously, chosen to believe the story told them by the villagers of their great beauty; the entire exchange not only foreshadows the plot, but the strength of Mary's powers of rationalization and Martin's romantic imagination.

seven counties of the east: Antrim, Down, Louth, Meath, Dublin, Wexford, and Waterford.

99 *two perches*: eleven yards.

101 *a thing wasn't right*: 'a thing that is uncanny, mysterious, supernatural' (Synge).

110 *playing shows*: 'playing little plays, or performing in circuses such as are seen in country fairs' (Synge).

115 *too cute a little fellow to be minding me at all*: 'too clever to take notice of me' (Synge).

125 *we don't want any . . . we are ourselves*: 'we are such fine-looking wonderful people that we are wonder enough for this place, and we don't wish you to do anything here that people would think of instead of us' (Synge).

129 *a still*: for illegally distilling whiskey (poteen).

141 *you've queer humbugging talk*: you are speaking oddly and deceivingly.

145 *the grave of the four beautiful saints?*: Synge records a story of the blind being cured by water from a holy well near the Church of the Four Beauties on Aran (*Prose* 56–7).

158 *a naggin*: a quarter-pint.

160 *the thatch*: probably a hiding-place in the bushes rather than the thatched roof of a building.

234 *the saint's a simple fellow, and it's no lie*: as in *Riders to the Sea*, Synge suggests that the well-meaning clergy are innocent and inexperienced in the ways of the world.

238 *Wonders is*: 'miracles are' (Synge).

270 *as the archangels below, fell out with the Almighty God*: 'the archangels down in hell that quarrelled or fought with the Almighty God' (Synge).

282 *God help you, but it's little you know of her at all*: Molly's unintentional irony in the customary phrase 'God help you' deepens the tone but also suggests how determined the blind couple have been to accept the villagers' mocking description of them.

301 *selvage*: edge.

315 *a bit of copper*: 'a few pence' (Synge).

336 *Cashla Bay*: an inlet on Galway Bay.

352 *the words of women and smiths*: 'This phrase is almost a quotation from an old hymn of Saint Patrick. In Irish folklore smiths were thought to be magicians, and more or less in league with the powers of darkness' (Synge).

354 *brave*: handsome.

359 *would do rightly*: 'would have the same effect' (Synge).

387 *Laus patri sit . . . est Hiberniae*: 'Praise be to the Father and to the Son with the Holy Spirit | Who by His gift of grace took pity on Ireland.'

393 *the black of his head*: the soot on his head (from the forge).

395 *the gamey eyes in him*: 'tricky, merry eyes' (Synge).

406 *a bad one*: 'an ugly man' (Synge).

430 *with your giggling, weeping eyes*: Martin's phrase foreshadows the details that will make everyone in Act 2 conscious of their appearance.

439 *the two of you*: 'Molly and Mary' (Synge).

454 *a wisp on any grey mare*: 'a tangle of dirty hair on any grey horse' (Synge). *on the ridge of the world*: anywhere in the world.

461 *what is that to you*: what good is that to you.

463 *never fit to rear a child to me itself*: never even fit to have a child.

471 *with their knees bled*: bleeding from going on their knees in prayer.

500 *Leave him go now*: let go of him now.

507 *Annagolan*: a townland in Wicklow, pronounced 'annagoulan, the "ou" as in "out" ' (Synge). *Laragh*: a village near Glendalough, 7 miles from Rathdrum.

508 *Glenassil*: perhaps Glendasan near Glendalough.

510 *the bed of the holy Kevin*: a stone cell on a cliff in Glendalough, commonly referred to as 'St Kevin's bed' after the founder of the medieval monastery.

2.5 *whacking your old thorns*: 'hacking, chopping, or cutting your sticks (of hawthorn)' (Synge).

14 *handy*: easily.

16 *fear*: chance.

25 *rake the ashes from the forge*: 'rake out ashes from under the forge' (Synge).

35 *a power of queer things*: 'a great many bad things' (Synge).

41 *a poor thing*: 'a miserable thing' (Synge).

48 *it's well for the blind don't be seeing*: 'it is a good fortune blind people have, for they do not see' (Synge).

55 *a hard thing*: 'a wretched thing' (Synge).

58 *it should be*: 'it must be' (Synge).

60 *slipping each way in the muck*: 'slipping in every direction in the mud' (Synge).

61 s.d. *pot-hooks*: hooks to hold the cauldrons over the fire.

72 *Let you not be tormenting yourself trying to make me afeard*: 'Don't be troubling yourself trying to frighten me!' (Synge).

73 *it's right now for you*: 'you ought to' (Synge).

94 *And she after going by*: 'When she has just gone by' (Synge).

96 *a sainted lady going . . . singing to themselves*: towards the end of rehearsals Synge was finally persuaded by the company to alter this line from the original, which read: 'a priest going where there'd be a drunken man in the side ditch talking with a girl.' See Introduction, p. xvi.

136 *dreepiness*: 'the red-nosed look people have when they have a cold in the head' (Synge).

141 *no call*: 'no right' (Synge).

145 *Rathvanna*: see note to *The Shadow of the Glen*, l. 104.

168 *coaxing*: 'flattering, wheedling' (Synge).

192 *speckled*: 'varied, beautiful' (Synge).

203 *with dry timber lining the roof*: i.e. boards instead of the humbler thatched cottage.

222 *Cahir Iveraghig and the Reeks of Cork*: the town of Cahircveen in County Kerry and the McGillicuddy Reeks, mountains on the border between Cork and Kerry; Cahir Iveraghig is pronounced 'kahir eevrau-ig the "au" as in caught' (Synge).

252 *a man is after looking out . . . of the world*: 'a man who has been for a long time looking at the bad weather and ugliness, which Martin now finds in the world' (Synge).

303 *a sight*: 'a great deal' (Synge); the Abbey Theatre prompt-book adds the stage direction '*Martin staggers back RC and rests head on wall*' (Nicholas Grene's edn. (1982), 63).

308 *an old wretched road woman*: 'a wretched old beggar woman' (Synge).

316 *does be soon turning the like of*: 'that soon turns the colour of' (Synge).

326 *welt*: 'blow' (Synge).

334 *It's making game of you she is*: 'She is making a fool of you' (Synge).

337 *let you raise your voice*: 'speak out loudly, cry out' (Synge).

374 *and it's fine care I'll be taking the Lord Almighty doesn't know*: the irony of Martin's double-edged prayer reflects the ambiguity over vision and knowledge he and Mary share throughout the play. Synge explained to his German translator: 'you are right in supposing that Martin wishes to deceive God, his theology—folk-theology—is always vague and he fears that even in Hell God might plague him in some new way, if he knew what an unholy joy Martin has found for himself.' (*Letters* i. 126).

3.3 *hard set*: 'I'll find it hard' (Synge).

6 *blink*: glimpse of light.

11 *what place is himself*: where my husband is.

16 *The devil mend . . .* : 'the devil cure', that is, 'make suffer', a variation on Dan's curse in *The Shadow of the Glen*, 156.

55 *a space*: 'a long time' (Synge).

71 *minding*: 'remembering' (Synge).

75 *the length of that*: 'so far as that!' (Synge).

90 *the like of me*: 'anything to equal me, anything so fine as myself' (Synge).

91 *cute thinking*: 'clever' (Synge).

95 *Kitty Bawn*: 'White Kitty' (Synge).

101 *In a short while*: 'Soon' (Synge).

117 *There's talking for a cute woman!*: 'that is grand talk (ironically) for a clever woman' (Synge).

123 *the eastern world*: 'He does not mean here in the east of Ireland, but away in the "eastern world", a sort of wonderland very often spoken of in Irish folk-tales' (Synge).

124 *the quality*: 'the rich people' (Synge).

129 *and great talking before we die*: 'She means that they will have a good time talking and quarrelling with each other as they were doing at the beginning of Act I' (Synge).

132 *would have*: 'who had' (Synge).

136 *the way*: 'so that' (Synge).

141 *the full river*: 'the flooded river' (Synge).

146 *the churches*: i.e. the Seven Churches of Glendalough.

152 *Will we be running off . . . ?*: 'Shall we run away' (Synge).

154 *sloughs*: 'bogs' (Synge).

156 *yeomen*: guards or militia.

165 *Would we have a right to be crawling*: 'Should we crawl' (Synge).

169 *It's hard set . . . and you fearing to see?*: 'I don't know what we should do! And isn't it a miserable thing to be blind so that you cannot even run away when you are afraid that your sight will be given to you?' (Synge).

218 *the way he'll be curing you now*: 'so that he will cure you now' (Synge).

220 *after seeing a while, and working for your bread*: perhaps only Martin could grasp the ironic significance of Timmy's echo of the Saint here.

224 *It's many a time*: 'It often happened that' (Synge).

238 *I'm not saying a word of penance, or fasting itself*: I will not insist on your making penance, or even fasting.

282 *till we'd be looking up in our own minds . . .* : Martin's counter-argument in praise of his own world to the Saint's praise of God reflects the age-old debate between pagan Oisin and Christian St Patrick.

366 *and be looking out day and night upon the holy men of God*: 'he will be looking himself at the holy men of God. (He is merely wheedling or flattering the saint, to hide his intention)' (Synge).

390 *Go on from this*: Be on your way from here.

407 *Go on now . . . of the Lord*: the Abbey Theatre prompt-book indicates how these lines are distributed among the cast: ' "Go on now, Martin Doul" (Girls) "Go on from this place" (Men) "Let you not be bringing great storms" (Timmy) "or droughts on us" (Mat Simon) "maybe, from the power of the Lord" (deleted)' (Grene's edn., 79).

417 *a slough of wet*: 'a wet quagmire or bog' (Synge).

The Playboy of the Western World

Preface 12 *Geesala, or Carraroe, or Dingle Bay*: in Northwest Mayo, Galway, and Kerry respectively, areas which Synge knew well; see *Works* ii. 237–343.

31 *Mallarmé and Huysmans . . . Ibsen and Zola*: in an article published in 1903 Synge dismisses Symbolist poet Stéphane Mallarmé (1842–98) and novelist Joris Karl Huysmans (1848–1907) as writers 'who make pitiful efforts to gain new effects by literary devices' (*Works* ii. 396); here he somewhat unfairly lumps Norwegian dramatist and poet Henrik Ibsen (1828–1906) with the French champion of naturalism, novelist Émile Zola (1840–1902), and in his Preface to *The Tinker's Wedding* further denounces Ibsen's use of realism.

Persons *a squatter*: someone illegally 'squatting' on land belonging to an absentee landlord.

Scene *a wild coast of Mayo*: a wild, infertile area along the north-west coast; see *Works* ii. 316 ff. for Synge's description of a tour through this 'district of the greatest poverty . . . a waste of turf and bog' while on a tour in 1905 for the *Manchester Guardian* with artist-illustrator Jack B. Yeats.

S.D. *shebeen*: a low wayside public-house, more usually used to describe an unlicensed house selling poteen.

S.D. *the usual peasant dress*: described by Synge in *Works* ii. 316 n. as 'a short red petticoat over bare feet and legs, a faded uncertain bodice'; but the Abbey Theatre production omitted the 'white or blue rag swathing the head'.

1.3 *a fine tooth comb*: possibly a comb to be used as an ornament in her hair, but more likely the kind required for combing out lice.

4 *creel cart*: cart with open or grated sides, usually used for carrying turf or fish.

9 *himself*: the man of the house, in this case Michael James.

11 *Castlebar*: the major market town of County Mayo.

26 *scruff of the hill*: the back of the hill, below the summit.

34 *Shaneen*: the suffix '-een' is frequently used to suggest 'little' or young or, as in this case, familiarity.

36 *Father Reilly's dispensation*: the 'sheepskin parchment' required because Pegeen and Shawn are second cousins.

43 *queer*: strange, odd, unworthy.

61 *that murderer?*: as we learn later, Pegeen dismisses the idea of asking the Widow Quin for help not because she has killed her husband, but because of contempt and perhaps even some sexual rivalry between the insider (Pegeen) and the outsider (the Widow).

65 *I'm after feeling a kind of fellow*: I overheard (but did not see) some strange fellow.

furzy ditch: bank overgrown with furze or gorse.

76 *Well, you're a daring fellow!*: used ironically here but again foreshadowing the frequency with which it will be applied seriously to Christy Mahon.

101 *the Stooks of the Dead Women*: rocks on the shore which Synge has transposed to Mayo from West Kerry; 'Do you see that sandy head? . . . that is called the Stooks of the Dead Women; for one time a boat came ashore there with twelve dead women on board her, big big ladies with green dresses and gold rings, and fine jewelries, and a dead harper or fiddler along with them' (*Works* ii. 264).

110 *the thousand militia*: soldiery, but perhaps the unemployed military from the Boer War (1899–1902).

bad cess to them!: ill luck to them!

154 *a penny pot-boy*: a poorly paid serving-man.

177 *polis*: police, pronounced with the emphasis on the first syllable.

183 *a bona fide*: a genuine traveller living at a distance of more than 3 miles and therefore exempt from licensing hours.

190 *wanting*: on the run from the law.

192 *broken harvest*: poor potato harvest.

193 *ended wars*: the Boer War of 1899–1902.

204 *a strong farmer*: a well-to-do farmer.

206 *tail-pocket*: the deep pocket of an old-fashioned swallow-tailed coat, which, with knee breeches, buckled shoes, and shillelagh, was the costume worn by the traditional stage Irishman.

216 *and he did what any decent man would do*: in the long struggle between peasants and landlords, homicide—especially of those responsible for evictions—was sometimes considered justifiable.

218 *The divil a one*: not one.

219 *agents*: landlords' agents responsible for evictions; Synge describes one in *Works* ii. 88–92.

224 *simple*: simple-minded.

226 *a puzzle-the-world*: an enigma to all, apparently one of Synge's own inventions.

227 *Dan Davies' Circus*: Synge describes a visit to one of these small travelling circuses in *Works* ii. 241–4.

the holy missioners: travelling preachers.

230 *strike golden guineas . . . coins*: that is, counterfeit coins.

234 *the holy Luthers of the preaching North*: Protestant preachers so violently anti-Catholic they might be guilty of any sin.

238 *Maybe he went fighting . . . quartered, and drawn*: early drafts refer explicitly to John MacBride, Maud Gonne's husband, who led a volunteer force to fight against the British in the Boer War, and to Colonel Lynch, who was executed for fighting against the British.

239 *Kruger*: Paul Kruger, president of the Transvaal Republic.

265 *mister honey*: my dear man.

276 *from the licence*: in an effort to avoid paying the dog licence.

279 *riz the loy*: raised the long narrow spade used for digging potatoes ('spuds').

305 *pitchpike*: two-pronged fork used for pitching hay or dung.

308 *the loosèd khaki cut-throats*: the discharged British soldiers who wore khaki during the Boer War.

356 *would wear the spirits from the saints of peace*: would make even the peaceful saints impatient.

360 *destroyed*: exhausted.

367 *a kind of a quality name*: an aristocratic name; the Mahons were a military family.

397 *Owen Roe O'Sullivan*: an eighteenth-century poet from Killarney whose collected songs were published by the Gaelic League in 1907 as part of their attempt to encourage recognition of native poets and the use of the Irish language.

the poets of the Dingle Bay: Pegeen's experience with 'the big world' extends only as far as the songs sung by wandering poets who travelled from one market town to another and perhaps from as far south as the Dingle peninsula in County Kerry.

411 *crusty*: bad-tempered.

435 *near got six months . . . fish*: almost got a six-months jail sentence for poaching salmon with a pitchpike.

439 *St Martin's Day*: 11 November.

446 *a gaudy officer*: an officer in a splendid uniform.

457 *not a one of them*: every one of them.

468 *did up a Tuesday*: got up on Tuesday.

496 *I've their word*: I've their orders.

516 *the penny poets singing in an August Fair*: at one time Synge had contemplated a ballad framework to the play, introducing a further character who sold ballads of Christy's story.

518 *himself*: her late husband, the Marcus Quin who told 'stories of holy Ireland'.

520 *overed*: recovered from.

525 *comrade*: partner, usually in marriage.

526 *let you a wink*: wink at you, flirt.

532 *cuteness*: acuteness, cleverness.

542 *without a tramp itself*: without even a wandering beggar.

544 *contriving*: scheming, planning.

551 *the elements of a Christian . . . kidney stew?*: grotesque and wild as this image is, it has its roots in a story told to Synge in West Kerry by his landlord, Philly Harris: 'about a woman from Cahirciveen who suckled a lamb at her own breast, and the doctor to whom she later served it as a meal "detected the elements of a Christian" in it' (D. H. Greene and E. M. Stephens, *J. M. Synge, 1871–1909* (1959), 150).

553 *sop of grass tobacco*: tuft of uncured tobacco leaf; the implication is that she has been on even more intimate terms with the French captain.

556 *rating*: scolding.

562 *God increase you*: may you prosper, a traditional blessing.

2.43 *Belmullet*: a small seaport 40 miles north-west of Castlebar.

47 *the man bit the yellow lady's nostril on the northern shore*: a reference to the sensational escape of James Lynchehaun who had been tried for assault—see James Carney, *The Playboy and the Yellow Lady* (1986).

95 *nursing a feast*: hoarding food for a feast.

164 *outlandish*: foreign.

167 *jobbing jockies*: casual workers who travel about breaking in horses.

169 *juries fill their stomachs . . . the English law*: jury members who accept bribes to bring down judgments attractive to the English landlords.

171 *What is it you're wanting?*: the public-house serves also as a small shop for local commodities.

179 *shift*: this first reference to a woman's undergarment seems to have gone unnoticed by the nationalists on opening night.

180 *the flood*: Noah's flood, only one of many Biblical references throughout the play; see Christy's references to 'Esau or Cain and Abel' (239–40).

181 *Killamuck*: perhaps a combination of Killala and Rosmuck.

207 *lepping the stones*: crossing by stepping-stones.

221 *frish-frash*: recorded by Synge in his notebooks as a mixture of Indian meal and raw cabbage 'boiled down as thin as gruel'.

225 *shut of jeopardy*: free of danger.

240 *Neifin*: a mountain north-west of Castlebar, the traditional spot for lovers' assignations in *Love Songs of Connacht*, one of many borrowings by Synge from Douglas Hyde for Christy's love speeches (Kiberd, 130–40).

Erris Plain: a barony or district in north-west County Mayo.

242 *Circuit Judges*: High Court judges who travel from town to town.

320 *the Western States*: the United States of America.

339 *hunters*: horses bred for fox-hunting, a sport common to the gentry.

365 *Kilmainham*: a well-known jail in Dublin.

377 *Michaelmas*: Feast of St Michael, 29 September.

turbary: the right to cut turf on land owned by someone else.

383 *on the long car . . . from Crossmolina or from Ballina*: both journeys of some 40 miles, requiring travel on the wagon used by postmen and commercial travellers.

393 *measuring the race-course while the tide is low*: races were held on the sands between posts measured for the purpose.

416 *not saluting at all*: not giving the customary greeting (variations on 'God save all here').

419 *An ugly young streeler with a murderous gob on him*: an ugly, slovenly young loiterer with a murderous mouth or look.

422 *harvest hundreds*: hundreds of men on their way to Sligo to take the boat to Glasgow for the harvest.

436 *You'd best be wary of a mortified scalp*: gangrene, a reflection on the way Marcus Quin (the Widow's husband) died.

510 *a kind of carcase that you'd fling upon the sea*: the way dead sheep and cattle were pushed over cliffs into the Atlantic.

523 *the love-light of the star of knowledge*: 'love . . . is like a star of knowledge on account of the way in which it opens our senses' (Hyde, *Love Songs of Connacht* (1893), 41).

524 *the holy Brigid*: one of Ireland's favourite saints, said to have been present at Christ's birth and to have returned to the Holy Land in time to be present at Christ's death.

526 *spavindy*: lame or halting from the spavin, a disease of the jock-joint.

549 *at the corner of my wheel*: beside her spinning-wheel.

3.11 *trick-o'-the-loop*: game in which the spectator must guess which is the centre loop in a leather belt without seeing either end.

12 *the cockshot-man*: man whose cheek and eye in an otherwise blackened face is the target for wooden balls thrown by competitors (see *Works* ii. 274 for Synge's description of this and other games held on the strand on a race day in West Kerry).

23 *an old Dane, maybe*: Dublin was first settled by the Danes.

121 *Belmullet*: a small seaport 48 miles north-west of Castlebar, where casual labourers catch the steamer for England (see *Works* ii. 325 ff.).

128 *again*: against.

148 *The post's cleared for them now!*: the crowd has cleared the path to the winning-post.

178 *It's maybe out of reason that man's himself*: maybe it's crazy to think that's who it is.

183 *the butt of my lug*: the lobe of my ear.

226 *would lick the scholars out of Dublin town*: would chase the students (of Dublin schools and Trinity College—which Synge himself attended) out of town.

242 *banns*: public notice of intention to marry.

249 *pacing Neifin in the dews of night*: see note to 2.240 above.

258 *till I'd feel . . . in his golden chair*: again there are parallels with Hyde's *Love Songs of Connacht* (Kiberd, 129), but see also Synge's poem 'Dread' (*Works* i. 40).

263 *when Good Friday's by*: when Lent is over.

271 *the Lady Helen of Troy*: Kiberd (139–41) notes the similarities between Christy and the nineteenth-century blind poet of Connacht much revered by Hyde and Lady Gregory, Anthony Raftery, who frequently mingled the Gaelic with the classical.

279 *the Owen or the Carrowmore*: the Owenmore River runs through Bangor Erris in north-west Mayo, a few miles from Lough Carrowmore.

290 *every jackstraw you have roofing your head*: every little straw in the roof over your head.

300 *till I'd marry a Jew-man with ten kegs of gold*: here Pegeen's romanticism draws upon folk tales 'of the Eastern world' in contrast to Christy's use of more local imagery.

318 *... All in a prison bound*: Michael James sings the popular ballad 'John McGoldrick and the Quaker's Daughter'; the county town of *Cavan* has held numerous political prisoners since the time of the Jacobite rebellions in the seventeenth century.

361 *with the wind upon my heart*: with the pain of heartburn.

380 *the plains of Meath*: the rich fertile region of the midlands.

388 *and it piled with poteen for our drink tonight?*: despite pride in his licensed premises, Michael James has had the forethought to bring in local illicit whiskey for the celebrations after the sports, and doesn't want the police around.

396 *Sneem*: about 150 miles further south, in a gentler part of Kerry.

418 *like an old braying jackass strayed upon the rocks?*: 'a man who is not married is no better than an old jackass ... he eats a bit in this place and a bit in another place, but he has no home for himself; like an old jackass straying on the rocks' (*Works* ii. 121).

468 *old hen*: influenza.

469 *cholera morbus*: fatal cholera.

481 *Keel*: a village on Achill, an island to the south, where Lynchehaun was sheltered from the police.

528 *from Binghamstown unto the plain of Meath*: from here (Binghamstown is 2 miles south of Belmullet) to the east of Ireland.

533 *a drift of ... their shifts itself maybe*: although attention was fastened on 'shifts', a word reminiscent of Parnell's relationship with Kitty O'Shea when anti-Parnellites waved shifts during his final campaign, it was likely the sexual implications of a flock of young women being paraded before Christy, made even more local by the interpolation of 'Mayo girls' by Willie Fay, the actor playing Christy, that provided the proof of immorality the first-night audience was expecting; see Introduction, pp. xvii–xviii.

563 *stretch you*: hang you.

587 *lift a lighted sod*: take up a piece of burning turf.

599 *hanging as a scarecrow for the fowls of hell*: the grisly image of buzzards feasting on carrion even in hell.

605 *I'll have a royal judgment ... courts of law*: the sentence of murder would require the lieutenant-governor's signature.

608 *crying out in Mayo . . . in their lacy kerchiefs*: an image from the hanging ballads still popular with the wandering ballad singers.

652 S.D. *breaking out into wild lamentations*: Pegeen's grief takes the form of traditional keening, in this case for the death of a dream.

Deirdre of the Sorrows

Draft Essay 12 *Walter Scott*: in his notes on aesthetics and style, Synge praised Sir Walter Scott (1771–1832), Scottish writer of historical novels, including *Kenilworth*, for 'dialogue where there is style formed of living language' (see Saddlemyer, 'A Share in the Dignity of the World' in R. Skelton and A. Saddlemyer (eds.), *The World of W. B. Yeats* (1965), 212).

13 *Westward Ho*: novel by Charles Kingsley (1819–75) set in Elizabethan times.

Promessi Sposi(?): historical novel by Alexander Manzoni (1785–1873).

20 *Browning, Rossetti*: Synge is probably thinking of the historical poetic dramas of English poet Robert Browning (1812–89), which had a brief popularity on the London stage in the mid-nineteenth century, rather than his better-known dramatic monologues; Dante Gabriel Rossetti (1828–82) included a number of poems on historical subjects in his *Ballads and Sonnets* (1881).

27 *Pelleas and Melisande*: a play by Belgian Symbolist poet and dramatist Maurice Maeterlinck (1862–1949) which was extremely popular in a production toured by the French actress Sarah Bernhardt and the English actress Mrs Patrick Campbell; Synge saw their performance in Dublin in 1905.

Persons *Lavarcham*: pronounced 'Lower'kem' (as in allow); in some versions of the story she has magical powers and can prophesy, hence 'a wise woman'.

Conchubor: pronounced 'Connahar' or, more often by Synge, 'Conor'.

Deirdre: pronounced 'Dare'dra'.

Naisi: pronounced 'Nee'shi'.

Ainnle: pronounced 'Awin'le'.

heroes of the Red Branch: the warriors of the Red Branch of Ulster were led by Cuchulain, ward or nephew of Conchubar; *Cuchulain of Muirthemne*, an English version of their exploits published by Lady Gregory in 1902, received mixed praise from Synge (see *Works* ii. 367–70), but clearly influenced him.

Scene *Slieve Fuadh*: the highest peak of the mountain-range in County Armagh; pronounced 'Sleeve Foo'a'.

Emain Macha: the High King's residence near Armagh, pronounced 'Evin Vaha'.

Opening S.D.: *press*: cupboard.

1.4 *later than the common*: later than usual.

5 *Usna*: pronounced 'Uish'na'.

8 *the gods send*: pray to the gods that.

14 *Who'd check her like was made to have her pleasure only*: 'who would restrain someone like her who was born to a life of pleasure.' The phrase 'her like' acts as a refrain throughout, emphasizing not only the uniqueness of Deirdre's beauty but of her story.

26 *a blue stew*: very cross; the difference in tone and idiom between the Old Woman, Conchubor's cook, and Lavarcham distinguishes their social class as well as their understanding of the subtleties of the situation.

36 *in his tempers*: in a bad temper.

68 S.D. *going to frame*: this is the moment at which the action Yeats refers to in his Preface, when Owen was to have taken the knife Conchubor used to cut himself free from threads of silk, would have been performed.

102 *and you old itself*: when you are so old.

113 *light and airy*: light-hearted and lively, even wayward.

127 *your duns and grey*: the peasant dress of homespun cloth which she is wearing.

133 *a man with his hair . . . split on it*: the words Deirdre uses to describe the tapestry she is working on (and the man she has seen on the hills) are taken by Synge from the Irish text he translated himself (see Introduction, p. ix).

140 *Three young men, and they chasing in the green gap of a wood*: Conchubor could not help but recognize Deirdre's reference to Naisi and his brothers in this hunting scene.

170 *Duns of Emain*: the hill-forts surrounding his residence.

181 *the five parts of Ireland*: the historic five kingdoms of Ulster, Munster, Leinster, Connaught, and Meath.

197 *a man has no lies*: a man who does not lie.

203 *Emer and Maeve*: two great queens, Emer who was wooed by Cuchulain, and Maeve, the queen of Connacht.

229 *it's no work the High King to be slipping on stepping stones*: it isn't suitable for the High King to risk slipping on stepping-stones through flooded pathways.

237 *a sight nearer*: a great deal sooner.

270 *away in your head?*: mad.

272 *Dundealgan*: Dundalk.

279 *Cuchulain*: hero of the Red Branch, pronounced 'Cuhoolin' or 'Cu-hul-lin'.

280 *Conall Cearneach*: one of the chief heroes of the Red Branch (pronounced 'Carnah').

283 *in her skin*: naked.

287 *the more astray*: mistaken, wandering in my mind.

325 S.D. *pulls her hair and cloak over her face*: one more indication that Lavarcham is herself a well-known figure in Conchubor's circle.

347. *Tara*: the seat of priest-kings in pre-Christian Ireland, in County Meath 6 miles south-west of Navan.

378 *Orion*: the constellation.

396 *Nessa and Rogh*: Nessa, mother of Conchubor and daughter of the king of Ulster, and Roigh (the more traditional spelling, pronounced 'rou', as in 'out'), father of Sualtim, Cuchulain's father and therefore part of the saga of the Red Branch.

403 *Fedlimid*: Conchubor's story-teller and soothsayer.

463 *Alban*: Scotland.

481 *from this out*: from now on.

492 *Brandon*: a mountain on the Dingle peninsula.

493 *in the course of a piece*: in a short time.

511 *By the sun . . . and moon*: Synge seems to have invented this ceremony, based on his own pantheistic tendencies; he provides a similar invocation in his early play *When the Moon Has Set*.

2.37 *I didn't care*: I wouldn't care.

70 *gamey*: frisky, lively.

94 *and it squeezing the crack in my skull*: Owen's own acknowledgement that he is 'half-cracked' or mad for love of Deirdre.

99 *Saxon*: an adjective used here as contemptuous dismissal.

100 *spancelled*: tied together, just one example of the violent animal imagery chastised by Deirdre.

106 *a queen in Tara*: perhaps a reference to the origins of Tara as the meeting-place of the High King and the fertility goddess who later gave her name to Maeve.

155 S.D. *Deirdre begins to net*: Deirdre is repairing one of the fishing nets used by the brothers, an indication of the life she has chosen instead of one more queenly.

161 *for there's no place . . . peace always*: an echo of the well-known Irish poetry of exile, with its paean to nature.

169 *from the princes' wives*: it was customary for royal children to be fostered in the households of princes.

178 *the Sons of Usna*: as sons of a king and well-loved warriors of the Red Branch, they deserve a better life.

200 *I've had a dread . . . wearied*: here Naisi echoes the fear Deirdre voices to Lavarcham earlier (2.54–59), and provides a reason for action differing from the traditional narrative which depends upon the supernatural occasion of a vision she experiences.

214 *Glen Masain*: the glens of Argyllshire here mentioned by Deirdre (Masain, da Ruadh) and the woods of Cuan are taken by Synge from the traditional lament, 'Deirdre's farewell to Alban'.

224 *the age of the eagle and the salmon and the crow of Britain*: considered by the Celts the oldest animals.

232 *Glen da Ruadh*: one of the glens of Argyllshire (pronounced 'roo'a'); see note to 2.214 above.

307 *he'll not credit your oath*: Owen, who is Conchubor's spy, has knowledge of the High King's plans and could warn them, but Naisi would not believe someone he suspects of vengeance.

371 *Cuan*: see note to 2.214 above.

3.27 *that's a trick*: in the traditional narrative Conchubor arranges for Fergus to be invited to a feast, which he is under *geis* (prohibition) never to refuse.

40 *dummies*: dumb persons.

62 S.D. *exultingly*: killing the king's messenger would have been treason.

98 *figuring*: imagining.

111 *the Red Branch House*: there were three royal courts at Emain, the Royal Branch, the Speckled Branch, and the Red Branch in which were stored the spoils of battle.

197 *knacky fancier*: ingenious or artful chooser.

215 *a game the like of yours*: a manner like yours.

263 *the madder and the stone-crop*: vegetable dyes of red and orange, colours which delighted Synge on Aran.

310 *let build rooms*: had rooms built.

368 *a torch of bog-deal*: resinous pine-wood dug out of the bog cast a great flame when lighted.

374 *a clean death was your share*: a common thread in the formal elegy, as in Maurya's lament at the end of *Riders to the Sea*.

432 *a thief and traitor*: by breaking his word or seal, thereby betraying Fergus as well as Naisi, Conchubor is no longer worthy of kingship.

460 *She will do herself harm*: despite this risk, all respect the formality of the keen.

463 *the High King who is your master*: Death.

GLOSSARY

above up there

ails is wrong with

banbhs young pigs (pronounced 'ban-nuvs' or 'bonnivs')

baronies divisions of the county

basking an adjectival form of the verb to bask, lying or sitting comfortably in the warmth

bedizened decked out gaudily

below down there

beyond over there

blackthorn walking-stick made from stem of blackthorn shrub

blather foolish talk, nonsense; used as both noun and verb, as in 'blathering'

bog moor or heath where turf or peat is cut

boghole soft place where peat has been cut

boreen narrow lane or passage between stone walls or high earth banks

butt bottom or end (of his tailpocket, of the ditch, of a rope, etc.)

call need or right

clack idle chatter

cleeve basket or hamper

cnuceen a little hill, pronounced 'knockeen'

comrade spouse

conceit liking or preference

cot cottage

creel large wicker basket, usually for fish or turf

creel cart cart with open or grated sides

curagh small canoe made of wickerwork covered with hides (or by Synge's time with tarred canvas), the shape varying from district to district, but usually keel-less with an upturned bow especially designed for the waves of Galway Bay

da father

darlint darling, wonderful

destroyed injured, bothered or exhausted, perhaps even ruined or driven mad, not necessarily as in TW 1.176, half-killed

ditch bank

doul blind, pronounced as in 'out'

dram-shop a public-house, where one can buy small quantities of whiskey and other spirits

dray a low cart without sides, for heavy loads such as beer-barrels

drift small flock

drouth or drought thirst or, as an adjective ('droughty'), thirsty

dun hill-fort, often in ancient times a fortified royal residence

easy comfortable or quiet

-een diminutive suffix, e.g. 'houseen', 'priesteen', 'Shaneen', 'supeen'; pronounced 'yeen'

felts fieldfares, thrushes

furze gorse

gaffer lad

gallous splendid

gripe of the ditch grasp or hollow of the ditch

griseldy 'grisly' (Synge), perhaps also grizzled or unshaven

haggard enclosure for stock

hap'worth a halfpenny's worth

hitch noose

hooker a small sailing cutter, commonly used off the west coast for transporting both people and cargo

hooshing lifting up or removing TW 2.209; encouraging POWW 3.147

in it there

itself even

keen a lament for the dead, used also as
  an active verb
kidnabbed kidnapped

lep leap or jump
liefer rather
louty loutish, thoughtless

making game of fooling, joking WS
  1.315; making a fool of TW 2.238,
  POWW 1.153
making mugs making faces
mitch off play truant
moiling drudging

pandied beaten like a schoolboy
parish public licensed public-house
parlatic paralytic from drink
paters paternosters, the Lord's Prayer
peelers policemen, nicknamed after Sir
  Robert Peel who established Ireland's
  first constabulary
pitching playing the game of pitch and
  toss, where the winner throws an object
  closest to a designated mark
playboy as used in POWW, a combination of trickster, athlete, performer,
  creator, seducer, and hero
porter malt beer sold in every public
  house
poteen illegally distilled whiskey, pronounced 'potyeen'
power of, a many, a great deal of

right duty, free claim

Samhain All Souls' Day or All-
  Hallowtide, 1 November, the beginning of winter and in pre-Christian
  times the Feast of the Dead, pronounced 'sow'in' (as in 'allow')
scribes of bog long stretches of waste-
  land, where turf-cutting took place
seamed wrinkled
shanty 'a tumbled down old house'
  (Synge)

shift chemise, a woman's undergarment
  like a slip, worn next to the skin and
  reaching to the knees
shut of rid of
skelping beating
skillets cooking utensils, usually with
  three or four feet and a long handle
slate beat
sluig hollow in muddy ground
small farmers poor farmers possessing
  very small farms, in contrast to 'strong'
  farmers, who were better off
sop of tuft
staggers staggering state of drunkenness
streeleen trail or stream of talk
sup a few drops or small quantity of
  liquid
swiggling swinging and wriggling

thraneen a withered stalk of grass, a
  worthless thing
topknot literally the tuft of feathers on a
  bird's head, hence here 'another
  feather in his cap'
tramper a tramp or vagrant
turf peat, a common fuel

Union the workhouse

wake the 'watching of the dead' before
  burial, frequently an occasion for all-
  night social gatherings
want need
warrant a certainty
wattle a little stick
western world in WS 1.295 and
  POWW the entire world we know as
  opposed to the world of folk and fairy
  tales (the 'eastern' world) except for
  POWW 2.389, when the reference is to
  the United States
whisht be silent
winkered mule mule with blinkers
wizendy wizened